Lecture Notes in Computer Scien

T0237915

Commenced Publication in 1973
Founding and Former Series Editors:
Gerhard Goos, Juris Hartmanis, and Jan van Leeuwen

Martin Leucker (Ed.)

Runtime
Verification

8th International Workshop, RV 2008
Budapest, Hungary, March 30, 2008
Selected Papers

 Springer

Volume Editor

Martin Leucker
Technical University Munich
Institute for Informatics I4
Boltzmannstr. 3
85748 Garching, Germany
E-mail: leucker@in.tum.de

Library of Congress Control Number: Applied for

CR Subject Classification (1998): D.2, D.3, F.3, K.6

LNCS Sublibrary: SL 2 – Programming and Software Engineering

ISSN   0302-9743
ISBN-10   3-540-89246-X Springer Berlin Heidelberg New York
ISBN-13   978-3-540-89246-5 Springer Berlin Heidelberg New York

Springer is a part of Springer Science+Business Media

springer.com

© Springer-Verlag Berlin Heidelberg 2008
Printed in Germany

Typesetting: Camera-ready by author, data conversion by Scientific Publishing Services, Chennai, India
Printed on acid-free paper   SPIN: 12539178   06/3180   5 4 3 2 1 0

Preface

These proceedings are compiled from revised submissions presented at RV 2008, the 8th International Workshop on Runtime Verification held on March 30, 2008 in Budapest, Hungary, as a satellite event of ETAPS 2008.

There were 27 submissions. Each submission was reviewed by at least three Program Committee members. The committee decided to accept nine papers. This volume also includes two contributions by the invited speakers Jean Goubault-Larrecq (LSV/ENS Cachan) on "A Smell of Orchids" and John Rushby (SRI) on "Runtime Certification".

We would like to thank the members of the Program Committee and the additional referees for their timely reviewing and lively participation in the subsequent discussion—the quality of the contributions herein is due to their efforts and expertise. We would like to thank the local organizers of ETAPS 2008 for facilitating this workshop. We would also like to thank the Technical University of Munich for their financial support. Last but not least, we thank the participants of RV 2008 for the stimulating discussions during the workshop and the authors for reflecting this discussion in their revised papers.

We acknowlege the effort of the EasyChair support team.

July 2008   Martin Leucker

Conference Organization

Program Chairs

Martin Leucker

Program Committee

Mehmet Aksit
Howard Barringer
Mads Dam
Bernd Finkbeiner
Klaus Havelund
Bengt Jonsson
Moonzoo Kim
Dejan Nickovic
Doron Peled
Mauro Pezze
Shaz Qadeer
Grigore Rosu
Gerardo Schneider
Henny Sipma
Oleg Sokolsky
Scott Stoller
Mario Suedholt
Serdar Tasiran
Stavros Tripakis
Yaron Wolfsthal

External Reviewers

Rahul Agarwal
Joachim Baran
Benedikt Bollig
Feng Chen
Nikhil Dinesh
Klaus Dräger
Tayfun Elmas
Ylies Falcone
Danny Harnik
Mark Hills
Shin Hong
Marcel Kyas
Nicolas Markey

Patrick Meredith
Mark Moulin
Christian Pfaller
Dmitry Pidan
Cristian Prisacariu
David Rydeheard
Christian Schallhart
Sven Schewe
Viktor Schuppan
Edi Shmueli
Haya Shulman
Volker Stolz
Alan Williams

Table of Contents

A Smell of ORCHIDS

Jean Goubault-Larrecq[1] and Julien Olivain[1,2]

[1] LSV, ENS Cachan, CNRS, INRIA
LSV, 61 avenue du président Wilson, F-94235 Cachan Cedex
{olivain,goubault}@lsv.ens-cachan.fr
[2] Above Security, Suite 203
1919 Lionel-Bertrand boulevard, Boisbriand, Québec, Canada, J7H 1N8
julien.olivain@abovesecurity.com

Abstract. ORCHIDS is an intrusion detection tool based on techniques for fast, on-line model-checking. ORCHIDS detects complex, correlated strands of events with very low overhead in practice, although its detection algorithm has worst-case exponential time complexity.

The purpose of this paper is twofold. First, we explain the salient features of the basic model-checking algorithm in an intuitive way, as a form of dynamically-spawned monitors. One distinctive feature of the ORCHIDS algorithm is that fresh monitors need to be spawned at a possibly alarming rate.

The second goal of this paper is therefore to explain how we tame the complexity of the procedure, using abstract interpretation techniques to safely kill useless monitors. This includes monitors which will provably detect nothing, but also monitors that are subsumed by others, in the sense that they will definitely fail the so-called shortest run criterion. We take the opportunity to show how the ORCHIDS algorithm maintains its monitors sorted in such a way that the subsumption operation is effected with no overhead, and we correct a small, but definitely annoying bug in its core algorithm, as it was published in 2001.

1 Introduction

It is a *lieu commun* that the security of computer systems and networks is more and more challenged by new threats. Viruses, worms, Trojan horses have been reported to infect computers since the early 1980s, network attacks such as denial of service, spoofing, defacing have been commonplace since the late 1980s, and new attacks keep coming up, either based on new principles such as phishing or keyloggers, or using older vulnerabilities. New applications create new opportunities for vulnerabilities. E.g., the advent of Web-based applications created new families of vulnerabilities such as SQL insertion, PHP insertion, or cross-site scripting.

It is harder and harder to maintain an acceptable level of security on computers and networks, while keeping the induced nuisance at an acceptable level to honest users. Static analysis and formal methods in general can certainly help increase the faith we can put in critical pieces of code, but they are far from being able to ascertain the global security of a whole computer system or network.

M. Leucker (Ed.): RV 2008, LNCS 5289, pp. 1–20, 2008.

A successful family of techniques in this respect is *intrusion detection*, whereby flows of system and network events are monitored in real time, and analyzed so as to detect attacks. Intrusion detection systems that also react against attacks are sometimes called intrusion *prevention* systems.

Definitions in this domain tend to be fuzzy, starting from the very notion of attack. *Anomaly detection* systems count as possible attack any significant statistical deviation from normal behavior. *Misuse detection* systems would check the flow of events against some security policy, raising an alert when the policy is violated, or against some database of attack signatures, raising an alert when one of the signatures is matched.

ORCHIDS [6] is an intrusion prevention system that was developed at LSV by the authors, starting from 2002. It was initially meant as a misuse detection system, whose originality was that it could detect complex attacks consisting of several events correlated over time. An example of such an attack is the `ptrace` attack [10,11], which we shall describe shortly in Section 2. We shall again use this attack to describe the ORCHIDS detection algorithm by means of an example run, in Section 3. In Section 4, we shall describe the core detection algorithm in more detail, repairing a bug in [13]. The point of this algorithm is to detect the shortest run by keeping all runs sorted with the lowest possible overhead—in particular, we *never* call any sort routine. The `ptrace` example, while impressive, remains simple-minded, for reasons we shall explain in Section 6. There, we shall illustrate how a single signature can detect whole families of attacks, and even some zero-day attacks. This is important to security practitioners.

ORCHIDS was presented at the CAV'05 conference [7], and its core algorithm is based on the one described in [13, Section 4]. In these papers, ORCHIDS was described as a model-checker for a specific temporal logic. However, somehow OR-CHIDS is better described as running monitors, with the twist that each monitor will spawn new monitors dynamically, to follow possible beginnings of attacks. Presenting this work at RV'08 is therefore quite apt indeed, and we must thank Martin Leucker and the organizers for inviting the first author to Budapest and allow him to give an overview of it.

2   The `ptrace` Attack Example

Let's concentrate on the `ptrace` attack [10,11]. This is a local-to-root exploit, i.e., it enables a user having local access to a host machine to get root privileges. This is a real attack, which has been used in practice. Patches have been available for some time, of course; none of the attacks presented here should be effective on up-to-date systems.

The main point in using the `ptrace` attack as an example is that it is witnessed by a flow of events that are all entirely uncharacteristic of any malicious activity in isolation: most events in an instance of the attack are calls to the `ptrace` system call, a perfectly benign system call used for all debugger-related activities. Rather, the *sequence* of events throughout the attack must be identified to isolate the attack. In other words, the `ptrace` attacks avoids detection by classical intrusion detection systems, which only match individual events against a database of word patterns.

To understand the attack, it is useful to realize what a modular operating system kernel, such as most versions of Linux, will do when a user program calls an unimplemented kernel functionality. See Figure 1, where the user program has pid 100, and the unimplemented functionality is the special case of the `socket` system call on the (never implemented, Linux specific) domain `AF_SECURITY`. The kernel will search for a kernel module implementing this, calling the `modprobe` utility to search and install the desired module. If the search fails, an error code is reported.

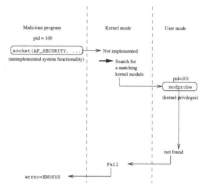

Fig. 1. Calling an unimplemented kernel functionality

While this is how this is meant to work, some versions of Linux suffer from a race condition (Figure 2(a)). While `modprobe` has started running, with kernel privileges, the kernel updates the owner tables to make `modprobe` root-owned instead of user-owned. So there is a small amount of time where the malicious user program has complete control over the kernel process `modprobe`: between timepoints ① and ②. The malicious program takes this opportunity to attach the `modprobe` process through the standard Unix debugging API function `ptrace`, and to insert a *shellcode* (a code of the intruder's choosing) inside it. When `modprobe` resumes execution, it will execute the shellcode with full root privileges (Figure 2(b)).

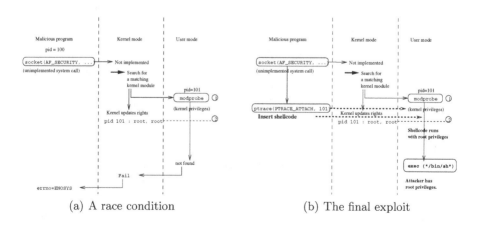

(a) A race condition   (b) The final exploit

Fig. 2. The `ptrace` Linux attack

3 Detecting the ptrace Attack

ORCHIDS can be made to detect this attack using the following signature:

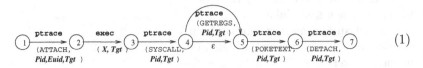

$$(1)$$

This can be thought as an automaton (a *monitor*), with starting state ①, and final state ⑦. Transitions are labeled with *patterns*, say ptrace(ATTACH, Pid, $Euid$, Tgt), meant to match single events such as ptrace(ATTACH, 57, 500, 58) (with the variable Pid mapped to 57, $Euid$ to 500, Tgt to 58; ORCHIDS actually uses explicit field selectors instead of patterns—we use patterns to simplify the exposition). Transitions can also be labeled with the symbol ϵ: these can be triggered without matching any event.

Patterns may contain variables, i.e., signatures have first-order capabilities. However, the main difference with standard monitors is that such an automaton is meant to match *subsequences* of the event flow, not the whole sequence of events. For example, the ptrace signature above should match the subsequence of the event flow shown in Figure 3 (see Section 3.2) consisting of events number 3, 4, 7, 8, 9, 12 with $Pid = 100$, $Euid = 500$, $Tgt = 101$. It should also match the sequence of events 3, 4, 7, 9, 12, omitting event 8 by choosing to go through the ϵ transition between states ④ and ⑤ instead of going through the transition labeled ptrace(GETREGS, Pid, Tgt). Note that it should also match the sequence of events 3, 4, 7, 8 (optional), 10, and 12, and also the sequence 3, 4, 7, 8 (optional), 11, and 12.

To fix ideas, let *events* be ground first-order terms over some set of function symbols (e.g., ptrace, exec). This signature includes numbers such as 100, 101, or 58 as constants, as well as symbolic values and character strings such as GETREGS. (Interpreting actual events, such as provided by the Linux kernel module Snare or other input modules, as terms, is essentially a parsing task.) *Patterns* are just first-order terms, not necessarily ground. We take the set $\mathcal{V}$ of variables to be the disjoint union of two countably infinite subsets, the set $\mathcal{V}_r$ of so-called *rigid* variables and $\mathcal{V}_f$ of *flexible* variables. Rigid variables such as Pid, $Euid$, or Tgt above are meant to match the same value over all events in a matching subsequence, while flexible variables may assume distinct values at each event. This is reminiscent of Manna and Pnueli [2]. ORCHIDS actually imposes a typing discipline on variables, events, and patterns, of which the distinction between rigid and flexible is just one aspect. We shall largely ignore the details of this typing discipline, except in Section 5.

Let $\mathcal{T}(\mathcal{V})$ be the set of all terms (patterns), $\mathcal{T}$ be the subset of all ground terms (events). We let fv(t) denote the set of free variables in t, $t\sigma$ denote the result of applying the substitution σ to t, where substitutions σ are finite maps $[x_1 := t_1, \ldots, x_n := t_n]$ with $x_1, \ldots, x_n$ pairwise disjoint variables—in which case the *domain* dom σ of σ is $\{x_1, \ldots, x_n\}$. Substitutions σ are meant to keep

1: **open** ("/etc/passwd", "r", 58, 500)
2: **ptrace** (ATTACH, 57, 500, 58)
3: **ptrace** (ATTACH, 100, 500, 101)
4: **exec** ("modprobe", 101)
5: **ptrace** (ATTACH, 100, 500, 101)
6: **exit** (58)

7: **ptrace** (SYSCALL, 100, 101)
8: **ptrace** (GETREGS, 100, 101)
9: **ptrace** (POKETEXT, 100, 101)
10: **ptrace** (POKETEXT, 100, 101)
11: **ptrace** (POKETEXT, 100, 101)
12: **ptrace** (DETACH, 100, 101)

Fig. 3. A typical event flow

the values of specific variables such as Pid or $Euid$ above. Let $\sigma \oplus \sigma'$ be the substitution with domain dom $\sigma \cup$ dom σ', mapping every $x \in$ dom σ' to $\sigma'(x)$, and every $x \in$ dom $\sigma \setminus$ dom σ' to $\sigma(x)$.

Given a substitution σ, a pattern p and a ground term t, we let $\sigma \vdash p \triangleleft t \Rightarrow \sigma \oplus \sigma'$, provided the most general matcher σ' of p against t exists, and $\sigma(x) = \sigma'(x)$ for every $x \in \mathcal{V}_r \cap$ dom $\sigma \cap$ dom σ' (i.e., we check that rigid variables do not change; flexible variables may be overwritten at will). In this case, we say that pattern p *matches* event t in σ, yielding $\sigma \oplus \sigma'$. E.g., ptrace(ATTACH, $Pid, Euid, Tgt$) matches ptrace(ATTACH, 57, 500, 58) (event number 2 in Figure 3) in the empty substitution, yielding $[Pid := 57, Euid := 500, Tgt := 58]$; ptrace(SYSCALL, Pid, Tgt) matches ptrace(SYSCALL, 100, 101) (event 7) in $[Pid := 100, Euid := 500, Tgt := 101]$ but not in $[Pid := 57, Euid := 500, Tgt := 58]$.

Each transition in a signature may be additionally labeled with a *guard*, which is an expression over the variables in $\mathcal{V}$ denoting a Boolean value. The actual syntax of guards is unimportant here. Letting $\mathcal{G}$ be the set of guards, we shall only assume that one may compute the finite set fv(g) of free variables in the guard g, and that we may evaluate a guard g in an environment σ to a Boolean value $[\![g]\!]\sigma$, as soon as fv$(g) \subseteq$ dom σ.

Signatures Σ are automata (Q, I, T, Δ), where Q is a finite set of *states*, $I \subseteq Q$ is the subset of *initial states*, $T \subseteq Q$ is the set of *final states*, and $\Delta \subseteq Q \times (\mathcal{T}(\mathcal{V}) \uplus \{\epsilon\}) \times \mathcal{G} \times Q$ is the *transition relation*. Any transition of the form (q_0, ϵ, g, q_1) is called an ϵ-*transition*. We assume that no ϵ-transition goes out of the initial state, i.e., that there is no transition of the form (q_0, ϵ, g, q_1) with $q_0 \in I$.

An *event flow* $t_{\bullet}$ is any finite or infinite sequence $t_1 t_2 \ldots t_i \ldots$ of events, i.e., of ground terms in $\mathcal{T}$. We are interested in finding specific subsequences of events with indices $i_1 < i_2 < \ldots < i_k$ $(k \geq 1)$: these subsequences are uniquely determined by the sets $\{i_1, i_2, \ldots, i_k\}$, which we call *subflows*. A *partial run* of an event flow $t_{\bullet}$ against a signature $\Sigma = (Q, I, T, \Delta)$ is a sequence $q_0, \sigma_0 \xrightarrow{i_1} q_1, \sigma_1 \xrightarrow{i_2} \ldots \xrightarrow{i_k} q_k, \sigma_k$, where $k \geq 1$, $q_0, q_1 \ldots, q_k$ are states in Q, $q_0 \in I$, σ_0 is the empty substitution, and there is an integer i_{k+1} such that for all j, $1 \leq j \leq k$, either there is a transition $(q_{j-1}, \epsilon, g, q_j) \in \Delta$ with $[\![g]\!]\sigma_{j-1}$ true and $i_j = i_{j+1}$ (go through the ϵ-transition, do not move in the event flow), or there is a transition $(q_{j-1}, p, g, q_j) \in \Delta$ with $p \neq \epsilon$, $\sigma_{j-1} \vdash p \triangleleft t_{i_j} \Rightarrow \sigma_j$, with $[\![g]\!]\sigma_j$ true, and $i_j < i_{j+1}$ (go through the transition, acquiring new values for variables, and proceed to some later point in the event flow). The subflow of such a partial run is the set of indices i_1, i_2, ..., i_k, with duplicates removed. We say that i_1 is its *birthdate*. A *complete run* is a partial run such that, additionally, $q_k \in F$.

ORCHIDS is in fact based on a more complex, and more expressive, language of signatures, with mutable variables, external system calls, and an embedded Prolog interpreter to maintain various databases: black lists, attacks that have succeeded in the past and that may be prerequisites to some others, neighboring relations between hosts in networks, equivalences between host names and between other services, and alert correlation information as in the M2D2 model [5]. However, the above simpler automata are enough to convey the essential ideas.

3.1 Shortest Runs

It is important to note that there is no unique complete run of a given event flow against a given signature in general, as we have seen above on the example of the ptrace attack: even the corresponding subflows are not unique.

An intrusion detection system cannot just report the *existence* of a matching subsequence (an attack): it should also collect, report enough information about the attack, and use it to react appropriately. Complete runs are enough information. On the other hand, it cannot report *all* matching complete runs either. This would flood the security administrator with too many alerts, prompting him to turn the intrusion detection system off, or to ignore its warnings. Instead, OR-CHIDS reports a *shortest run* [13] among all matching subsequences starting at a given event. The definition is as follows. For any subflows $i_1 < i_2 < \ldots < i_k$ and $j_1 < j_2 < \ldots < j_\ell$ $(k, \ell \geq 1)$, we let $(i_1, i_2, \ldots, i_k) \preceq (j_1, j_2, \ldots, j_\ell)$ iff $i_1 = j_1$ (the subflows have the same birthdate), $i_k \leq j_\ell$ (the first one stops earlier than the second one), and $(i_1, i_2, \ldots, i_k)$ is lexicographically smaller than $(j_1, j_2, \ldots, j_\ell)$.

On subflows with a given, fixed birthdate i_1, $\preceq$ is a total well-founded ordering, so any non-empty family F of subflows with the same birthdate i_1 has a unique smallest element wrt. $\preceq$. This is the *shortest subflow* of F. By extension, a *shortest run* of a flow $t_\bullet$ against a signature Σ with birthdate i_1, is a complete run whose subflow is shortest, among all subflows of complete runs against Σ with birthdate i_1.

ORCHIDS will only return shortest runs, taken as canonical representatives of all runs against a given signature Σ with a given birthdate i_1. Another view is to say that ORCHIDS considers all runs against the same signature Σ and starting at the same position as equivalent. Pouzol and Ducassé [9] consider more general notions of equivalence. However, the efficiency of the algorithm of Section 4 owes a lot to our particular definition of equivalence. While the latter is fixed in ORCHIDS, experience shows that it is adequate. It was argued in [13] that the shortest run against a given signature with birthdate i_1, was in a sense the most informative one, and experience again has vindicated this stance. We discuss this briefly.

First, shortest runs are shortest in the intuitive sense that they can be reported as soon as one run succeeds that matches the given signature. A simple example is the signature ①—A→②—A→③, with some arbitrary event A, and the event flow AAAAA...AA. While matching runs with birthdate $i_1 = 1$ include all pairs $1, n$ for all $n \geq 2$, only the pair $1, 2$ counts as shortest. This guarantees that the intrusion detection system will react as soon as some matching run is encountered.

Second, and more subtly, consider the signature shown on the right, and the event flow ACDCDCDCB. Any shortest run with birthdate $i_1 = 1$ must end at $i_k = 9$, on the final B. Candidates are $1, 9$, which only matches the initial A and the final B; or $1, 2, 3, 9$, which additionally matches the first CD, going around the loop between states ② and ③; or $1, 4, 5, 9$; or $1, 4, 7, 9$... we invite the reader to check that the shortest run is $1, 2, 3, 4, 5, 6, 7, 9$: contrarily to what the adjective "shortest" may suggest, the shortest run contains as many relevant events as permitted to describe a matching attack.

Returning to the `ptrace` attack signature (1), and the example event flow of Figure 3, the only matching runs have birthdate $i_1 = 3$, and the only shortest run is $3, 4, 7, 8,$ $10, 12$. Note that the optional event 8 is included, although it would be allowed to skip it, by going through the ϵ-transi-

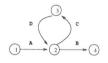

tion from ④ to ⑤, instead of that labeled `ptrace(GETREGS, Pid, Tgt)`. The latter transition would be irrelevant without the shortest run semantics. Here, it instructs ORCHIDS to report an event of the form `ptrace(GETREGS, Pid, Tgt)` in a matching attack, in case one is indeed present.

3.2   Running ORCHIDS on the `ptrace` Signature

Let us simulate an execution of ORCHIDS of the signature (1) against the example event flow of Figure 3. This will give us an opportunity to illustrate the salient features of the ORCHIDS algorithm, which we shall explain in more detail in Section 4. Here ORCHIDS will try to match just one signature; in normal use, it will try to match all signatures in a given signature database at the same time.

Initially, ORCHIDS reads event 1. Since (1) does not contain any pattern matching an **open** event, we skip to event 2, $t = \texttt{ptrace(ATTACH}, 57, 500, 58)$. The pattern $p = \texttt{ptrace(ATTACH}, Pid, Euid, Tgt)$ matches this, i.e.: $\sigma_0 \vdash p \triangleleft t \Rightarrow [Pid := 57, Euid := 500, Tgt := 58]$. So ORCHIDS produces the partial run $①, \sigma_0 \overset{2}{\to} ②$ $[Pid := 57, Euid := 500, Tgt := 58]$, where σ_0 is the empty substitution.

Think of these partial runs as being *threads* running in parallel, of a single program that tries several ways of matching subflows against the signature (1). (Threads will actually be partial runs, plus some extra information, but we shall equate the two concepts for now.) Such threads will be put in a queue. Currently, this queue only contains thread (i) below (i.e., signature (1), at state ②), with substitution $[Pid := 57, Euid := 500, Tgt := 58]$, and the subflow of the corresponding partial run contains just 2. From now on, we write subflows with visible spaces $\lrcorner$ to make explicit those events that were not taken into account; e.g., we write $\lrcorner 2 \lrcorner \lrcorner 5\ 6$ instead of $\{2, 5, 6\}$.

(i) ①—ptrace→●—exec→○—ptrace→○—ptrace(GETREGS Pid,Tgt)→○—ptrace→○—ptrace→○ $[Pid := 57, Euid := 500, Tgt := 58]$ $\lrcorner 2$

In other words, ORCHIDS is considering event 2 as the first event of a possible attack.

Now ORCHIDS reads event 3, and decides to create a new thread (ii). Indeed, event 3 is also matched by the first pattern of the signature (1), so might also be the beginning of a possible attack. The current state of the thread queue is now:

(i) [diagram] $\quad [Pid := 57, Euid := 500, Tgt := 58] \quad \llcorner 2 \lrcorner$

(ii) [diagram] $\quad [Pid := 100, Euid := 500, Tgt := 101] \quad \llcorner\llcorner 3$

ORCHIDS has to *spawn* this new thread. Otherwise, it might miss an attack. If ORCHIDS had not spawned this new thread, there would be opportunities for intruders to launch so-called *masking attacks*. In other words, to start fake attack beginnings so as to lead the intrusion detection system on a false track. ORCHIDS cannot know whether there is indeed an attack starting at event 2 (first thread), or at event 3 (second thread), or none, but needs to consider both possibilities. Similar behavior is typical of modern multi-event intrusion detection systems, e.g., chronicles [4], or GnG [15].

ORCHIDS now reads event 4, i.e., the `exec` event launching the instance of `modprobe` where the shellcode will eventually be inserted. The thread queue is now:

(i) [diagram] $\quad [Pid := 57, Euid := 500, Tgt := 58] \quad \llcorner 2 \lrcorner\lrcorner$

(ii) [diagram] $\quad [Pid := 100, Euid := 500,$
$\qquad Tgt := 101, X := \text{"modprobe"}] \quad \llcorner\llcorner 3\ 4$

where the second thread has advanced to state ③, and is waiting on an event matching $\texttt{ptrace}(\texttt{SYSCALL}, Pid, Tgt)$. The first thread does not advance, since the value of Tgt (here, 101) does not match the one it already got (58).

If this seems natural to you, you have probably missed something—or you're clever. To avoid masking attacks, ORCHIDS should also have launched a third thread:

[diagram] $\quad [Pid := 100, Euid := 500, Tgt := 101] \quad \llcorner\llcorner 3 \lrcorner$

Indeed, it may be the case that the `exec` event 4 was only used to mount a masking attack again. If this is the case, we should spawn the thread above, which would disregard event 4 in the hope of finding a later `exec` event which would be the right one.

ORCHIDS does not spawn this thread, because it is able to show that this is useless. It is not that this thread has no chance of eventually detecting an attack: this would not be true. But, if this new thread eventually detects an attack, the corresponding subflow will never be shortest: if the new thread detects an attack at some event n, with subflow $\llcorner\llcorner 3 \ldots n$, then thread (ii) will have detected an attack at event n too, with subflow of the form $\llcorner\llcorner 3\ 4 \ldots n$. Now notice that the latter is strictly smaller in the $\preceq$ ordering, hence is more informative. We can therefore safely ignore the above, useless, thread: we say that thread (ii) *subsumes* the above thread. This is an example of a *green cut*, see Section 5. Such green cuts are crucial to the efficiency of ORCHIDS.

ORCHIDS now reads event 5, which may against be the beginning of a `ptrace` attack. So ORCHIDS launches a new thread:

(i) $[Pid := 57, Euid := 500, Tgt := 58]$ ␣2␣␣␣

(ii) $[Pid := 100, Euid := 500,$
        $Tgt := 101, X := \text{"modprobe"}]$ ␣␣3 4␣

(iii) $[Pid := 100, Euid := 500, Tgt := 101]$ ␣␣␣␣5

Event 6 is irrelevant, and event 7 advances thread (ii):

(i) $[Pid := 57, Euid := 500, Tgt := 58]$ ␣2␣␣␣␣␣

(ii) $[Pid := 100, Euid := 500,$
        $Tgt := 101, X := \text{"modprobe"}]$ ␣␣3 4␣␣7

(iii) $[Pid := 100, Euid := 500, Tgt := 101]$ ␣␣␣␣5␣␣

Again, there is no need to create another thread that would consider the possibility that thread (ii) might not advance, because it would be subsumed by (ii), i.e., it would violate shortest runs. Event 8, `ptrace(SYSCALL, 100, 101)`, matches the `ptrace(SYSCALL, `Pid, Tgt`)` pattern of the non-ϵ-transition of thread (ii) from state $④$ to $⑤$. Again thanks to the shortest run trick, ORCHIDS does not need to consider spawning a new copy of thread (ii) that would remain in state $④$. More importantly, ORCHIDS does not need to consider spawning a new copy of thread (ii) that would advance to state $⑤$: again, ORCHIDS detects that this would be subsumed. The thread queue is now therefore:

(i) $[Pid := 57, Euid := 500, Tgt := 58]$ ␣2␣␣␣␣␣␣

(ii) $[Pid := 100, Euid := 500,$
        $Tgt := 101, X := \text{"modprobe"}]$ ␣␣3 4␣␣7

(iii) $[Pid := 100, Euid := 500, Tgt := 101]$ ␣␣␣␣5␣␣

Reading event 9, ORCHIDS decides to advance thread (ii) to state $⑥$. Again, ORCHIDS is able to show that it would be useless to spawn a copy of thread (ii) that would wait at state $⑤$, because it would be subsumed. ORCHIDS will then ignore events 10 and 11 in thread (ii), although they would be relevant (we let the reader rewrite the signature so that it captures *all* relevant `ptrace(POKETEXT, ...)` events), and will reach the final state $⑦$ with thread (ii), and subflow ␣␣3 4␣␣7 8 9␣␣12.

At this point, ORCHIDS' thread queue still contains threads (i) and (iii). These may be indicative of attacks starting at event 2, resp. 5, and which haven't been completed yet. For the moment, where we have just read event 12, ORCHIDS reports an alert. We decided to have ORCHIDS kill the offending user's processes (with pid 100, and all descendants), and to close his account. Such retaliation measures have sometimes been described as characteristic of intrusion *prevention* systems, as opposed to intrusion detection systems. They are needed: a typical shellcode will insert some form of trapdoor into the system, such as setting the setuid bit on one of the user's process, to allow him to become root at any later time, without running the attack again.

The actual signature ORCHIDS uses to detect the ptrace attack is a bit more complicated. While ORCHIDS really reports and retaliates at state ⑦, this state is not final, and the real signature has added transitions. This allows ORCHIDS to track down all events done by the shellcode (with pid obtained in variable Tgt, here 101) until it exits (which it will eventually do, if only because ORCHIDS sent it a KILL signal). This allows a security engineer to analyze the inserted shellcode and its effects—this is called *forensic analysis*—and to take appropriate corrective countermeasures.

4   The Core Algorithm

The core algorithm that ORCHIDS uses, and which we have illustrated in Section 3.2, is based on the algorithm of [13, Figure 6]. However, the latter algorithm contains a bug, which the first author found 6 months after the paper was published. We take the opportunity to describe a correct algorithm, with a simpler presentation.

As far as simplifications go, first, we don't consider green cuts for now, in particular those related to shortest runs: see Section 5. Also, we consider only one signature $\Sigma = (Q, I, T, \Delta)$, although the extension to more is straightforward. Finally, we assume Σ does not contain any ϵ-transition. Removing ϵ-transitions is done mostly as in standard finite-state automata, and only requires that we can form the conjunction $g_1 \wedge g_2$ of two guards g_1 and g_2, so that $[\![g_1 \wedge g_2]\!]\sigma$ is true if and only if $[\![g_1]\!]\sigma$ and $[\![g_2]\!]\sigma$ are both true: whenever Σ contains two transitions (q_1, p, g_1, q_2) and $(q_2, \epsilon, g_2, q_3)$, add the transition $(q_1, p, g_1 \wedge g_2, q_3)$ unless it is already present. When the signature is saturated under applications of this rule, remove all ϵ-transitions.

The main idea of the algorithm is to keep the thread queue sorted, and to traverse this queue in such a way that the first thread with a given birthdate i_1 and signature Σ that reaches a final state in the queue is shortest. Then, we remove all other threads with the same birthdate i_1 and Σ from the queue—we *kill* these threads.

Intuitively, it should be enough to keep all threads sorted in the lexicographic ordering of the corresponding subflows, but this is wrong. Imagine the current thread queue contains threads corresponding to subflows 1 2 3, 1 2␣, and 1␣3. If event 4, the next event to be considered, led each of these to a final state, then we would have to pick the lexicographically smallest subflow among 1 2 3 4, 1 2␣4, and 1␣3 4: this is 1 2 3 4. Observe that $\{1, 2, 3, 4\} <_{lex} \{1, 2, 4\} <_{lex} \{1, 3, 4\}$, where $<_{lex}$ is lexicographic ordering. Before event 4, we would therefore like the threads to be ordered as 1 2 3, then 1 2␣, then 1␣3. This way, no reordering will have to happen when adding 4 to each subflow. However, 1 2 3 is certainly not smaller, lexicographically, than 1 2␣, i.e., $\{1,2\}$! So we have to maintain the thread queue in some different ordering. This was recognized in [13, Theorem 4.11], where an ordering $<_i$ is defined for this purpose, for each event position i. (In the example, $i = 3$.) The right ordering is given by: for every subflows $D, D' \subseteq \{1,\ldots,i\}$, $D <_i D'$ if and only if D and D' have the same least element, and $D \cup \{i+1\} <_{lex} D' \cup \{i+1\}$. Roger and the first author [13] use a more complex, equivalent formula (up to the condition on least elements). Let $\leq_i$ be the reflexive closure of $<_i$, i.e., $D \leq_i D'$ if and only if $D = D'$ or $D <_i D'$.

Say that a list of partial runs $R_1, R_2, \ldots, R_m$ is $\leq_i$-*sorted* if and only if $R_j \leq_i R_k$ implies $j \leq k$. We aim at keeping queues of partial runs sorted, with minimal algorithmic effort. Whenever we read event number $i + 1$, starting from a $\leq_i$-sorted thread queue $R_1, R_2, \ldots, R_k$, we must create a $\leq_{i+1}$-sorted thread queue of all possible *extensions* of the runs R_j, $1 \leq j \leq k$, as predicted by the semantics of signatures, and all possible partial runs *starting* at event $i + 1$.

Extensions are defined as follows. Let $R = q_0, \sigma_0 \xrightarrow{i_1} q_1, \sigma_1 \xrightarrow{i_2} \ldots \xrightarrow{i_k} q_k, \sigma_k$ be a partial run, with subflow included in $\{1,\ldots,i\}$, and R' a partial run with subflow included in $\{1,\ldots,i,i+1\}$. We say that R' *extends* R at position $i + 1$ if and only if either $R' = R$ (wait without taking a transition), or $R' = q_0, \sigma_0 \xrightarrow{i_1} q_1, \sigma_1 \xrightarrow{i_2} \ldots \xrightarrow{i_k} q_k, \sigma_k \xrightarrow{i+1} q_{k+1}, \sigma_{k+1}$, where there is a transition $(q_k, p, g, q_{k+1}) \in \Delta$ with $p \neq \epsilon$, $\sigma_k \vdash p \triangleleft t_{i+1} \Rightarrow \sigma_{k+1}$, and with $[\![g]\!]\sigma_{k+1}$ true (go through the transition, acquiring new values for variables, and proceed to some later point in the event flow). In the latter case, R' extends R *non-trivially, through* the *outgoing* transition (q_k, p, g, q_{k+1}). Remember we assume Σ does not contain any ϵ-transition, so we can safely ignore them.

A partial run *starts* at event $i+1$ if and only if it is of the form $q_0, \sigma_0 \xrightarrow{i+1} q_1, \sigma_1$, where $q_0 \in I$, σ_0 is the empty substitution, and there is a transition $(q_0, p, g, q_1) \in \Delta$ with $\sigma_0 \vdash p \triangleleft t_{i+1} \Rightarrow \sigma_1$, and with $[\![g]\!]\sigma_1$ true.

Given a $\leq_i$-sorted list of partial runs $R_1, R_2, \ldots, R_m$, we must produce a $\leq_{i+1}$-sorted list $R'_1, R'_2, \ldots, R'_n$ of all partial runs extending some R_j, $1 \leq j \leq m$, or starting at $i + 1$. In the case of extensions of the partial runs R_j, the idea of the algorithm of [13] is to enumerate each R_j in turn, and to list the partial runs R'_k that extend R_j, starting with those that extend R_j non trivially. For example, starting from the partial runs 1 2 3 $<_3$ 1 2␣$<_3$ 1␣3 (where we identify partial runs with their subflows), imagine each has both trivial and non-trivial extensions at position 4. We start with 1 2 3, and output 1 2 3 4 first, then 1 2 3␣. Going on with 1 2␣, we output 1 2␣4, then 1 2␣␣. Eventually, this algorithm will output the partial runs 1 2 3 4, 1 2 3␣, 1 2␣4, 1 2␣␣, 1␣3 4, and 1␣3 ␣. We let the reader check that this is $\leq_4$-sorted.

However, there is a bug, which occurs whenever two partial runs are generated that induce the *same* subflow. Imagine for example that we must generate two partial runs with subflow 1␣3 4, on reading event 4. The above algorithm lists them in an arbitrary order. However, it may be that the first one will eventually lead to a complete run such as 1␣3 4␣6, and that the second one will lead to another complete run such as 1␣3 4 5 6... and 1␣3 4␣6, the first one, is then not shortest.

ORCHIDS uses a corrected algorithm, where partial runs are first grouped in *blobs*, i.e., non-empty sets of threads with the same subflow. Each blob therefore has a unique associated subflow. Then, blobs are $\leq_i$-sorted, in the sense that the associated subflows are $\leq_i$-sorted. In other words, a list of blobs $B_1, B_2, \ldots, B_m$ is $\leq_i$-*sorted* if and only if $D_j \leq_i D_k$ implies $j \leq k$, for all $1 \leq j, k \leq m$, writing D_j for B_j's subflow.

More precisely, at position i, ORCHIDS produces a $\leq_i$-sorted list $B_1, B_2, \ldots,$ B_m. On reading event number $i + 1$, ORCHIDS produces the queue described in Proposition 1 below, obtained by listing all partial runs starting at $i + 1$ in a unique blob B'_0, and dealing with partial runs from B_j by first listing all non-trivial extensions of partial runs from B_j, in a new blob B'_{2j-1} that will precede the blob B'_{2j} of the (unique) trivial extension. In other words, the corrected algorithm works as above, except it needs to consider blobs instead of single partial runs.

Proposition 1. *Let $B_1, B_2, \ldots, B_m$ be a $\leq_i$-sorted list of blobs, and assume all the subflows of each B_j, $1 \leq j \leq m$, are contained in $\{1, \ldots, i\}$. Let B'_0 be the set of all partial runs starting at $i+1$, B'_{2j-1} be the set of all non-trivial extensions to partial runs in B_j, B'_{2j} be the set of all trivial extensions to partial runs in B_j, $1 \leq j \leq m$. Then the queue obtained from $B'_0, B'_1, B'_2, \ldots, B'_{2m-1}, B'_{2m}$ by eliminating those B'_js that are empty is $\leq_{i+1}$-sorted, and their subflows are contained in $\{1, \ldots, i, i + 1\}$.*

Proof. Assume that $B'_0, B'_1, B'_2, \ldots, B'_{2m-1}, B'_{2m}$ is not $\leq_{i+1}$-sorted. Let D'_j be the subflow of B'_j, for all j, and D_j be the subflow of B_j. Then there are j', k' with $0 \leq k' < j' \leq 2m$ and $D'_{j'} \leq_{i+1} D'_{k'}$. Note that $k' \neq 0$, since the birthdate of any partial run in B'_0 is $i + 1$, which is different from all other birthdates. Write $k' = 2k - \delta_k$ and $j' = 2j - \delta_j$, where δ_k, δ_j are 0 or 1, and $k \leq j$. If $k = j$, then $k' < j'$ implies $\delta_k = 1$, $\delta_j = 0$, so that $D'_{k'} = D_k \cup \{i + 1\}$ (the partial runs of $B'_{k'} = B'_{2k-1}$ are non-trivial extensions of those of B_k), and $D'_{j'} = D_k$ (those of $B'_{j'} = B'_{2j} = B'_{2k}$ are trivial extensions). But $D_k \cup \{i + 1\} <_{i+1} D_k$, so $D'_{k'} <_{i+1} D'_{j'}$, contradiction.

So $k < j$. Then $D_{k'}$ equals D_k, possibly with $i + 1$ added, and $D_{j'}$ equals D_j, possibly with $i+1$ added. Since $B_1, B_2, \ldots, B_m$ is $\leq_i$-sorted, it is impossible that $D_j \leq_i D_k$, i.e., that $D_j \cup \{i+1\} \leq_{lex} D_k \cup \{i+1\}$. Since $\leq_{lex}$ is a total ordering, we must have $D_k \cup \{i + 1\} <_{lex} D_j \cup \{i + 1\}$. Write the elements of D_k as $i_1 < i_2 < \ldots < i_p$ (with $i_p < i+1$), those of D_j as $j_1 < j_2 < \ldots < j_q$ (with $j_q < i+1$, and $j_1 = i_1$). Let $i_{p+1} = i + 1$, $j_{q+1} = i + 1$. Since $D_k \cup \{i+1\} <_{lex} D_j \cup \{i+1\}$, for some ℓ between 1 and $\min(p+1, q+1)$, $i_1 = j_1$, $i_2 = j_2$, $\ldots$, $i_{\ell-1} = j_{\ell-1}$, and $i_\ell < j_\ell$. Now $\ell \neq p + 1$, else $i + 1 = i_\ell < j_\ell \leq j_{q+1} = i + 1$. So $\ell \leq p$. But then $D_{k'} \cup \{i+2\}$, which is composed of $i_1, i_2, \ldots, i_p$ (optionally $i_{p+1} = i+1$) and $i+2$, is lexicographically smaller than $D_{j'} \cup \{i+2\}$, which is composed of $j_1, j_2, \ldots, j_q$ (optionally $j_{q+1} = i + 1$) and $i + 2$. That is, $D_{k'} <_{i+1} D_{j'}$, contradiction. $\square$

While we have equated threads with partial runs until now, *threads* are in fact pairs of a partial run R and an outgoing transition (q_k, p, g, q_{k+1}). One may think of a thread as *waiting* on a particular transition to fire. In general, there may be several threads with the same partial run, waiting on different transitions in the same blob. From now on, call *thread queue* at position i a $\leq_i$-sorted list of blobs, composed of such threads. At the moment, this organization of blobs in threads rather than in partial runs only leads to a minor modification in the core algorithm. This will become important in Section 5.

Additionally, ORCHIDS maintains a set $Kill$ of birthdates of partial runs that have reached their final state, to kill non-shortest runs. On reading event $i + 1$, ORCHIDS first resets $Kill$ to $\emptyset$. ORCHIDS runs through the threads R in $B_1, B_2, \ldots, B_m$ as described in Proposition 1, with two modifications. First, whenever a thread with run R' is produced in one of the new blobs $B'_{j'}$, $0 \leq j' \leq 2m$, that reaches a final state, ORCHIDS adds the birthdate i_1 of R' to $Kill$. This is a shortest complete run. Second, ORCHIDS kills all other threads with the same birthdate i_1 by simply ignoring the threads in $B_1, B_2, \ldots, B_m$ whose birthdate are in $Kill$ when their turn comes.

ORCHIDS also ignores a number of other threads, see Section 5. Note that the actual thread queue, consisting of subsets of the blobs of Proposition 1, will also remain $\leq_i$-sorted at each event number i, guaranteeing that the unique complete run that will reach a final state (with given birthdate and signature) indeed has a shortest subflow.

Finally, we didn't say what ORCHIDS did on reaching a final state. It might seem obvious that this would be the right point to emit a report, warning the security administrator that an attack has just successfully completed, and to take active countermeasures. This is in fact wrong, and confuses two roles for final states. One of these roles is recognizing that enough information has been collected to conclude that some attack was indeed under way. The other role is to terminate ORCHIDS monitoring, and kill the corresponding threads. These two roles are distinct. The actual signature we use for `ptrace` has more states. State ⑦ is not final, and is the state at which ORCHIDS takes corrective actions—here, ORCHIDS will emit an attack report, store it into a secured database of successful fatal attacks, kill the offending attacking process (whose pid is in Pid) and all its descendants, securely close the attacker's account (whose id is in $Euid$) through an SSH connection to the attacked machine. (We assume that ORCHIDS runs on a different, dedicated host, for obvious security reasons.) However, killing subprocesses and closing user accounts takes some time, in particular if this is done through a remote SSH connection, so the shellcode has some time to do harm. The actual `ptrace` signature we use in ORCHIDS has additional states following ⑦, whose purpose is to trace and record all subsequent events done by the shellcode. This allows later, precise forensic analysis of the attack, and is crucial both for repairing the attacked host and for acquiring information on emerging viruses and worms.

5   Cuts, Green Cuts, Red Cuts

By *cut*, we mean any optimization or construction allowing one to kill threads. Cuts are important to be able to bound the number of active threads at any given position in the event flow. Following Prolog conventions [1], we distinguish between *green cuts*, which preserve the semantics, and *red cuts*, which don't. We first describe green cuts based on the notion of monotonic variables. These cuts are green, because they eliminate threads that will provably *never* reach a final state. Some other green cuts allow one to kill threads that may reach a final state, but if they do, the corresponding subflow will never be shortest. We have already seen an example of this in Section 3.2. We explain this in a second subsection. We argue for red cuts in the final subsection.

Green Cuts I: Monotonicity and Generalized Timeouts. The *monotonicity* cuts we describe now are typically justified by the need for *timeouts*, although they are not limited to the latter. Timeouts are needed to eliminate proliferating threads. Otherwise, attacker might mount denial-of-service attacks against the intrusion prevention system itself. Instead, it is necessary to kill threads that have exceeded a certain quota in terms of time or number of events. Naturally, this opens the door to *slow attacks*, i.e., to attacks that would evade detection by taking a long time to complete, and by generating events that are far away from each other in the event flow. A security administrator has to define suitable timeouts, as a result of a compromise between avoiding denial-of-service attacks and detecting slow attacks.

Enough freedom should be given to the security administrator to tune timeout information. We said that timeout information may be some combination of elapsed time and number of events. We may also take into account other time fields: the time at which a given event happened on a remote host, the time at which it was sent to the intrusion prevention system, the time at which it was received, the time at which it was logged. These are usually available as different time fields in the incoming events.

Instead of designing a specific notation for timeouts, it is simpler and more versatile to just use the guards $g \in \mathcal{G}$ for this purpose. For example, assuming the rigid variable T_0 holds the time at which the first event in the current partial run was logged and I_0 holds its position, the flexible variable $\$t$ holds the time at which the current event was logged, and the flexible variable $\$i$ holds the event position (obtained through pattern-matching), the guard $\$t < T_0 + 60 \wedge \$i < I_0 + 30\,000$ states that we wish to continue to monitor the given possible attack for at most 60 seconds and at most 30 000 events.

Such guards by themselves are not enough to reduce the number of threads. However, recognizing that a guard will always be false in the future allows us to disregard it entirely. We accomplish this in ORCHIDS by subdividing the **int** type of integers (and other numerical types) into those of values that are *monotonic* (non-decreasing over time), *antitonic* (non-increasing over time), *constant* (i.e., both monotonic and antitonic), and *arbitrary*. We also equate Boolean values as the subtype consisting of 0 (false) and 1 (true) for this purpose. Such monotonicity information can be formalized by using the familiar 4-element lattice **Four** of subsets of $\{\uparrow, \downarrow\}$ ordered by inclusion: $\emptyset$ means arbitrary, $\{\uparrow\}$ monotonic, $\{\downarrow\}$ antitonic, and $\{\uparrow, \downarrow\}$ means constant. Numerical types τ_i also include a monotonicity information, in **Four**, e.g., $\texttt{int}/\{\downarrow\}$.

Specific fields in events are marked as monotonic, such as time fields, or event numbers. Formally, each function symbol f comes with a typing rule, e.g., stating that any term $f(t_1, \ldots, t_n)$ gives each t_i some type τ_i, $1 \leq i \leq n$. To simplify the presentation, assume that all variables have type int/m for some monotonicity information m, and that the types τ_i mentioned earlier are either $\text{int}/\emptyset$, or $\text{int}/\{\uparrow\}$—in which case we say that i is a *monotonic position*. Given a pattern p and a set V of variables (denoting variables that are already bound to some value), let $\Gamma[p, V]$ be the typing context of all bindings $x : \tau$, where either x is rigid and in V and $\tau = \text{int}/\{\uparrow, \downarrow\}$ (rigid variables, once bound, will remain constant), or x is flexible and occurs in p at some monotonic position, and $\tau = \text{int}/\{\uparrow\}$. Guards are typed using typing rules that include:

$$\frac{m \supseteq m'}{\text{int}/m <: \text{int}/m'} \qquad \frac{}{\tau <: \tau} \qquad \frac{\Gamma \vdash t : \tau \quad \tau <: \tau'}{\Gamma \vdash t : \tau'}$$

$$\frac{}{\Gamma, x : \tau \vdash x : \tau} \qquad \frac{(c \text{ numerical constant})}{\Gamma \vdash c : \text{int}/\{\uparrow, \downarrow\}} \qquad \frac{\Gamma \vdash t_1 : \text{int}/m_1 \quad \Gamma \vdash t_2 : \text{int}/m_2}{\Gamma \vdash t_1 + t_2 : \text{int}/(m_1 \cap m_2)}$$

$$\frac{\Gamma \vdash t_1 : \text{int}/m_1 \quad \Gamma \vdash t_2 : \text{int}/m_2}{\Gamma \vdash t_1 < t_2 : \text{int}/(\overline{m}_1 \cap m_2)} \qquad \frac{\Gamma \vdash t_1 : \text{int}/m_1 \quad \Gamma \vdash t_2 : \text{int}/m_2}{\Gamma \vdash t_1 \wedge t_2 : \text{int}/(m_1 \cap m_2)}$$

In the last rules, we use the fact that Boolean values are considered as integers, and we take the convention that $\overline{\uparrow} = \downarrow$, $\overline{\downarrow} = \downarrow$, $\overline{m} = \{\overline{s} \mid s \in m\}$. Using the typing rules above, it is easy to see that we can derive $\$t : \text{int}/\{\uparrow\}, \$i : \text{int}/\{\uparrow\}, T_0 : \text{int}/\{\uparrow, \downarrow\}, I_0 : \text{int}/\{\uparrow, \downarrow\} \vdash \$t < T_0 + 60 \wedge \$i < I_0 + 30\,000 : \text{int}/\{\downarrow\}$. This implies that the guard $g = (\$t < T_0 + 60 \wedge \$i < I_0 + 30\,000)$ is antitonic, in particular that if it is false at event position i, it will remain false at every later position. This is a consequence of the following, easily proved proposition, with $t = g$. We assume the evaluation function $[\![\_]\!]\sigma$ to behave as expected, e.g., $[\![t_1 + t_2]\!]\sigma = [\![t_1]\!]\sigma + [\![t_2]\!]\sigma$.

Proposition 2. *Assume that event fields are marked monotonic or arbitrary, and that monotonic fields of events t_i are integers that are non-decreasing in i. For any pattern p, substitution σ, and term t, if $\Gamma[p, \text{dom } \sigma] \vdash t : \text{int}/m$ is derivable, and if $\sigma \vdash p \triangleleft t_i \Rightarrow \sigma_i$, then for every $j > i$ such that $\sigma \vdash p \triangleleft t_j \Rightarrow \sigma_j$, $[\![t_i]\!]\sigma_i$ and $[\![t_j]\!]\sigma_j$ are integers, $[\![t_i]\!]\sigma_i \leq [\![t_j]\!]\sigma_j$ if $\uparrow \in m$, and $[\![t_i]\!]\sigma_i \leq [\![t_j]\!]\sigma_j$ if $\downarrow \in m$.*

ORCHIDS implements this as follows. Recall that one may think of each thread, with partial run $R = q_0, \sigma_0 \overset{i_1}{\to} q_1, \sigma_1 \overset{i_2}{\to} \ldots \overset{i_k}{\to} q_k, \sigma_k$, as *waiting* on a transition (q_k, p, g, q_{k+1}) to fire. If $\sigma_k \vdash p \triangleleft t_i \Rightarrow \sigma'$ for some substitution σ' but $[\![g]\!]\sigma' = 0$ (false), and if $\Gamma[p, \text{dom } \sigma_k] \vdash g : \text{int}/\{\downarrow\}$ is derivable, then ORCHIDS kills the thread, i.e., removes it from its blob (and removes the blob from the queue if it becomes empty): not only does this transition fail to fire at position i, it will *never* fire.

Green Cuts II: Predicting Non-Shortest Runs. The algorithm of Section 4 kills all threads with a given birthdate and signature, once a corresponding (shortest) complete run has been found. However, as we have illustrated in Section 3.2, ORCHIDS also kills some threads *in advance*, knowing that they cannot be completed to a shortest run. This is crucial to the performance of

ORCHIDS. Otherwise, we would accumulate useless threads, only to kill them en masse when one of them completes, if ever.

Returning to the example of Section 3.2, the first case this happened was on reading event 4, where we decided that it was useless to spawn the thread with subflow $\_\_3\_$, since it would be subsumed by thread (ii), with subflow $\_\_3$ 4. In this example, most states only have one outgoing transition, so that we had only one thread per partial run. Hence, we equated threads with partial runs. In general, we should be careful that threads are partial runs *waiting* on a given transition. Here, before reading event 4, we had a thread (ii), with a partial run of subflow $\_\_3\_$, waiting on transition $(②, \texttt{exec}(X, Tgt), 1, ③)$. The core algorithm should in principle create two threads from the latter when reading event 4 ($\texttt{exec}(\texttt{"modprobe"}, 101)$). One would advance this thread to one with subflow $\_\_3$ 4, waiting on $(③, \texttt{ptrace}(\texttt{SYSCALL}, Pid, Tgt), 1, ④)$. The other (the trivial extension of the partial run) would decide to continue waiting on a later event matching $\texttt{exec}(X, Tgt)$. As we have already argued, the latter is useless.

It would be wrong to think that all trivial extensions of a partial run R are subsumed by any non-trivial extension of R, i.e., that it is always useless to wait when a transition could be fired. Although the case does not happen in the example of Section 3.2, consider the signature $① \xrightarrow[\,(\,Tgt\,)\,]{\texttt{start}} ② \xrightarrow[\,(\,Tgt, X\,)\,]{\texttt{action}} ③ \xrightarrow[\,(\,X\,)\,]{\texttt{final}} ④$, and the event flow 1: $\texttt{start}$ (58); 2: $\texttt{action}$ (58, A); 3: $\texttt{action}$ (58, B); 4: $\texttt{final}$ (B). On reading event 2, while in state $②$, both the trivial extension $1\_$ (with $Tgt := 58$) and the non-trivial extension $1\ 2$ (with $Tgt := 58$, $X := A$) have to be considered. The point is that we don't know whether A is the right value for X that will lead to a subflow that matches the signature. And indeed, the only such subflow is 1_3 4, with $Tgt := 58, X := B$. We may say that, at state $②$, the value of X still has to be discovered. On the contrary, in the $\texttt{ptrace}$ example, the value of rigid variable Tgt has already been discovered at state $②$, while the value of X, which we discover at this point, will never be used by any later guard.

This is formalized as follows. Given a computable property $P(\Gamma, g)$ of a typing context Γ and a guard g, we say that P *holds at all reachable transitions* from Γ and the transition (q, p, g, q'), inductively, if and only if $P(\Gamma, g)$ holds and P holds at all reachable transitions from $\Gamma \oplus \{x : \texttt{int}/\{\uparrow, \downarrow\} \mid x \in \text{fv}(p')\}$ and (q', p', g', q'') for all outgoing transitions (q', p', g', q''). This is meant to say that $P(\Gamma', g')$ holds whenever we reach a transition (q', p', g', q''), where Γ' is Γ, with all variables bound in-between assumed constant. Let $\Gamma\langle p, V\rangle$ be the typing context of all bindings $x : \tau$, where: if x is in V and not a flexible variable in $\text{fv}(p)$, then $\tau = \texttt{int}/\{\uparrow, \downarrow\}$; if x is flexible and occurs in p at some monotonic position, then $\tau = \texttt{int}/\{\uparrow\}$; otherwise, $\tau = \texttt{int}/\emptyset$.

Proposition 3. *Assume that event fields are marked monotonic or arbitrary, and that monotonic fields of events t_i are integers that are non-decreasing in i.*

Let $R = q_0, \sigma_0 \xrightarrow{i_1} q_1, \sigma_1 \xrightarrow{i_2} \ldots \xrightarrow{i_k} q_k, \sigma_k$ be a partial run, with subflow included in $\{1, \ldots, i\}$, and where q_k is not final. Let (q_k, p, g, q_{k+1}) be some outgoing transition, assume that $\sigma_k \vdash p \triangleleft t_{i+1} \Rightarrow \sigma_{k+1}$, and that P holds at all reachable transitions from $\Gamma\langle p, \text{dom } \sigma_k\rangle$ and (q_k, p, g, q_{k+1}), where $P(\Gamma', g')$ is the property: $\Gamma' \vdash g' : \texttt{int}/\{\downarrow\}$

is derivable. For any complete run $q_0, \sigma_0 \overset{i_1}{\to} q_1, \sigma_1 \overset{i_2}{\to} \ldots \overset{i_k}{\to} q_k, \sigma_k \overset{i_{k+1}}{\to} q_{k+1}, \sigma'_{k+1} \overset{i_{k+2}}{\to} \ldots$ $\overset{i_m}{\to} q_m, \sigma'_m$ *with* $i+1 < i_{k+1}$, *there is a strictly shorter complete run* $q_0, \sigma_0 \overset{i_1}{\to} q_1, \sigma_1 \overset{i_2}{\to}$ $\ldots \overset{i_k}{\to} q_k, \sigma_k \overset{i+1}{\to} q_{k+1}, \sigma_{k+1} \overset{i_{k+2}}{\to} \ldots \overset{i_m}{\to} q_m, \sigma_m.$

Proof. (Sketch.) I.e., we can build a strictly shorter run by firing the transition (q_k, p, g, q_{k+1}) at event position $i + 1$ instead of waiting for some later position i_{k+1}. The assumption $\sigma_k \vdash p \lhd t_{i+1} \Rightarrow \sigma_{k+1}$ ensures that we can indeed fire this at position $i + 1$. All further transitions, from q_{k+1} to q_{k+2} to ... to q_m are the same in both runs. This may change variable bindings, from σ'_{k+1} to σ_{k+1}, ..., and from σ'_m to σ_m. But, by the typing condition, this can only make the value of guards increase. Since all guards were made true by $\sigma'_{k+1}, \ldots, \sigma'_m$, the same guards are made true by $\sigma_{k+1}, \ldots, \sigma_m$. □

So, under the assumptions of Proposition 3, it is safe to advance along the transition (q_k, p, g, q_{k+1}), *without* spawning a thread waiting on a later event position for the same transition. Note that, as a particular case, the assumptions of Proposition 3 are satisfied whenever p only binds rigid variables, and those that were not in dom σ_k are free in no guard occurring later in the signature. This is what we illustrated in Section 3.2.

Such green cuts are, as we have said, crucial to the performance of ORCHIDS. Totel *et al.* have already recognized the importance of timeouts, and shown [15, Figure 7] that with a timeout value of 1 s on a user machine, the number of plans (similar to our threads) culminated to a few hundreds. We worked together in 2002, in the framework of the French RNTL project DICO, and evaluated our respective algorithms by comparing numbers of threads throughout several event flows, both artificial and real. On E. Totel's main signature example, which was meant to test the limits of multi-event intrusion detection systems, our algorithm never maintained more than 6 threads in the queue. Our worst case was on a real flow of 31 467 events, in which we had introduced two attack subflows, one on `sendmail` and one on `rpcinfo`, with interleaved events, and very far apart: our algorithm culminated to 19 threads, with an average of 7.1. (We didn't rely on any timeout.) Analysis showed that this good performance was a direct consequence of the green cuts described here, which allow us to kill threads that will violate shortest runs, *in advance*. We have also run ORCHIDS on the LSV network, in normal operation, during six months in 2005. It caught some attack attempts (mostly IP range probing), while only consuming a few minutes of system time total.

Red Cuts. By red cut, we mean any feature designed to kill threads arbitrarily, possibly missing some attacks. This is in analogy with Prolog's cut "!" [1]. While the concept may seem ugly, it is definitely required in practice. For example, remember that the complete `ptrace` signature has more transitions after state ⑦ than shown in (1), which collect actions done by the intruder before its processes are killed and its account closed. On reaching state ⑦, we use a red cut to instruct ORCHIDS to kill all threads with the same birthdate and signature.

So we collect intruder actions for only one instance of the attacks that succeeded with the same birthdate.

Red cuts are important, in general, to avert denial-of-service attacks against the intrusion prevention system. They allow a more direct control on the number of generated threads. Notably, they allow us to implement a form of the **Without** operator of Totel *et al.* [15], an effective tool to control the growth of the thread queue. This allows one to monitor one signature Σ_1, provided some other signature Σ_2 does not match in-between. For example, this allows us to monitor what a given process does, while it is alive, i.e., while no `exit` event is recorded by this process. This is implemented in ORCHIDS by running threads that monitor both Σ_1 and Σ_2. Once a complete run for Σ_2 is found, a red cut is issued that kills all pending instances of both Σ_2 and Σ_1.

6   Detecting Families of Attacks

The `ptrace` attack example may give the wrong impression that ORCHIDS requires one signature for each attack, requiring high maintenance overhead. Instead, one may write signatures that detect attacks by their effects, e.g., illicitly acquiring root privileges. In ORCHIDS, this is done by using the `pidtracker` signature, which has three states. There are transitions labeled with patterns matching calls to `fork`, `vfork`, `execve`, `setgid32`, and `setresuid32`, from state ① to ①. The latter two primitives are the only ones (in Linux) that may legitimately change one of the variants of the user id (i.e., user id, effective user id, saved user id), and these transitions are used to track all changes to these user ids by a given process (whose pid is stored in some rigid variable Pid). The first three primitives are monitored to track down all created processes. Even without red cuts, the shortest run semantics guarantees that no such call will be missed.

Additionally, there is a transition from ① to ②, tracking all calls made by the process with pid Pid with some user id different from the one obtained through tracking the events above. This detects any system call done with an unexpected user id, typically with user id 0 (root) while the process was normally running under a non-root user id. Finally, there is a transition from ① to ③, tracking calls to `exit` by process Pid, with a red cut to kill all threads monitoring the same process Pid.

The `pidtracker` rule is a practical way to detect instances of the `do_brk` attack [14], a vicious local-to-root attack in which the intruder repeatedly calls `do_brk` to allocate all available memory until kernel space is mapped into user space, and the process rights table in kernel space is modified to obtain root privileges. This is vicious in the sense that the only characteristic events of this attack are calls to `do_brk`, and a flurry of `SIGSEGV` signals. None of these are logged in any event logging system, for technical reasons. So a characteristic event subflow for this attack would be empty! And the `do_brk` attack has already been used, with disastrous effects: crackers used it to infect the Savannah servers (the master servers of the GNU distribution) and the Debian Linux master servers in 2004. Once the infection was suspected, these servers had to be turned down for manual inspection of all packages, and this took several weeks.

The `pidtracker` signature detects that an attack such as `do_brk` has succeeded as soon as the offending process invokes the next system call. An added benefit of this signature is that it will detect *all* such local-to-root attacks. It is important that signatures be able to detect whole *families* of attacks, to decrease the maintenance overhead of the signature base. In this case, we discovered in 2005 that the `pidtracker` signature, unchanged, would catch the newer but similar `map`, `munmap`, `mremap` attacks.

This also shows that, contrary to popular belief, it is possible to detect *zero-day attacks*, i.e., attacks which are launched before an advisory is made public. To wit, the `pidtracker` rule caught the recent Linux `vmsplice` attack [12], an attack published less than two months before our presentation at RV'08. (By the way, this attack gets completely undetected by the SELinux security enhancement to Linux, under standard reference policies, in `ENFORCED` mode.)

7 Conclusion

There is much more that could be said about ORCHIDS, in particular from a perspective more geared towards security administrators. One strand would have been to expand on the fact that ORCHIDS is both able to detect bad behavior (attacks described through signatures), or deviation from good behavior (where "good" is defined through some security policy, of which the setuid model of Section 6 was a simple example). Another would have been to show how ORCHIDS, originally a misuse detection system, can also work as an anomaly detection system: adding statistical classifiers to ORCHIDS is essentially a matter of adding an event logging module that outputs statistical data in the form of events, which ORCHIDS can then match. We could also have demonstrated how ORCHIDS detects complex, *network* attacks such as the `mod_ssl` attack [3], using such a statistical module [8]. Instead, we have chosen to center our presentation on algorithmic issues, taking the opportunity to describe both the core algorithm and the notion of cuts—in particular the *green* cuts that are so central to the efficiency of ORCHIDS—in as clear and intuitive a way as possible. We hope to have demonstrated how efficient multi-event intrusion prevention was possible, and how much monitor technology was relevant to this task. ORCHIDS is freely available under the Cecill 2 (GPL) license [6].

References

1. Clocksin, W., Mellish, C.: Programming in Prolog. Springer, Heidelberg (1981)
2. Manna, Z., Pnueli, A.: The Temporal Logic of Reactive and Concurrent Systems. Springer, Heidelberg (1991)
3. McDonald, J., A.L. Digital Ltd., The Bunker: OpenSSL SSLv2 malformed client key remote buffer overflow vulnerability (July 2002),
   http://www.securityfocus.com/bid/5363

4. Morin, B., Debar, H.: Correlation of intrusion symptoms: An application of chronicles. In: Vigna, G., Krügel, C., Jonsson, E. (eds.) RAID 2003. LNCS, vol. 2820, pp. 94–112. Springer, Heidelberg (2003)
5. Morin, B., Mé, L., Debar, H., Ducassé, M.: M2D2: A formal data model for IDS alert correlation. In: Wespi, A., Vigna, G., Deri, L. (eds.) RAID 2002. LNCS, vol. 2516. Springer, Heidelberg (2002)
6. Olivain, J.: ORCHIDS—real-time event analysis and temporal correlation for intrusion detection in information systems (2004),
http://www.lsv.ens-cachan.fr/orchids/
7. Olivain, J., Goubault-Larrecq, J.: The Orchids intrusion detection tool. In: Etessami, K., Rajamani, S.K. (eds.) CAV 2005. LNCS, vol. 3576, pp. 286–290. Springer, Heidelberg (2005)
8. Olivain, J., Goubault-Larrecq, J.: Detecting subverted cryptographic protocols by entropy checking. Research Report LSV-06-13, Laboratoire Spécification et Vérification, ENS Cachan, France, 19. pages (June 2006)
9. Pouzol, J.-P., Ducassé, M.: Formal specification of intrusion signatures and detection rules. In: Cervesato, I. (ed.) 15th IEEE Computer Security Foundations Workshop (CSFW 2002), pp. 64–76. IEEE Comp.Soc.Press, Los Alamitos (2002)
10. Purczyński, W.: Linux ptrace/execve race condition vulnerability. BugTraq Id 2529 (March 2001), http://www.securityfocus.com/bid/2529
11. Purczyński, W.: Linux kernel privileged process hijacking vulnerability. BugTraq Id 7112 (March 2003), http://www.securityfocus.com/bid/7112
12. Purczyński, W., qaaz.: Linux kernel prior to 2.6.24.2 'vmsplice_to_pipe()' local privilege escalation vulnerability (February 2008),
http://www.securityfocus.com/bid/27801
13. Roger, M., Goubault-Larrecq, J.: Log auditing through model checking. In: 14th IEEE Computer Security Foundations Workshop (CSFW 2001), pp. 220–236. IEEE Computer Society Press, Los Alamitos (2001)
14. Starzetz, P.: Linux kernel 2.4.22 do_brk() privilege escalation vulnerability, K-Otik ID 0446, CVE CAN-2003-0961 (December 2003),
http://www.k-otik.net/bugtraq/12.02.kernel.2422.php
15. Totel, E., Vivinis, B., Mé, L.: A language driven IDS for event and alert correlation. In: Deswarte, Y., Cuppens, F., Jajodia, S., Wang, L. (eds.) Security and Protection in Information Processing Systems, IFIP 18th World Computer Congress, TC11 19th International Information Security Conference, pp. 209–224. Kluwer, Dordrecht (2004)

Runtime Certification*

John Rushby

Computer Science Laboratory
SRI International
333 Ravenswood Avenue
Menlo Park, CA 94025, USA

Abstract. Software often must be certified for safety, security, or other critical properties. Traditional approaches to certification require the software, its systems context, and all their associated assurance artifacts to be available for scrutiny in their final, completed forms. But modern development practices often postpone the determination of final system configuration from design time to integration time, load time, or even runtime. Adaptive systems go beyond this and modify or synthesize functions at runtime.

Developments such as these require an overhaul to the basic framework for certification, so that some of its responsibilities also may be discharged at integration-, load- or runtime.

We outline a suitable framework, in which the basis for certification is changed from compliance with standards to the construction of explicit goals, evidence, and arguments (generally called an "assurance case"). We describe how runtime verification can be used within this framework, thereby allowing certification partially to be performed at runtime or, more provocatively, enabling "runtime certification."

1 Introduction

Runtime verification, whose technology provides for automated construction of monitors for formally specified properties [1], can be considered from two viewpoints: one sees it as a form of testing, performed as part of pre-deployment verification activities, while the other sees it as a form of post-deployment monitoring. From the latter viewpoint, the ability to generate monitors that guarantee certain properties can be seen as valuable evidence that might be considered in certification.

Traditional approaches to certification are based on adherence to standards or guidelines and do not readily embrace new technologies, such as runtime verification. But other trends, such as the use of adaptive systems for greater resilience, create situations where runtime verification and monitoring could be particularly valuable. Hence, there is increasing interest in alternative approaches to certification that can better exploit new technical opportunities, as well as accommodate

---

* This work was supported by National Science Foundation Grant CNS-0720908 and by NASA Cooperative Agreement NNX08AC64A.

M. Leucker (Ed.): RV 2008, LNCS 5289, pp. 21–35, 2008.

new hazards. Within suitable new frameworks, some of the evidence required for certification can be achieved by runtime monitoring—by analogy with runtime verification, this approach can, somewhat provocatively, be named "runtime certification."

We do not argue that runtime methods should replace traditional, pre-deployment methods of assurance and certification. Rather, the argument is that traditional methods have become sufficiently effective that accidents seldom occur within the anticipated operating envelope of the system concerned, so that attention has turned to attempting to maintain safe control in unanticipated circumstances, such as those involving major structural damage. Software that attempts to maintain control in these circumstances is necessarily adaptive, and possibly heuristic. The role of runtime verification in these circumstances is first, through assumption monitoring and anomaly detection to contribute to the detection of novel circumstances and, second, to check that any attempted recovery or adaptive control does not violate essential safety properties. It is also possible that technology related to runtime verification can extend its contribution from analysis toward synthesis of safe methods for adaptive control.

More controversially, runtime verification can contribute to detection and recovery from software failure. This is controversial because certified software in a critical system should not fail, and methods for "software fault tolerance" such as n-version programming have not been particularly successful and have fallen into disfavor. However, serious software-induced incidents have been observed in certified critical systems (we describe some involving commercial airplane later in the paper) and there is concern that these may become more significant as systems become more complex and evolve into systems-of-systems. An example is Next-Generation Air Traffic Control, where the software of different airplanes will interact to operate as a distributed system for maintaining separation without the ground-based supervision employed today. Experience suggests that the primary source of software failure will be violations of assumptions under which it was constructed and certified. Some of these violated assumptions may be due to oversights, some to unanticipated circumstances, and some to "software aging," where software remains constant while the environment in which it operates undergoes change [2].

This paper is organized as follows. The next section outlines an emerging new framework for certification, which we refer to as an "assurance case." The three sections that follow suggest how the framework of an assurance case can guide runtime monitoring for assumptions, anomalies, and safety, respectively. Section 6 considers diagnosis and recovery from failures detected by monitoring, and the final section provides a summary and conclusion.

2   Assurance Cases

Certification is a judgement that deploying a given system in a given context will not pose unacceptable risks of adverse consequences. The intellectual foundation for certification rests on three elements: *claims*, *evidence*, and *argument*. The claims identify the adverse consequences to be considered and the degree of risk considered acceptable; evidence comprises the results of analyses, reviews, and tests; the argument makes the case, based on the evidence, that the claims are satisfied.

The traditional approach to certification may be called "standards based" and largely requires (or strongly recommends) that system development follows prescribed processes (e.g., DO-178B [3] for airborne software) and generates specified evidence (e.g., MC/DC tests [4]). The standards-based approach focuses on evidence: the claims and the argument are largely implicit. Thus, it is not immediately clear whether the evidence from MC/DC testing is intended to support an argument for adequate testing, or one for high-quality requirements, or one for absence of unintended function. Standards-based certification can be very effective in fields where change is relatively slow, so that extensive experience can support the efficacy of the recommended processes and evidence. However, it is less appropriate when rapid innovation leads to systems that are very different to those anticipated in the standard, and it can inhibit the introduction of new assurance methods that provide novel kinds of evidence.

An emerging alternative to standards-based certification is known as a "safety case" [5]. In a safety case, the claims, evidence, and argument for assurance are presented explicitly and are evaluated by the certifying authority or some delegated third party. The exact form of the assurance case is a matter for negotiation by the parties involved, but must generally conform to a given outline (e.g., [6,7]). The advantage of the safety-case approach is that it focuses on the specifics of the system under consideration, and hence can tailor the methods of assurance appropriately (for this reason, it is sometimes referred to as a *goal-based* approach to assurance). The idea that certification should be based on explicit goal-based argumentation began in the UK (following inquiries into several disasters in the petro-chemical industry), and is becoming widely accepted—for example, it is a principal recommendation in a recent report of the National Research Council [8]—and it is now being generalized from safety, so that one hears of "dependability cases," "security cases," and general "assurance cases," which is the term we will use.

Assurance cases are attractive to runtime verification because they not only provide a flexible framework in which we may construct arguments to be discharged by evidence from runtime verification, but the assurance argument can be a source of properties to be monitored at runtime. We explore these topics in the following sections.

3   Runtime Assumption Monitoring

Certification is ultimately a human judgement that might not—or perhaps should not—be reduced to a completely formal or mechanized process. For this reason, some proponents of goal-based assurance look to Toulmin [9] rather than classical logic in framing assurance cases [10]; Toulmin stresses *justification* rather than *inference*. Toulmin's model of argument has the following six elements (from [11]), which are also portrayed in Figure 1.

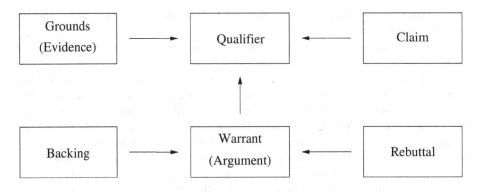

Fig. 1. Toulmin's Model of Argument

Claim: This is the expressed opinion or conclusion that the arguer wants accepted by the audience.

Grounds: This is the evidence or data for the claim.

Qualifier: An adverbial phrase indicating the strength of the claim (e.g., certainly, presumably, probably, possibly, etc.).

Warrant: The reasoning or argument (e.g., rules or principles) for connecting the grounds to the claim.

Backing: Further facts or reasoning used to support or legitimate the warrant.

Rebuttal: Circumstances or conditions that cast doubt on the argument; it represents any reservations or "exceptions to the rule" that undermine the reasoning expressed in the warrant or the backing for it.

The *claim, grounds,* and *warrant* of Toulmin's approach correspond to the claim, evidence, and argument of an assurance case. The overall structure will often be hierarchical, with the (sub)claim at one level providing the grounds (evidence) at a higher level. Toulmin's *qualifier, backing,* and *rebuttal* find no direct correspondence in an assurance case and, in fact, represent elements in Toulmin's rejection of formal logic.

The case that Toulmin advances against formal logic has some appeal when the topics of discourse are ethics, or aesthetics, say, but it is less persuasive for the topic of certification. There may certainly be areas of doubt in an assurance case, and human judgement and experience may be the appropriate recourse, but these doubts concern our ignorance of the true state of affairs (i.e., facts), rather than genuine judgements (where differences—on aesthetics, for example—cannot be resolved by facts, and reasonable people may come to different conclusions), so the presence of uncertainty need not lead us to reject formal logic.[1] Furthermore, Toulmin's use of adverbial *qualifiers* ("presumably," "possibly" and so on) rather than the "proves" ($\vdash$) or "models" ($\models$) of classical logic precludes use of automated tools such as theorem provers and model checkers.

---

[1] Although even within formal logic, there are controversies about the treatment of probabilistic uncertainty in evidential reasoning [12, 13].

An alternative to expressing doubts and partial knowledge in the qualifier is to express these as explicit assumptions in the hypotheses to a theorem (i.e., using qualifier "proves"). Thus, the elements of an assurance case could be (mechanically analyzed) theorems of the form

$$A_1, \ldots, A_n, S \vdash R$$

where $A_1, \ldots, A_n$ are the assumptions under which the system or design S satisfies requirements or claim R. Toulmin's *backing* and *rebuttal* and can likewise be represented by further assumptions and by additional case analysis, respectively.

Once we have made assumptions explicit, we can subject them to analysis in the same way as other claims: we can ask whether they can be substantiated by subsidiary arguments and evidence, in what circumstances might they be invalidated (cf. fault-tree analysis), and what might be the consequences if they are false (cf. failure modes and effects analysis). And, of course, we can sometimes check them at runtime. We do not describe here how to generate suitable monitors for runtime assumption verification—we suggest use of existing languages and frameworks for runtime verification, such as EAGLE or RULER [14] and Monitoring-Oriented Programming (MOP) [15]—but we note that one of the strengths of runtime verification is that it provides technology to synthesize monitors automatically from their formal descriptions.

Our central point is that construction of formal arguments in support of assurance cases helps make assumptions explicit—and in a form that makes them available for runtime verification. Runtime detection of an assumption violation is not necessarily a harbinger of imminent system failure or safety violation, for the assumption might not be required for the specific execution scenario in progress (but then the assurance case could have been refined by a sharper analysis). Suitable responses to an assumption violation could range from merely logging it and waiting for a more definite indication of trouble, to proactively initiating some repair or fault recovery activity. We consider these in Sections 5 and 6, respectively, but first we consider other kinds of runtime "early warning" or anomaly detection.

4   Runtime Anomaly Detection

Not all assumptions can be verified at runtime. For example, one of the most serious in-flight incidents due to software occurred to a Boeing 777, registration 9M-MRG, near Perth, Australia, on 1 August 2005 [16]. The air data inertial reference unit (ADIRU) performed a restart in circumstances where two of its accelerometers were faulty—whereas the restart algorithm assumed at most one accelerometer would be faulty. The outcome was a series of wild excursions as the autopilot responded to essentially random inputs from its ADIRU. It is not always feasible to detect faulty components (if it were, fault tolerance would be easy), so direct assumption monitoring would not have been feasible in this case.

An alternative to monitoring assumptions and properties that are explicit in the requirements or in the assurance case is to monitor for properties learned by "experience": that is, we check that the system is behaving "as usual." This idea has its roots in methods for intrusion detection in computer security [17], which were subsequently refined to detect infections by computer viruses. An activated virus causes a program to change its behavior—as does an activated fault or violated assumption; hence, it is plausible that methods for detecting anomalies caused by viruses may also detect manifestations of a developing problem.

Most modern methods for anomaly detection work by constructing a model of the normal behavior of the software, in terms, for example, of the invariants that it maintains, or the execution paths that it follows. A program's execution paths can represented as a context-free grammar or, more crudely, as a set of digraphs on monitored control points (i.e., the set of all pairs of monitored control points—which are often system calls—that are encountered consecutively). The program is monitored in execution and an anomaly alarm is raised whenever execution departs from the recorded model. Following the lead of Wagner and Dean [18], models are often generated by automated formal analysis: for example, an overapproximation to the set of expected execution paths can be constructed using static analysis, and invariants also can be generated in this way.

However, our context for anomaly detection is rather different than that of computer security, and this makes models constructed by static analysis less useful. In computer security, the context is a program that has been changed by activation of a virus, whereas our context is an unchanged program whose behavior has been changed by violation of an assumption (which we can think of as a bug if the assumption is unrecorded). Thus, in our context, static analysis will generate its models from a program in which the bug or faulty assumption is already present, and monitoring will therefore be ineffective. We need, instead, to generate models from bug-free representations of the program.

One way to do this is to generate models from the behavior of the program during test. Critical software is subjected to very thorough testing (e.g., MC/DC coverage in the case of DO-178B Level A) so that models generated from tests should be very accurate, but they will not include faulty behaviors due to activated bugs or violated assumptions—for if those were to arise in test, they would be detected and fixed. The dynamic analyzer Daikon [19] can synthesize invariants from behavior observed in test, and digraphs or other compact representations of observed control flow can be constructed by monitoring test executions. By these means, we can build models that allow runtime monitoring to detect when software behavior departs from that observed during test. Monitoring execution against control flows encountered during test is related to the "vital coded processor" used in railway signaling [20] and is also suggested in the IEC 61508 standard [21, Part 7, page 159].

Violation of an invariant or control flow derived from tests may indicate a genuine error, or simply an untested scenario. If the latter is considered the more likely, then logging the anomaly, rather than initiating repair or fault recovery, may be the most suitable response. Logs of detected anomalies then provide a way to identify inadequately tested or poorly documented cases, and also provide information for *post-deployment testing* and *cooperative bug isolation* [22].

5   Runtime Safety Monitoring

Runtime monitoring for assumptions and anomalies can give early warning that things may be going wrong, but monitoring requirements and safety properties should provide more definitive indications of trouble or, dually, more assurance that the system is operating safely. However, this expectation must be tempered by consideration of the sources of the monitored properties.

Obvious sources for properties to monitor are the requirements for the software concerned. The problem with this choice is that critical software is developed and assured to exacting standards that provide rather effective guarantees that requirements—particularly low-level requirements—will be satisfied. For example, flight-critical software is generally developed and assured according to the guidelines DO-178B Level A [3]. These demand construction of high- and low-level software requirements and rigorous testing of the code against these requirements; in particular, tests generated from the low-level software requirements must achieve MC/DC coverage on the code [4]. These development and assurance processes seem very effective in producing software that is correct with respect to its requirements. Furthermore, these requirements are generally at the unit level and the correctness of the software is often robust at this level; that is to say, there may be problems present at the system level, but individual software units will still be operating correctly according to their unit-level requirements.

Thus, there is unlikely to be much benefit in monitoring requirements at or below the unit level: not only is critical software generally correct with respect to this level of specification, but larger problems may not be manifested at this level. Instead, we need to monitor properties that more directly relate to the safe functioning of the system, and that are more likely to be violated when problems are present—and this invites the question of how might we obtain such properties.

Certification guidelines such as DO-178B offer rather little support in this enterprise because the goal of assurance for the software development process is to establish that the delivered software exactly matches (i.e., is *correct* with respect to) its requirements, rather than that it is safe. Thus Conmy [23] and Amey and Hilton [24] argue that DO-178B is about software correctness, not system safety ("there is no relation of the software to the system hazards, the developer can only state that the whole box has been tested to level A") and Ankrum and Kromholz [25] find no clear link between desired system properties and many of the evidence artifacts required by DO-178B.

However, the system-level arguments and certification evidence for airplane safety are based on various kinds of system and safety analysis such as hazard analysis, failure modes and effects analysis, and fault tree analysis (e.g., [26,27]), and these penetrate down into subsystems and the top-level requirements for the software. Thus, although it is not couched in these terms, the upper levels of assurance for airplane safety, and possibly other classes of systems, too, already have much in common with the notion of a safety or assurance case, as introduced in Section 2.

Thus, we envisage that with modest amendments to current practices for system development and assurance, it will be feasible to introduce elements of a formal assurance case, and that this will yield explicit safety claims that can be subjected to runtime monitoring. Runtime monitoring for critical properties is not new: the idea of a "reference monitor" for security was introduced in 1972 [28]. Later, Rushby analyzed the general class of properties that can be *guaranteed* by monitoring [29], and this analysis was developed further by Wika and Knight [30] and, for the case of security properties, by Schneider [31]. Reduced to essentials, these analyses demonstrate that only safety (as opposed to liveness [32]) properties can be ensured by monitoring.

In this regard, it is worth recalling another serious in-flight incident due to software. An Airbus A340-642, registration G-VATL, suffered a fuel emergency on 8 February 2005 [33]. The plane was over Europe on a flight from Hong Kong to London when two engines flamed out. The crew found that the tanks supplying those engines were empty and those for the other two engines were very low. They declared an emergency and landed at Amsterdam. The subsequent investigation reported that two Fuel Control Monitoring Computers (FCMCs) are responsible for pumping fuel between the tanks on this type of airplane. The two FCMCs cross-compare and the "healthiest" one drives the outputs to the data bus. In this case, both FCMCs had known faults (but complied with the minimum capabilities required for flight); unfortunately, one of the faults in the one judged healthiest was the inability to drive the data bus. Thus, although it gave correct commands to the fuel pumps (there was plenty of fuel distributed in other tanks), these were never received. Backup systems were not invoked because the FCMCs indicated that not both were failed.

Monitoring low-level requirements for the FCMCs would not detect this problem, since faulty requirements were the root of the problem. At the top level, the failure was a *loss of function*, so that the high-level requirement most directly violated was a liveness property: one that says "something good"—i.e., pumping fuel—eventually happens. As noted above, monitoring is effective only for safety properties: ones that say "something bad" does not occur, so it might seem that monitoring would not be effective for this example.

This conundrum is easily solved: most critical systems perform some kind of real-time control function, and a liveness property constrained by a deadline becomes a safety property. For example, "the fuel pumps should activate at least once per hour" is a safety property that can be monitored. In all likelihood, there are many other safety properties suitable for monitoring in this system (e.g., those concerning the acceptable distribution of fuel among the different tanks, or minimum levels in the tanks feeding the engines).

The other classes of major system faults—that is, *malfunction* and *unintended function*—are safety properties and should be suitable for runtime safety monitoring. Other properties that seem suitable for monitoring are interfaces and invariants for distributed algorithms (in the spirit of *interface automata* [34]) and cooperatively maintained data structures (in the spirit of *robust data structures* [35]). Although these may be below the level of properties cited in an assurance case, they do relate to component interactions, and so assurance of their health is a valuable benefit.

6 Diagnosis, Recovery, and Mitigation

Runtime verification for assumptions, anomalies, and safety properties can deliver strong evidence for an assurance case and, ultimately, for certification. As we noted in the introduction, a principal driver for adoption of these techniques is the desire to maintain safe control in the presence of unanticipated events. The idea is that control will be maintained by various "adaptive" methods, and that runtime verification will provide some assurance that these are operating safely. However, runtime verification derives from formal methods and closely related techniques from this field could provide assured mechanization for some of the "adaptive" tasks—such as diagnosis, and recovery or mitigation of unplanned events—that currently often use ad-hoc methods.

The component whose monitor raises an alarm may not be the source of the fault. Given some symptoms in the form of alarms from software health monitors, *fault diagnosis* is the problem of identifying the source and nature of the fault. Early approaches to fault diagnosis in physical systems used rule-based "expert systems" but these proved fragile and modern methods are based on model-based reasoning "from first principles" [36].

The idea of model-based diagnosis is to perturb a model of the system until the modeled behavior matches that observed. The diagnosis is then derived from the perturbation. Models can range from simple graphs representing connectivity among components to interacting state machines. Models are perturbed by replacing the standard model of a component by one that is faulty; each component is generally provided with a set of fault models (or a single model that can manifest different faults under control of a set of Boolean "switches"), that may range from very specific kinds of fault to a generic "something's wrong," which may be represented by a fully nondeterministic state machine, or communication of a distinguished "bad" data value. The preferred diagnosis is generally one that accounts for the observed symptoms with the smallest number of postulated faults. Calculation of a diagnosis is performed using methods related to model checking, which effectively reduce the problem to one that can be solved using techniques from automated deduction such as SAT or SMT solving. More elaborate diagnostic methods can take probabilities into account, and the underlying methods of deduction then involve Markov decision processes, which can be solved by Monte Carlo methods or by model counting [37].

Much of the research in diagnosis is concerned with the challenge of making exactly the correct identification of the underlying fault. However, although there may be many possible faults, the number of possible reconfigurations or other mitigating actions may be rather few. For the case of jet engines, which were the target of NASA's pioneering Faultfinder system [38], there are just four possible actions: do nothing, reduce power, shut the engine down, or discharge its fire extinguisher. There is no point in performing diagnosis to greater precision than that required to identify the appropriate mitigation. Thus, we propose that diagnosis should be performed in tandem with the search for an appropriate mitigation. Some mitigations (e.g., reconfigurations) can be found through an extension to model-based diagnosis ([39] was the first to propose this), while others require methods akin to AI planning, or program synthesis.

Local mitigations for faults that are attributed to software include retrying a computation, reverting to a checkpointed state, or performing a reset or reboot [40]. Sometimes it will be preferable to adjust input data rather than the system state (cf. *data diversity* [41]): for example, if a sensor sample provokes overflow or division by zero, then we can perturb it slightly, or substitute a previous value (e.g., from a prior iteration in a cyclic control loop). Alternatively, we may be able to reconfigure the system so that a faulty software component is replaced by a diverse alternate. *Recovery blocks* [42] provide a systematic framework for such reconfigurations; alternates may perform graceful degradation rather than exactly reproduce the behavior of the failed primary, and a final alternate may be verified to guarantee some safe minimal functionality (this is *provably safe programming* [43]; a similar idea appears in monitoring-oriented programming and in the work of Sha [44]).

Local mitigations such as those described above require additional implementation mechanism, add complication, and are of uncertain effectiveness. In some cases, the mitigation may be more hazardous than the fault. For example, on 12 May 1997, hard-coded anomaly detection and mitigation caused the display system (EFIS) of American Airlines Flight 903 (an Airbus A300) to go blank: the indicated roll rate of more than 40 degrees/second was considered implausible, and so a bus reset was performed. In fact, the pilots were attempting recovery from a major upset and the roll rate was real; the loss of all instruments at this critical time jeopardized the recovery.

Just as we believe that runtime monitoring will be performed most effectively against properties derived from a system-level assurance case, so we suspect that diagnosis and mitigation will best be performed at the system level also. Safety critical systems such as airplanes already contain massive, well-designed redundancy to protect against anticipated hardware faults, and it will often be possible to invoke this so that safe operation may continue in the presence of unanticipated events or software faults. For example, in the case of the 777 ADIRU problem, we could switch the autopilot to a different source of air data. Even when redundant components have identical designs and are running identical software, their internal state and sensor inputs are likely to differ slightly. Hence, the circumstances that provoke failure in one component (e.g., two faulty accelerometers) may not be present in another, and the same assumptions and the same software that has failed in one component may continue to operate perfectly well in the other.

Diagnosis at the system level may involve a number of steps (e.g., to see if the symptoms persist when various components are reset or shut down) and mitigation may also require several steps rather than a simple reconfiguration. In these cases, we need to synthesize a multi-step *program* of action and the appropriate framework for doing this is supervisory controller synthesis, introduced by Ramadge and Wonham [45]. Controller synthesis can be formulated as a game between the controller and its environment: the controller seeks a strategy to maintain or achieve a given property no matter how the environment behaves. Simple instances, such as certain kinds of AI planning, can be reduced to SAT solving—for example, when the system is deterministic with respect to the inputs and the task is to find a sequence of inputs that places the system in some specific state. In more complicated cases, the controller must really be a strategy that reacts to the environment rather than a simple sequence or a schedule. In this situation, the controller synthesis problem can be solved using techniques derived from model checking [46].

The advantage of a formal, model-based approach to mitigation is that it can consider multiple possible diagnoses and calculate the best overall response. The model can also be cognizant of system-level safety properties, so that we can be sure that an action that seems reasonable at the local level does not have adverse consequences at a higher level (as in the case of American Flight 903). Above all, correctness of the formally synthesized approach is guaranteed, relative to the model. Thus, assurance and certification can focus on the models employed, unlike more heuristic methods whose behavior must be determined experimentally.

It is likely that mitigations undertaken at the system level will require participation by the human operators (e.g., to power-cycle a subsystem or to switch to a backup system). In these cases it will be important that the recovery and mitigation procedures communicate effectively with the operators so that they understand the possible states of the system, the available courses of action, and the reasons behind those recommended. One way to do this is to include an explicit representation of the information available to the operators as part of the model that drives the search for diagnosis and mitigations. The feasibility of doing this is supported by [47], which shows how pilots' *mental models* can be represented and used in formal analysis to help avoid mode confusion and other forms of automation surprise, and to guide selection of information presented to the pilots.

7   Summary and Conclusion

There is extensive prior work on runtime monitoring for assurance and for error detection and recovery (e.g., [48,49]). The main novelty in the approach proposed here is use of an assurance case as the source of monitored properties.

Runtime monitoring of safety properties related to an assurance case can provide potent evidence to support the case. Such runtime evidence is most useful in adaptive systems that attempt to maintain safe control in unanticipated circumstances that are beyond those considered in the standard design and predeployment certification of the system. Assurance delivered by runtime monitoring can therefore contribute to certification of systems that follow a "never give up" strategy, in the spirit of autonomic and resilient systems [50].

Unanticipated circumstances and violation of assumptions may cause even certified software to fail. Monitoring for assumptions—also derived from an assurance case—and for anomalies—which may be regarded as departures from behaviors encountered in test—can give early warning that problems are at hand, while monitoring for safety properties can give assurance that those problems are being contained or, dually, that they are not and that recovery should be attempted. Formal methods related to runtime verification can provide automated techniques for diagnosis, mitigation, and recovery. These methods for monitoring, analysis, and synthesis are driven by formal models, so their assurance can focus on the models. This may be contrasted with ad-hoc methods, where assurance must often be obtained experimentally.

Complex modern systems, such as airplanes, increasingly incorporate sophisticated functions for sensing, monitoring, and managing the "health" of the system; in airplanes these functions are called *Integrated Vehicle Health Management* (IVHM). We hope the techniques proposed here will contribute to the effectiveness and to the assurance and certification of IVHM systems, and to the emerging field of *software health management*.

Acknowledgment. I appreciate helpful discussions on these topics with Robin Bloomfield and Bev Littlewood of City University, and with my SRI colleagues Bruno Dutertre, Bob Riemenschneider, and Hassen Saïdi.

References

1. Havelund, K., Rosu, G.: Efficient monitoring of safety properties. Software Tools for Technology Transfer 6(2), 158–173 (2004)
2. Parnas, D.: Software aging. In: 16th International Conference on Software Engineering, pp. 279–287. IEEE Computer Society, Sorrento (May 1994)
3. Requirements and Technical Concepts for Aviation Washington, DC: DO-178B: Software Considerations in Airborne Systems and Equipment Certification, This document is known as EUROCAE ED-12B in Europe (December 1992)
4. Chilenski, J.J., Miller, S.P.: Applicability of modified condition/decision coverage to software testing. Issued for information under FAA memorandum ANM-106N:93-20 (August 1993)
5. Bishop, P., Bloomfield, R.: A methodology for safety case development. In: Safety-Critical Systems Symposium, Birmingham, UK (February 1998), http://www.adelard.com/resources/papers/pdf/sss98web.pdf
6. UK Ministry of Defence: Interim Defence Standard 00-56, Issue 3: Safety Management Requirements for Defence Systems. Part 2: Guidance on Establishing a Means of Complying with Part 1 (December 2004)
7. Safety Regulation Group, UK Civil Aviation Authority: Air Traffic Services Safety Requirements, CAP 670 (2005)
8. Jackson, D., Thomas, M., Millett, L.I.: Software for Dependable Systems: Sufficient Evidence? National Academies Press, Washington (May 2007)
9. Toulmin, S.E.: The Uses of Argument. Cambridge University Press, Cambridge (2003); Updated edition (the original is dated 1958)

10. Bishop, P., Bloomfield, R., Guerra, S.: The future of goal-based assurance cases. In: DSN Workshop on Assurance Cases: Best Practices, Possible Obstacles, and Future Opportunities, Florence, Italy (July 2004), http://www.aitcnet.org/AssuranceCases/agenda.html

11. Adelman, L., Lehner, P.E., Cheikes, B.A., Taylor, M.F.: An empirical evaluation of structured argumentation using the Toulmin argument formalism. IEEE Transactions on Systems, Man, and Cybernetics—Part A: Systems and Humans 37(3), 340–347 (2007)

12. Fitelson, B.: Studies in Bayesian Confirmation Theory. PhD thesis, Department of Philosophy, University of Wisconsin, Madison (May 2001), http://fitelson.org/thesis.pdf

13. Joyce, J.M.: On the plurality of probabilist measures of evidential relevance. In: Bayesian Epistemology Workshop of the 26th International Wittgenstein Symposium, Kirchberg, Austria (August 2003), http://www.uni-konstanz.de/ppm/kirchberg/Joyce_1.pdf

14. Barringer, H., Rydeheard, D., Havelund, K.: Rule systems for run-time monitoring: From Eagle to RuleR. In: Sokolsky, O., Taşıran, S. (eds.) RV 2007. LNCS, vol. 4839, pp. 111–125. Springer, Heidelberg (2007)

15. Monitoring-Oriented Programming (MOP) home page, http://fsl.cs.uiuc.edu/index.php/Monitoring-Oriented_Programming

16. Australian Transport Safety Bureau: In-flight upset event, 240 km northwest of Perth, WA, Boeing Company 777-200, 9M-MRG, Reference number Mar2007/DOTARS 50165. aair200503722.aspx. (August 1, 2005) (March 2007), http://www.atsb.gov.au/publications/investigation_reports/2005/AAIR/aair200503722.aspx

17. Denning, D.E.: An intrusion-detection model. IEEE Transactions on Software Engineering 13(2), 222–232 (1987)

18. Wagner, D., Dean, D.: Intrusion detection via static analysis. In: Proceedings of the Symposium on Security and Privacy, pp. 156–168. IEEE Computer Society, Oakland (May 2001)

19. Ernst, M.D., Cockrell, J., Griswold, W.G., Notkin, D.: Dynamically discovering likely program invariants to support program evolution. IEEE Transactions on Software Engineering 27(2), 99–123 (2001)

20. Chapront, P.: Vital coded processor and safety related software design. In: Frey, H.H. (ed.) Safety of Computer Control Systems (SAFECOMP 1992), Zurich, Switzerland, International Federation of Automatic Control, pp. 141–145 (October 1992)

21. International Electrotechnical Commission Geneva, Switzerland: IEC 61508— Functional Safety of Electrical/Electronic/Programmable Electronic Safety-Related Systems (March 2004)

22. Liblit, B.: Cooperative Bug Isolation. Winning Thesis of the 2005 ACM Doctoral Dissertation Competition. LNCS, vol. 4440. Springer, Heidelberg (May 2007)

23. Conmy, P.: Safety Analysis of Computer Resource Management Software. PhD thesis, Department of Computer Science, University of York, UK (2005)

24. Amey, P., Hilton, A.J.: Practical experiences of safety- and security-critical technologies. Ada User Journal 22(1) (March 2001)

25. Ankrum, T.S., Kromholz, A.H.: Structured assurance cases: Three common standards. In: High-Assurance Systems Engineering Symposium (HASE 2005). IEEE Computer Society, Heidelberg (2005)

26. Society of Automotive Engineers: Aerospace Recommended Practice (ARP) 4754: Certification Considerations for Highly-Integrated or Complex Aircraft Systems (November 1996)
27. Society of Automotive Engineers: Aerospace Recommended Practice (ARP) 4761: Guidelines and Methods for Conducting the Safety Assessment Process on Civil Airborne Systems and Equipment (December 1996)
28. Anderson, J.P.: Computer security technology planning study. Technical Report ESD-TR-73-51, US Air Force (October 1972) (Two volumes)
29. Rushby, J.: Kernels for safety? In: Anderson, T. (ed.) Safe and Secure Computing Systems, pp. 210–220. Blackwell Scientific Publications, Malden (1989)
30. Wika, K.G., Knight, J.C.: On the enforcement of software safety policies. In: COMPASS 1995 (Proceedings of the Tenth Annual Conference on Computer Assurance), Gaithersburg, MD, IEEE Washington Section, pp. 83–93 (June 1995)
31. Schneider, F.: Enforceable security policies. ACM Transactions on Information and System Security 3(1), 30–50 (2000)
32. Alpern, B., Schneider, F.B.: Defining liveness. Information Processing Letters 21(4), 181–185 (1985)
33. UK Air Investigations Branch: AAIB Special Bulletin S1/2005: Airbus A340-642, G-VATL (2005),
http://www.aaib.dft.gov.uk/cms_resources/G-VATL_Special_Bulletin1.pdf
34. de Alfaro, L., Henzinger, T.A.: Interface automata. In: Proceedings of the Ninth Annual Symposium on Foundations of Software Engineering (FSE), Association for Computing Machinery, pp. 109–120 (2001)
35. Taylor, D.J., Morgan, D.E., Black, J.P.: Redundancy in data structures: Improving software fault tolerance. IEEE Transactions on Software Engineering 6(6), 585–594 (1980)
36. Reiter, R.: A theory of diagnosis from first principles. Artificial Intelligence 32, 57–95 (1987)
37. Williams, B.C., Ingham, M., Chung, S.H., Elliott, P.H.: Model-based programming of intelligent embedded systems and robotic space explorers. Proceedings of the IEEE 91(3), 212–237 (2003)
38. Abbott, K.H., Schutte, P.C., Palmer, M.T., Ricks, W.R.: Faultfinder: A diagnostic expert system with graceful degradation for onboard aircraft applications. In: Proceedings, 14th Symposium on Aircraft Integrated Monitoring Systems, Friedrichshafen, W. Germany (September 1987)
39. Crow, J., Rushby, J.: Model-based reconfiguration: Toward an integration with diagnosis. In: Proceedings, AAAI 1991, Anaheim, CA, vol. 2, pp. 836–841 (July 1991)
40. Grottke, M., Trivedi, K.: Fighting bugs: Remove, retry, replicate, and rejuvenate. IEEE Computer, 107–109 (February 2007)
41. Ammann, P.E., Knight, J.C.: Data diversity: An approach to software fault tolerance. IEEE Transactions on Computers 37(4), 418–425 (1998)
42. Anderson, T., Kerr, R.: Recovery blocks in action: A system supporting high reliability. In: Proceedings of the 2nd International Conference on Software Engineering, pp. 447–457. IEEE Computer Society, San Francisco (1976)
43. Anderson, T., Witty, R.W.: Safe programming. BIT 18, 1–8 (1978)
44. Sha, L.: Using simplicity to control complexity. IEEE Software 18(4), 20–28 (2001)
45. Ramadge, P.J.G., Wonham, W.M.: The control of discrete event systems. Proceedings of the IEEE 77(1), 81–98 (1989)
46. Pnueli, A., Rosner, R.: On the synthesis of a reactive module. In: 16th ACM Symposium on Principles of Programming Languages, pp. 179–190 (1989)

47. Rushby, J.: Using model checking to help discover mode confusions and other automation surprises. Reliability Engineering and System Safety 75(2), 167–177 (2002)
48. Bauer, A., Leucker, M., Schallhart, C.: Model-based runtime analysis of distributed reactive systems. In: Proceedings of the Australian Software Engineering Conference (ASWEC 2006), Sydney, Australia, pp. 243–252 (April 2006)
49. Lee, I., Kannan, S., Kim, M., Sokolsky, O., Viswanathan, M.: Runtime assurance based on formal specifications. In: Proceedings of International Conference on Parallel and Distributed Processing Techniques and Applications, Las Vegas, NV, pp. 279–287 (June 1999)
50. Hollnagel, E., Woods, D.D., Leveson, N. (eds.): Resilience Engineering, Ashgate (2005)

Model-Based Run-Time Checking of Security Permissions Using Guarded Objects*

Jan Jürjens

Computing Department, The Open University, GB
http://www.jurjens.de/jan

Abstract. In this paper we deal with the application of run-time checking to enforce requirements which, because of their nature, cannot be
enforced statically. More specifically, it deals with the problem how to
control access to objects within an object-oriented system at run-time in
a way that enforces an overall security policy. It aims to improve on the
ad-hoc (and often untrustworthy) way it is currently done in practice by
automatically generating the run-time checks from a model-based specification of the system that captures the security policy. Concretely, the
models are expressed in the UML security extension UMLsec, and the
run-time checks that are generated for Java programs rely on GuardedObjects.

1 Introduction

A commonly used security concept is permission-based access control, i.e. asso-
ciating entities (e.g., users or objects) in a system with permissions and allowing
an entity to perform a certain action on another entity only if it owns the necessary permissions. Designing and enforcing a correct permission-based access
control policy (with respect to the general security requirements) is very hard,
especially because of the complex interplay between the system entities. This is
aggravated by the fact that permissions can also be delegated to other objects
for actions to be performed on the delegating object's behalf.

Especially dynamic access control mechanisms such as provided by Java since
the JDK 1.2 security architecture [Gon99] in the form of GuardedObjects can be
difficult to administer since it is easy to forget an access check. If the appropriate access controls are not performed, the security of the entire system may
be compromised. Additionally, access control may be granted indirectly and unintentionally by granting access to an object containing the signature key that
enables access to another object.

In this paper, we present an approach for the integration of run-time checks
to enforce permissions into early design models, in particular for object-oriented
design using UML. We both describe static modelling aspects, where we introduce owned and required permissions and capabilities for their delegation into

---

* This work was partially funded by the Royal Society within the project Model-based
Formal Security Analysis of Crypto Protocol Implementations.

M. Leucker (Ed.): RV 2008, LNCS 5289, pp. 36–50, 2008.

class diagrams, and dynamic modelling aspects. Dynamic modelling aspects are characterized by the use and delegation of permissions within a interaction of the system objects, modelled as a sequence diagram. To gain confidence in the correctness of the permission-based access control policy, we define checks for the consistency of the permission-related aspects within the static and dynamic models and between these models. For the implementation as run-time checks, we show a way to transfer permissions using cryptographic certificates and provide a formal analysis. We also address the realization of the run-time checks in Java using GuardedObjects. We demonstrate our approach at the example of a model of an instant message service.

The work presented here is part of a more general approach towards model-based security engineering visualized in Fig. 1 a) (see [Jür04]).

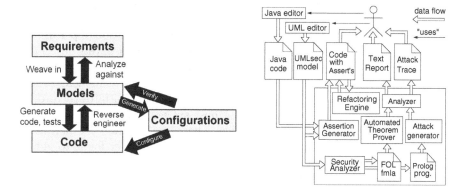

Fig. 1. a) Model-based Security Engineering; b) Model-based Security Tool Suite

2   Run-Time Checks for OO Security Permissions

Objects in object-oriented systems usually interact with each other in the following way: one object becomes an actor and performs an action on another (passive) object. The passive object will be changed or activated by these actions. Activation means that the entity will also become an actor in order to perform actions on other entities.

In security-critical systems, it is crucial to have control over the execution of the actions. For this purpose, the execution of the actions is controlled by permissions. An actor is only allowed to initiate actions on certain objects when he owns the associated permissions.

In the context of such a model, we denote objects which own or define permissions as *permission-secured* objects. Permission-secured objects are the smallest entities on which permissions can be defined. Not every object in a system must be a permission-secured object. The permissions are attached to the actions that can be performed on an object. It is possible to define several permissions, which must all be owned for performing an action. In the following, we write the names of objects, classes and methods in *italics*, and denote permissions and corresponding model annotations in sansserif.

As an example, we consider a simple file. There is the permission-secured object *file*. The file defines two protected actions: *read*, which is protected by the permission read, and *write*, protected by the permission write and the permission read. These permissions are valid for the whole *file* object. We assume the protection of lower levels like lines or characters is not possible.

There are two types of owning permissions: there are permissions which are defined statically, but there is also the possibility to delegate permissions to other objects. Delegation is necessary to enable an activated object to fulfil the jobs an actor has given to it, but where the activated object itself does not have the necessary rights.

In this case, it should be possible for the delegate to act in the name of the actor. For this purpose, it is necessary to restrict the given permissions to the ones actually needed, to limit security risks. It is also necessary that it is always recognizable that the delegate acts in commission. Therefore re-delegation of permissions to other objects is an important issue. It is possible that the delegating object does not know the final delegate at delegation time.

An example for a re-delegation is the use of an account statement printer. The account owner wants to get his account statement and initiates the process. As he is not able to enquire the banking host system himself, he charges the account statement printer with doing this. Therefore, he gives the permission for reading the account information to the machine, in order for it to get the information in behalf of the account owner.

As we regard this example in more detail, it turns out that it is suitable to restrict this authorization because of two aspects:

– The printer should be able to make use of the authorization only once. If it is possible to use the authorization more than once, the printer can print the owners account balance to every other customer.
– There should be a timeout, after which the authorization expires. If there is no timeout, it is possible that the printer makes use of the authorization after the customer has left the bank.

3   Run-Time Checks for Security Permissions with UMLsec

To model the permission-based security aspects of a system, we must identify the permission-secured objects. The smallest entities on which actions may be executed are the objects. Thus, every object that is defined in a system may be a permission-secured object.

The next step is to define the protected actions. The usual way to change an object's state from the outside is to invoke a corresponding method. So it is necessary to treat method invocations as security-critical actions and thus to protect methods by permissions.

Another way of changing an object's state is to read or write public attributes directly. Although public attributes are not a good way of object design, reading and writing them must also be regarded as an action. While it is possible to restrict access to public variables at the modelling level of a system, it is not possible to do so in common object oriented programming languages. The best way to cope with this problem is to use only private variables in combination with *get* and *set* methods.

Let us reconsider the file system example. In this case, we can model two objects: a *file* object and a *line* object, where the *file* object is an aggregation of many *line* objects. The only way to access the *line* objects is to use the methods of the corresponding *file* object. The methods of the *file* object are protected by permissions, whereas the methods the *line* object places at the *file* object's disposal are not. As these methods are only available to the *file* object, it is not necessary to make the *line* object a permission-secured object.

In a first step, we will look at the static description of the permissions in an system model. After that, we describe the permission-related aspects of the dynamic interaction of the system regarding the activities the system is designed for.

3.1   Static Definitions

First, we describe the static aspects of an integration of permission-based security into UML models. For this purpose, we consider class diagrams and deal with the following questions:

- Which classes define permission-secured objects?
- Which permissions will be assigned to these objects at instantiation time? These permissions are the same for all objects instantiated from the same class.
- Which methods (and public attributes) will be protected by permissions?
- What kinds of permissions are these?
- Which of the assigned permissions may be delegated? How can one define to which type of objects they may be delegated?

First of all, the permission-secured objects will be identified by marking classes that define or own permission objects with the stereotype « permission−secured ». If an object owns certain permissions on other objects at instantiation time, this is also stated at this place. A tagged value is associated with the « permission − secured » stereotype consisting of a list of tuples structured as follows: {permission = [(*class*, permission)]}. The first parameter of the tuple indicates the class on which the permission is valid. The second parameter names the permission.

Methods and public attributes to which access is restricted are marked with the stereotype « permissioncheck » and an associated tagged value containing the list of permissions needed for access ({permission = [permission]}). This list is only a simple list naming the permissions. The association to classes is given by the class implementing the method or containing the attribute. To allow objects of certain classes classified as reliable unrestricted access to particular methods and public variables, it is possible to associate a second tag to the stereotype « permission_check ». The tagged value {no_permission_needed = [*class*]} indicates that objects of the named classes need no permissions for access.

Although delegation is a dynamic process, which comes into effect at execution time, at this point of view it is of interest which permissions can be delegated at all, and if so, to which class of objects these permissions may be delegated.

Classes that can delegate at least some of their permissions have the following tag: {*delegation* = [(*class, permission, role/class*)]}. The first two parameters name the permission which is delegated together with the class it belongs to. The third parameter names the class to which the permission can be delegated.

The last aspect to be regarded in the static class definition is inheritance. Definitions belonging to the modelling of permissions are inherited in the same way as all other definitions are inherited. Redefining a method or an attribute makes it necessary to also redefine the stereotypes and tags for permission modelling.

Now let us describe the example of the Instant Messaging Service which will be used to illustrate the definitions in the remainder of this paper. The class diagram for this example contains the *SubscriptionClient* and the *InstantMessenger* on the client side, which define permission-secured objects. The class *SubscriptionClient* contains the permission subscribe on objects of class *SubscriptionServer* and the permission receive on objects of class *InstantMessenger*. In the model, this is reflected by the tagged value {permission=[(*SubscriptionServer*, subscribe), (*InstantMessenger*, receive)]}. The latter permission is marked for delegation to objects of class *Forwarder*. This is defined by the tag {*delegation* = [(*InstantMessenger, receive*, [*Forwarder*])]}.

On the server side, there are the classes *SubscriptionServer* and *Forwarder*. The class *SubscriptionServer* gets the permission forward on objects of class *Forwarder*. The access to the method *subscribe()* is guarded by the permission subscribe. This is stated by the stereotype « permission_check » and the tag {permission = [subscribe]}. For calling the method *checkLogin()*, the possession of the permission checkLogin is necessary. The class *Forwarder* defines the method *forward(msg, receiver)*, which is guarded by the permission forward.

3.2   Dynamic Definitions

In this section, the point of view on the system changes to the modelling of interactions between the objects instantiated from the classes defined above. For that purpose, we identify and model workflows.

For workflow modelling in UML, activity diagrams are used, where activities are assigned to the objects. It is possible to depict the interaction of several objects solving one problem regarding the causal and temporal dependencies.

For the description of used and needed permissions, we often need more detailed information than activity diagrams can offer. The main problem arises from the possibility to combine a number of single actions into one activity, which is connected with a number of objects. For coping with permissions in an automated way, one needs to identify the objects communicating with each other clearly. This means that for every single action we must be able to name the sender and the receiver to coordinate the necessary permissions. This information easily gets lost when aggregating actions to activities. For this reason it is only possible to use activity diagrams to catch the workflow whereas for further use the workflow must be converted to a sequence diagram. In a sequence diagram one can identify caller and callee in every single step of communication, which allows to assign the permissions to the sent messages.

For refinement of the workflow, a sequence diagram is created, allowing to specify the connection between permissions and messages by regarding the exchange of messages between objects. In a first step, we define which of the objects are permission-secured objects, using the same stereotype « permission − secured » as in the class diagram. To this stereotype, we attach the permissions the object owns on other objects, utilizing tagged values. These tags are defined the same way as in the class diagrams, by {permission = [($object$, permission)]}. In contrast to the class diagram, here the first parameter of the tuple means no longer a class but a concrete object on which the permission is valid. Additionally, the ability for delegation of certain permissions is stated by a tag as well ({delegation = [(class, permission, role/class)]}).

Permissions which are needed for executing a method – or in other words for sending a message successfully – are attached directly to the message which is to be protected by these permissions. To signalize that a message is protected by permissions, the message is marked with the stereotype « permission_check », where the permissions are named as tagged values ({permission = [permission]}).

The delegation is performed by emitting and passing on certificates, which are formally defined as 7-tuples

$$\text{certificate} = (e, d, c, o, p, x, s)$$

with emittent e, delegate d, class c of the delegate, object o, permission p which is valid on o, expiration timestamp x and sequence number s.

A certificate contains the following information:

- Who is delegating a permission? The emittent e is named in the certificate; he is signing the certificate.
- To whom is the permission to be delegated? For the definition of the delegate, there are two possibilities, depending on the relation between emittent and delegate. If the emittent knows the delegate at emission time of the certificate, he can name him explicitly (field d in the certificate). Otherwise, he can name the class c the delegate must be an instance of to make use of this certificate. In this case, d has the value *null*. In our example, the emittent never knows the delegate, thus the latter (more general) type of certificate is used.
- Which permission is to be delegated? The permission to be delegated is defined by two parameters: the permission p and the object o on which this permission is valid.
- For how long is the permission to be delegated? As it is not possible to define a contiguous time in sequence diagrams, it is also not possible to make temporal

restrictions on the validity of certificates. Time will be approximated by the number of messages to be sent, starting at zero with the first message. Thus, if a certificate is valid unrestrictedly, this parameter is set to -1.

- What about the sequence number? The sequence number s is contained in the certificate to avoid that it is used several times. The sequence number of certificates which are defined by the same parameter values must differ. It is also necessary that the number is the same if a certificate is passed along several objects. For defining a certificate which might be used more than once, this parameter is to be set to -1.

In the sequence diagram, messages where permission certificates are sent are marked by the stereotype « certification », where a 7-tuple representing a certificate will be directly attached as an tagged value. The parameters of this tag correspond to the definition above.

4   Statically Verifying the Run-Time Checks in UMLsec

In this section, we explain how one can statically verify the run-time checks that can be specified on the UMLsec model level (as explained in the previous section) against security requirements. This is supported by the security checkers provided within the UMLsec tool suite [Too08, JY07, JS08] (Fig. 1 b).

4.1   Consistency between Class and Sequence Diagrams

As class diagrams and sequence diagrams are linked very closely to each other regarding the security permissions, it is necessary to check the consistency of the definitions made in these two diagrams.

In the class diagram, classes are assigned permissions on other classes. The definitions made there have to correspond to the definitions of the objects instantiated out of these class definitions. This means that objects must not have been assigned definitions, which are not contained in the corresponding class definition. It is only admissible to define less permissions in the sequence diagram than in the class diagram.

The definitions for delegation are treated in a similar way, with some restrictions. In the sequence diagram, only permissions can be delegated for which this possibility is defined in the class diagram. Besides that, it is necessary that the permission which is to be delegated is present, which means that it is not only defined in the class definition, but also in the object definition.

The next thing to check is the definition of methods. The permissions needed to execute a single method are defined in the class diagram. It is necessary that these definitions fit the definitions of the sequence diagrams. The method calls are defined as messages there. Attached to these messages are the permissions which are necessary to force the receiver to execute the message in the desired way. Therefore, it is necessary that these permissions are consistent with the ones defined in the receiver's class definition.

4.2   Dynamic Checking of the Sequence Diagram

Are all permissions assigned in a system in a way that the processes modeled in the sequence diagram are able to be completed? This is the next question to solve. If an object should be able to send a message, it must own all permissions necessary for that action. Permissions which are assigned statically are not a problem (addressed by the consistency checks described above), but permissions assigned dynamically by delegation are:

- A permission certificate must be received before it can be used, which means both using the permission included in the certificate and passing on the certificate to other objects.
- The emittent of a certificate must be able to create the certificate. This means that he must own the permission statically and the permission must be released for delegation.
- A certificate must be valid at time of use. The loss of validity will be defined by a time stamp in the certificate.
- A certificate which is defined for being used only once looses validity by being used, so no object can use it again.

In the sequence diagram for the instant messaging service the object *Sender* calls the method *forward()* of *ForS* where the permission forward is needed. As the object *Sender* does not own this permission, it is delegated by an certificate which is passed on by the message *create()*:

$$\{certificate = (SubS, null, ForS, forward, InstantMessenger, -1, -1)\}$$

Because of lack of this permission, *SubSender*, the sender of this message, cannot create this certificate must receive it from *SubS* by sending *subscriptionConfirmation()*. *SubS* owns the permission and is able to delegate it. One can see this by the tags assigned to this object:

- {permission = [(ForS, forward)]}
- {delegate = [(ForS, forward, InstantMessenger)]}

The period of validity has not been considered in this example, because no time stamp is available. Also, the certificates may be used more than once.

5   Run-Time Checks for Permission Delegation

A permission is a message consisting of *permission* and *identifier* (of the object the permission is valid on). The object owning the permission will be specified by appending the object's public key. Therefore it is impossible for any other object to use this permission. A *certificate* is defined as a triple consisting of the identifier followed by the permission and the public key of the user of the *certificate*.

For signing the permissions, there is a trusted instance in the system called security authority (SA). This instance releases all permissions and passes them on to the objects at their instantiation time. It is not possible to change the definition of a permission once signed by this authority.

So the a certificate defining a permission will be formally defined as follows: $Sign(identifier{::}permission{::}K_{legitimate}, K_{SA}^{-1})$.

To enable the delegation of permissions, passing on the permission is not enough. The delegating object must issue a certificate containing the permission and restrictions for its use. In addition, the certificate contains the public key of the owner of the permission. This allows other objects to prove that this object originally was the owner of the permission. The certificate is be signed with the private key of the permission's owner:

$$Sign(K_{legitimate}{::}Sign(object{::}permission{::}K_{legitimate}, K_{SA}^{-1}){::}[properties], K_{legitimate}^{-1})$$

Making use of a delegated permission is only allowed for objects which are implementing the properties of the properties-list.

Here, we now have to deal with the usual Dolev-Yao attacker model:

- The intruder can save all messages sent between objects.
- Messages can be deleted by the intruder, so that the receiver is not able to get a specific message
- The intruder is able to insert messages into the communication between objects
- By combination of these threats, the intruder is able to manipulate messages.

As usual, one makes use of cryptography to try to avoid such attacks by encrypting messages. In the case of security permissions it must be ensured that only the legitimate object is able to make use of a permission. Although by the definition of permissions it is guaranteed that only legitimate objects are able to create certificates for granting permissions, it is possible for intruders to obtain such a certificate in order to use the included permission. This threat can only be avoided by using an additional encryption mechanism for transmitting these certificates.

For proving such a modelling we enhance the UML model by cryptographic functions given in Table 1 for producing a protocol for secure communication between the objects following [Jür04]. The security check for this protocol is done automatically using the first-order predicate logic automated theorem prover e-Setheo. For this, the protocol is converted into predicates in the TPTP-syntax following the formal semantics for UML given in [Jür04].

We explain the modelling of such a protocol by the example of the instant messaging service. For simplification, only the communication between sender and server will be regarded. In the communication with the receiver, it is assumed that the *Forwarder ForS* obtained the permission receive on the receiver-object before using it.

In Figure 2, the corresponding sequence diagram is shown. The notation for cryptographic expressions used in this diagram is given in Table 1. For better readability, the messages contain names of functions (such as subscribe or conf),

Table 1. Notation for cryptographic expressions

$inv(k)$	Inverse key of k; a message, encrypted with key k can be decrypted by $inv(k)$.
$sign(E,inv(k))$	The message E is signed with the inverse key $inv(k)$.
$enc(E,k)$	The message E is encrypted with the key k.
$conc(E1,E2)$	A message consists of two concatenated single messages E1 and E2.
$fst(E)$	Inversion of conc(E1,E2); gives back the first element E1 of the concatenation.
$snd(E)$	Inversion of conc(E1,E2); gives back the second element E1 of the concatenation.
$ext(E, k)$	Extracts the message E out of a message signed message with the inverse key $inv(k)$ of k.
$dec(E, inv(k))$	Decrypts the message E out of a message encrypted message with the inverse key $inv(k)$ of k.

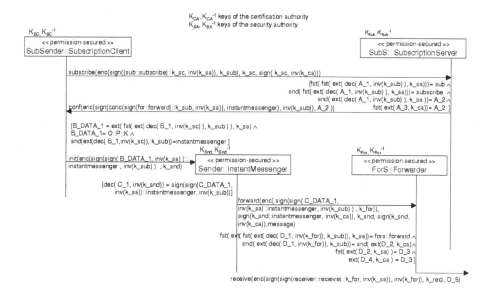

Fig. 2. Delegation protocol

indicating their purpose. On the receiving side, the components of the received messages are referred to by A_1, A_2 and A_3 (parameters of the subscribe message), respectively by B_i, C_i, and D_i (parameters of the messages conf, init and forward). Note that the protocol in Figure 2 is only considered as an example to demonstrate our approach, not necessarily as an optimal solution for the situation at hand.

As specified in Figure 2, the object *SubSender* connects to the server *SubS* and delivers the necessary certificate $sign(conc(conc(SubS,subscribe),K_{SC})$, $inv(K_{SA}))$ to the Server, which was signed by the security authority with key $inv(K_{SA})$. It is encrypted with the public key K_{Sub} of *SubS* to ensure that only *SubS* can access the message. When *SubS* gets the message, it checks the permission and the certification of the public key. If the check is successful, an acknowledgement is sent back to *SubSender* that contains a permission certificate allowing an object of class *InstantMessenger* to send messages to the Forwarder *ForS*. This certificate consists of the following parameters:

– The permission, signed by the security authority,
– The name of the class *InstantMessenger*, so that only objects of that class are able to use the permission,

For a secure transmission, the certificate is encrypted with the public key K_{SC} of *SubSender*.

SubSender analyzes the message. It expects a permission and a restriction to the class *InstantMessenger*. If the certificate fulfills these recommendations, the object Sender is initialized. For transmission, the certificate is encrypted with the public key K_{SND} of Sender.

The Sender object uses this permission certificate to send a message to *ForS* in order to transmit it to *Receiver*. For transmission, the certificate to *ForS* is signed with $inv(K_{SND})$ and encrypted afterwards with K_{FOR}, the public key of *ForS*. The kind of class is also attested using a certificate emitted by the certification authority. This certificate will be attached to the message.

ForS checks the contained permission *conc(ForS, forward)*, and whether the sender of the message identified itself as an object of class *InstantMessenger*, by comparing the declaration in the certificate to the certificate of the certification authority. If these checks are successful, the message is passed on to the *Receiver*.

6   Run-Time Checks in Java GuardedObjects

We now explain how this permission model can be realized in a concrete object oriented programming language such as Java.

In the JDK 1.0 security architecture, the challenges posed by mobile code were addressed by letting code from remote locations execute within a *sandbox* offering strong limitations on its execution. However, this model turned out to be too simplistic and restrictive. From JDK 1.2, a more fine-grained security architecture is employed which offers a user-definable access control, and the sophisticated concepts of signing, sealing, and guarding objects [Gon99].

A protection domain [SS75] is a set of entities accessible by a principal. In the JDK 1.2, permissions are granted to protection domains (which consist of classes and objects). Each object or class belongs to exactly one domain.

The system security policy set by the user (or a system administrator) is represented by a policy object instantiated from the class java.security.Policy. The security policy maps sets of running code (*protection domains*) to sets of access permissions given to the code. It is specified depending on the origin of the code (as given by a URL) and on the set of public keys corresponding to the private keys with which the code is signed.

There is a hierarchy of typed and parameterised access permissions, of which the root class is java.security.Permission and other permissions are subclassed either from the root class or one of its subclasses. Permissions consist of a target and an action. For file access permissions in the class FilePermission, the targets can be directories or files, and the actions include read, write, execute, and delete.

An access permission is granted if all callers in the current thread history belong to domains that have been granted the said permission. The history of a thread includes all classes on the current stack and also transitively inherits all classes in its parent thread when the current thread is created. This mechanism can be temporarily overridden using the static method doPrivileged().

Also, access modifiers protect sensitive fields of the JVM: For example, system classes cannot be replaced by subtyping since they are declared with access modifier final.

The sophisticated JDK 1.2 access control mechanisms are not so easy to use. The granting of permissions depends on the execution context (which however is overridden by doPrivileged(), which creates other subtleties). Sometimes, access control decisions rely on multiple threads. A thread may involve several protection domains. Thus it is not always easy to see if a given class will be granted a certain permission.

This complexity is increased by the new and rather powerful concepts of signed, sealed and guarded objects [Gon99]. A SignedObject contains the (to-be-)signed object and its signature. It can be used internally as an authorisation token or to sign and serialise data or objects for storage outside the Java runtime. Nested SignedObjects can be used to construct sequences of signatures (similar to certificate chains).

Similarly, a SealedObject is an encrypted object ensuring confidentiality.

If the supplier of a resource is not in the same thread as the consumer, and the consumer thread cannot provide the access control context information, one can use a GuardedObject to protect access to the resource. The supplier of the resource creates an object representing the resource and a GuardedObject containing the resource object, and then hands the GuardedObject to the consumer. A specified Guard object incorporates checks that need to be met so that the resource object can be obtained. For this, the Guard interface contains the method checkGuard, taking an Object argument and performing the checks. To grant access the Guard objects simply returns, to deny access is throws a SecurityException. GuardedObjects are a quite powerful access control mechanism. However, their use can be difficult to administer [Gon99]. For example, guard objects may check the signature on a class file. This way, access to an object may be granted indirectly (and possibly unintentionally) by giving access to another object containing the signature key for which the corresponding signature provides access to the first object.

To get access to the encapsulated Object, the requesting object calls the method getObject() of the GuardedObject. In a second step, it is checked if the accessing object owns the permissions defined by the GuardObject. If it does, the method returns the reference of the encapsulated Object. The requesting object can now call any method on this object by using this reference.

The Guard normally checks the permissions by using the Java AccessController. This object reads the class of which the requesting object in an instance off the execution stack. The classes are linked to their code sources and protection domains, to which the permissions are also assigned. This means in particular that all objects of the same class own the same permissions. For permissions assigned at instantiation time this is certainly right, but if one wants to allow the delegation of permissions at run-time (as in our approach), this may lead to different sets of permissions for objects of the same class.

For this reason, it is necessary to enhance this method of permission checking. For delegating permissions dynamically, it is necessary that every object manages its certificates it received for delegation on its own. If such permissions should be considered, they must be given to the GuardedObject as a parameter when invoking the method getObject(). The Guard must thus be enhanced that it not only checks the static permissions but also the permissions contained in the certificates.

It must be ensured that an object is not able to use "foreign" certificates to get access to another object. For that reason, the object references that the getObject() method produces may be secured by an asymmetric key.

If there is a permission to be delegated to a certain class, the relevant instance of the class will be referenced in the certificate. For checking that the callers' class and the named class in the certificate coincide, the callers' class will be read from the execution stack. Is there at least one certificate which is emitted for a specific object, a reference to this object must be saved in the certificate. To check the permission, the object's public key will be requested, and the reference of the encapsulated object will be encrypted with this key.

For using the reference, the caller must decode it using the corresponding private key. Since unauthorized objects do not have the appropriate private key, they are not able to decode the reference.

Another problem of the Guarded Objects in Java is that the caller gets either no or complete access to an object after the permission check. To achieve restricted access to objects, we cannot give back the real reference to an object, but build a wrapper object around the encapsulated object, having only the methods the caller has the permission for calling. These wrapper objects are the only ones which call the original object. This means that there must be created a wrapper class for all possible combinations of methods.

Note that there is one problem not to be solved by these modifications: Does one object get the reference to an encapsulated object the owner of the reference may pass it to unauthorized objects. This simply means that trusted objects must be developed in a trustworthy way.

We illustrate our approach with the example of a web-based financial application. Two (fictional) institutions offer services over the Internet to local users: an Internet bank, Bankeasy, and a financial advisor, Finance. To make use of these services, a local client needs to grant the applets from the respective sites certain privileges.

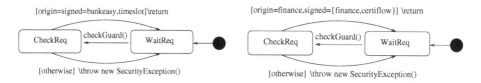

Fig. 3. Statechart FinGd resp. ExcGd

(1) Applets that originate at and are signed by the bank can read and write the financial data stored in the local database, but only between 1 pm and 2 pm (when the user usually manages her bank account).

(2) Applets from (and signed by) the financial advisor may read an excerpt of the local financial data created for this purpose. Since this information should only be used locally, they additionally have to be signed by a certification company, CertiFlow, certifying that they do not leak out information via covert channels.

(3) Applets originating at and signed by the financial advisor may use the micro-payment signature key of the local user (to purchase stock rate information on behalf of the user), but this should only be granted five times a week.

Financial data sent over the Internet is signed and sealed to ensure integrity and confidentiality. Access to the local financial data is realised using GuardedObjects. The access controls are realised by Guard objects such as FinGd, ExpGd, whose behaviour is specified in Figures 3 (we assume that the condition timeslot is fulfilled if and only if the time is between 1pm and 2pm).

Using the security checkers provided within the UMLsec tool suite [Too08, JY07, JS08] (Fig. 1 b), we can now, first, check that the specification given by UML diagrams is secure in the following sense: The specification given by UML diagrams for the guard objects does not grant any permissions not implied by the access permission requirements given in (1)–(3). Second, the tool implements the generation of the Java run-time checks in form of Guards.

7   Related Work

Despite a lot of work on formally verifying abstract specifications of security-critical systems, there is so far comparatively little work on making a link to the implementation level. For example, [GD04] explains how to verify a cryptographic protocol written in an abstract imperative language against security properties. Work on formal verification of access control policies includes [SYSR06]. The difference to ours is that that paper deals with static verification, while the paper here has the goal to generate run-time checks. Work on run-time verification in Java includes [HR04, KVK+04]. Note that the current work is not run-time verification in the special sense of verification against temporal logic, but only in the wider sense of verification that is not performed at compile-time but at run-time. Instead of using temporal logic, we make use of

UML statecharts to specify the properties for which run-time checks should be
generated, and we make use of the GuardedObjects that are readily available in
Java. The current work is an extension of a model-based security-engineering approach [Jür04, Jür05] from the specification level to incorporate run-time checks
for security permissions.

8   Conclusion

We presented an approach for application of run-time checking to enforce access
control requirements at run-time in a way that enforces an overall security policy.
Our approach is an improvement on the ad-hoc and error-prone way GuardedObjects are manually created and used in practice. It generates the run-time
checks from a UMLsec specification of the system that captures the security
policy, thereby reducing the risk for error.

References

[GD04]   Giambiagi, P., Dam, M.: On the secure implementation of security pro-
            tocols. Sci. Comput. Program. 50(1-3), 73–99 (2004)
[Gon99]   Gong, L.: Inside Java 2 Platform Security – Architecture, API Design,
            and Implementation. Addison-Wesley, Reading (1999)
[HR04]   Havelund, K., Rosu, G.: An overview of the runtime verification tool Java
            PathExplorer. Formal Methods in System Design 24(2), 189–215 (2004)
[JS08]   Jürjens, J., Schreck, J.: Automated analysis of permission-based security
            using UMLsec. In: Fiadeiro, J.L., Inverardi, P. (eds.) FASE 2008. LNCS,
            vol. 4961. Springer, Heidelberg (2008)
[Jür04]   Jürjens, J.: Secure Systems Development with UML. Springer, Heidelberg
            (2004)
[Jür05]   Jürjens, J.: Sound methods and effective tools for model-based security
            engineering with UML. In: ICSE. IEEE, Los Alamitos (2005)
[JY07]   Jürjens, J., Yu, Y.: Tools for model-based security engineering: Models
            vs.code. In: 22nd IEEE/ACM Int. Conf. Autom. Softw. Eng. ACM,
            New York (2007)
[KVK+04]   Kim, M., Viswanathan, M., Kannan, S., Lee, I., Sokolsky, O.: Java-MaC:
            A run-time assurance approach for Java programs. Formal Methods in
            System Design 24(2), 129–155 (2004)
[SS75]   Saltzer, J., Schroeder, M.: The protection of information in computer
            systems. Proceedings of the IEEE 63(9), 1278–1308 (1975)
[SYSR06]   Sasturkar, A., Yang, P., Stoller, S.D., Ramakrishnan, C.R.: Policy analy-
            sis for administrative Role Based Access Control. In: CSFW, pp. 124–138.
            IEEE, Los Alamitos (2006)
[Too08]   Security verification tool (2001-2008),
            http://computing-research.open.ac.uk/jj/umlsectool

Synthesizing Monitors for Safety Properties: This Time with Calls and Returns*

Grigore Roşu[1], Feng Chen[1], and Thomas Ball[2]

[1] Department of Computer Science, University of Illinois at Urbana-Champaign
[2] Microsoft Research, Redmond

Abstract. We present an extension of past time LTL with call/return atoms, called PTCARET, together with a monitor synthesis algorithm for it. PTCARET includes abstract variants of past temporal operators, which can express properties over traces in which terminated function or procedure executions are abstracted away into a call and a corresponding return. This way, PTCARET can express safety properties about procedural programs which cannot be expressed using conventional linear temporal logics. The generated monitors contain both a local state and a stack. The local state is encoded on as many bits as concrete temporal operators the original formula has. The stack pushes/pops bit vectors of size the number of abstract temporal operators the original formula has: push on begins, pop on ends of procedure executions. An optimized implementation is also discussed and is available to download.

1 Introduction

Theoretically speaking, it appears to be straightforward to monitor properties expressed as past time linear temporal logic (PTLTL) formulae, since the fixpoint semantics of the temporal operators gives a direct deterministic automaton. The practical challenge in monitoring PTLTL formulae stays in how to do it *efficiently*, both time-wise and memory-wise, so that the added runtime overhead to the observed system is minimal. Since in a real-life runtime verification application there could be millions of monitor instances living at the same time, each observing tens of millions of events (see, e.g., [1,4] and [6,7] for numbers and evaluations of runtime verification systems on large benchmarks), every bit of memory or monitor processing time may translate into significantly higher runtime overhead, to an extent that the overall use of runtime verification in a particular application may become unfeasible. For example, in many cases it may not be a good idea to generate an actual deterministic automaton as a monitor, because that may have an exponential or worse size; instead, a non-deterministic automaton performing an NFA-to-DFA construction on the fly saving space exponentially may be more appropriate, or even a monitor that does not store any automaton at all, but has an efficient way to generate the next state on-the-fly.

---

* Supported by NSF CCF-0448501, NSF CNS-0509321, NASA ARMD safety Program and Air Force STTR phase I award (Topic Number AF07-T019, Proposal Number F074-019-0162).

Havelund and Roşu proposed a monitor synthesis algorithm PTLTL) formulae φ [9]. The generated monitors implement the recursive semantics of PTLTL using a dynamic programming technique, and need $O(|\varphi|)$ time to process each new event and $O(|\varphi|)$ total space. Roşu proposed an improved monitor synthesis algorithm for PTLTL in [12] (un unpublished technical report) which, using a divide-and-conquer strategy, generates monitors that need $O(k)$ space and still $O(|\varphi|)$ time, where k is the number of temporal operators in φ.

Alur *et al.* gave an extension of linear temporal logic (LTL) with calls and returns [2], called CARET. Unlike LTL, CARET allows for matching call/return states in linear traces, allowing to express program trace properties not expressible using plain LTL. In particular, one can express properties on the execution stack of a program, such as "function g is always called from within function f", or structured-programming safety policies such as "each method must release before it terminates all the locks that it acquired during its execution", or even properties that are allowed to be temporarily violated, such as "user u never directly accesses the passwords file (but may access it through system procedures)". Because of allowing such important and desirable safety properties to be formally stated at the same time faithfully including LTL, CARET can be a more attractive temporal logic then LTL, provided of course that the complexity of checking programs against CARET formulae does not make it unfeasible.

We define a past time variant of CARET, called PTCARET, show by examples its usefulness in expressing a series of safety properties involving calls of functions/procedures, and then propose a monitor synthesis algorithm for properties expressed as PTCARET formulae. Motivated by practical reasons, PTCARET distinguishes call/return states from begin/end states: the former take place in the caller's context, while the latter take place in the callee's. This simple and standard distinction allows more flexibility and elegance in expressing properties, but requires an additional (but reasonable) constraint on traces: calls always immediately precede begins, and ends always immediately precede returns.

PTCARET conservatively extends PTLTL by adding abstract variants of temporal operators, namely "abstract previously" and "abstract since". The semantics of these operators is that of their corresponding core PTLTL operators "previously" and "since", but on the *abstract* trace obtained by collapsing executed functions or procedures into only two states, namely the caller's state at the call of the invoked function or procedure and the caller's state at its corresponding return. In other words, from the point of view of the abstract temporal operators, the intermediate states generated during function executions are invisible. Of course, the standard temporal operators continue to "see" the whole trace.

The monitors generated from PTCARET formulae using the proposed algorithm have both a monitor state and a monitor stack, so they can be regarded as push-down automata; however, both the monitor states and the data pushed onto stacks are calculated online, on a by-need basis. The monitor state is encoded on as many bits as standard past time operators in the original formula, while the monitor stack pushes/pops as many bits of data as abstract temporal operators in the original formula. If no abstract temporal operators are used in a

PTCARET formula, that is, if the PTCARET formula is a PTLTL formula, then its generated monitor is identical to that obtained using the technique in [12]. In other words, not only is PTCARET a conservative extension of PTLTL, but the proposed monitor synthesis algorithm conservatively extends the best known, provably optimal monitor synthesis algorithm for PTLTL.

The proposed PTCARET monitor synthesis algorithm has been implemented and is available to download and experiment with via a web interface at [3]. The rest of the paper is structured as follows: Section 2 discusses PTCARET as an extension of PTLTL; Section 3 introduces useful derived operators and shows some examples of PTCARET specifications. Section 4.2 discusses our monitor synthesis algorithm, including its implementation. Section 5 concludes the paper.

2   PTLTL and PTCARET

We here recall past time linear temporal logic (PTLTL) and define its extension PTCARET. For simplicity, we assume only two types of past operators, namely "previously" and "since". Other common or less common temporal operators can be added as derived operators. PTLTL contains only the usual, standard variants of temporal operators, while PTCARET contains both standard and abstract variants. We follow the usual recursive semantics of past time LTL and adopt the simplifying assumption that the empty trace invalidates any atomic proposition and any past temporal operator; as argued in [9], this may not always be the best choice, but other semantic variations regarding the empty trace present no difficulties for monitoring and can easily be accommodated.

Definition 1. *Syntactically,* PTLTL *consists of formulae over the grammar*

$$\varphi ::= true \mid a \mid \neg\varphi \mid \varphi \wedge \varphi \mid \circ\varphi \mid \varphi\, \mathcal{S}\, \varphi,$$

where a ranges over a set A of state predicates. *Other common syntactic constructs can be defined as derived operators in a standard way: false is ¬true, ◇φ ("eventually in the past") is true S φ, □φ ("always in the past") is ¬(◇¬φ)), etc.*

LTL's models, even for its safety fragment, traditionally are *infinite traces* (see, e.g., [11]), where a trace is a sequence of *states*, where a state is commonly abstracted as a set of atomic predicates in A. According to Lamport [10], a *safety property* is a set of such infinite traces (properties are commonly identified with the sets of traces satisfying them) such that once an execution "violates" it then it can never satisfy it again later. Formally, a set of infinite traces Q is a safety property if and only if for any infinite trace u, if $u \notin Q$ then there is some finite prefix w of u such that $wv \notin Q$ for all infinite traces v.

It can be shown that there are as many safety properties as real numbers [12]. Unfortunately, any logical formalism can define syntactically only as many formulae as natural numbers. Thus, any logical formalism can only express a small portion of safety properties. In LTL, a common way to specify safety properties is as "always past" formulae, that is, as formulae of the form □φ

($\Box$ is "always in the future"), where φ is a formula in PTLTL. There are two problems with identifying the problem of monitoring a PTLTL specification φ with checking the running system against the LTL safety formula $\Box\varphi$: on the one hand, LTL has an infinite trace semantics, while during monitoring we only have a finite number of past states available, and, on the other hand, once the LTL formula $\Box\varphi$ is violated then it can never be satisfied in the future. However, a major use of monitoring is in the context of recoverable systems, in the sense that the monitor can trigger recovery code when φ is violated, in the hope that φ will be satisfied from here on. For these reasons, we adopt a slightly modified semantics of past time LTL, namely the one on finite traces borrowed from [9]:

Definition 2. *A (program)* state *is a set of atomic predicates in A; let s, s', etc., denote states, and let ProgState denote the set of all states. A* trace *is a finite sequence of states in ProgState*; let w, w', etc., denote traces, and ϵ denote the empty trace. If $w \neq \epsilon$, that is, if $w = w's$ for some trace w' and some state s, then we let prefix(w) denote the trace w' and call it the* (concrete) prefix *of w, and let last(w) denote the state s. The satisfaction relation $w \models \varphi$ between a trace w and a PTLTL formula φ is defined recursively as follows:*

$$
\begin{aligned}
&w \models true && \text{is always true,} \\
&w \models a && \text{iff } w \neq \epsilon \text{ and } a \in last(w), \\
&w \models \neg\psi && \text{iff } w \not\models \psi, \\
&w \models \psi \wedge \psi' && \text{iff } w \models \psi \text{ and } w \models \psi', \\
&w \models \circ\psi && \text{iff } w \neq \epsilon \text{ and } prefix(w) \models \psi, \\
&w \models \psi \mathcal{S} \psi' && \text{iff } w \neq \epsilon \text{ and } (w \models \psi' \text{ or } w \models \psi \text{ and } prefix(w) \models \psi \mathcal{S} \psi').
\end{aligned}
$$

We next introduce PTCARET as an extension of PTLTL. Syntactically, it only adds abstract versions of the two temporal operators "previously" and "since" to PTLTL; semantically, some special atomic predicates corresponding to calls, returns, begins and ends of functions/procedures need to be assumed, as well as some natural and practically reasonable restrictions on traces.

Definition 3. PTCARET *syntactically extends* PTLTL *with: "$\varphi ::= \cdots \mid \overline{\circ}\varphi \mid \varphi \overline{\mathcal{S}} \varphi$." The former is called "abstract previously" and the latter "abstract since".*

The semantics of abstract previously and since are defined exactly as the semantics of their concrete counterparts, but on an abstract version of the trace from which all the intermediate states of the terminated function or procedure executions are erased. In order for this erasure, or abstraction, process to work, we need to impose some constraints on traces that are always satisfied in practice.

Definition 4. *In* PTCARET, *the set of atomic predicates A contains four special predicates:* call, begin, end, *and* return. *A state contains at most one of these and is called call, begin, end, or return state if it contains the corresponding predicate.* PTCARET *traces are constrained to the following restrictions:*

(1) any call state, except when the last one, must be immediately followed by a begin state, and any begin state must be immediately preceded by a call state;

(2) any end state, except when the last one, must be immediately followed by a return state, and any return state must be immediately preceded by an end.

For a trace w as above, we let $\overline{w}$ denote its abstraction, which is obtained by iteratively erasing contiguous subtraces $s_b w' s_e$ of w in which s_b is a begin state, s_e is an end state which is not the last one in w, and w' contains no begin or end states. One more restriction is imposed on PTCARET traces:

(3) the abstractions of PTCARET traces contain no return states which are not immediately preceded by call states.

Call and return states occur in the caller's context. Thus, call/return states can contain other predicates which may not be possible to evaluate in the callee's context during runtime monitoring. The begin/end states are generated in the callee's context, at the beginning and at the end of the execution of the invoked function, respectively. Similarly, for some common programming languages, begin/end states may contain other predicates that cannot be evaluated in the caller's context. The original CARET logic [2] did not distinguish between call and begin states or between end and return states. We included all four of them in PTCARET for the reasons above and also because most trace monitoring systems (e.g., Tracematches [1,4] and MOP [6,7]) make a clear distinction between these four types of states.

Fig. 1 (A) shows a PTCARET trace. To better reflect the call-return structure of the PTCARET trace, states are placed on different levels: states on the higher level are generated in the caller's context while those on the lower level are generated in the callee's. The vertical dotted lines connect the corresponding call-begin and end-return pairs. Fig. 1 (B) shows the abstraction of that trace: if w ends with the state pointed by $\Downarrow$, $\overline{w}$ contains only the circled states.

Restrictions *(1)* and *(2)* on PTCARET traces are very natural. One source of doubt though can be the sub-requirements that any return state must be preceded by an end state, and that any begin state must be preceded by a call state. While a return or a begin can indeed happen in any programming language only after a corresponding end or call state, respectively, one may argue that monitoring of a property should be allowed to start at any moment, in particular in between call and begin, or in between end and return states. While our synthesized monitors from PTCARET formulae (see Section 4.2) can be easily adapted to start monitoring at any moment in the trace, for the sake of a smoother and

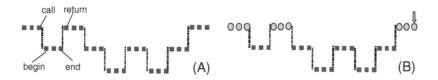

Fig. 1. PTCARET trace (A) and abstraction (B). $\Downarrow$: end of w, ■: w state, ○: $\overline{w}$ state.

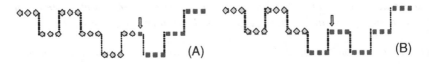

Fig. 2. $\overline{prefix}(w)$ on two traces, (A) and (B). ⇓: the end of w, ◇: state in $\overline{prefix}(w)$.

simpler development of the theoretical foundations of PTCARET, we assume that any PTCARET trace starts from the beginning of the program execution and thus satisfies the above-mentioned restrictions. Restriction *(3)* ensures that a trace does not contain return states that do not have corresponding matching call states, also a natural restriction on complete traces.

Our definition of trace abstraction above is admittedly operational, but we think that it captures the desired end/begin matching concept both compactly and intuitively. Alternatively, we could have followed the CARET style in [2] and define the matching begin state of an end state as the latest begin state containing a balanced number of begin/end states in between.

Definition 5. *For a non-empty* PTCARET *trace* w, *let* $\overline{prefix}(w)$, *called the abstract prefix of* w *(not to be confused with the abstraction of the prefix of* w, $\overline{prefix(w)}$*), be either* $prefix(w)$ *if* $last(w)$ *is not a return state, or otherwise the prefix of* w *up to and including the corresponding matching call state of* $last(w)$ *if it is a return state; formally, if* $last(w)$ *is a return state then* $\overline{prefix}(w)$ *is the trace* $w's_c$, *where* $w = w'w''$ *for some* w'' *with* $\overline{w''} = s_c s_r$, *where* s_c *and* s_r *are call and return states, respectively.*

Fig. 2 illustrates $\overline{prefix}(w)$ on two traces, with the down arrow pointing to the ends of the traces. In Fig. 2 (A) we assume that w ends with a state that is not a return (the arrow points to a call state) and in Fig. 2 (B) w ends with a return state (the states of the corresponding $\overline{prefix}(w)$ are marked with diamonds).

Definition 6. *The satisfaction relation between a* PTCARET *trace* w *and a* PT-CARET *formula* φ *is defined recursively exactly like in* PTLTL *for the* PTLTL *operators, and as follows for the two abstract temporal operators:*

$$w \models \overline{\circ}\psi \qquad \textit{iff} \quad w \neq \epsilon \textit{ and } \overline{prefix}(w) \models \psi,$$
$$w \models \psi\overline{\mathcal{S}}\psi' \quad \textit{iff} \quad w \neq \epsilon \textit{ and } (w \models \psi' \textit{ or } w \models \psi \textit{ and } \overline{prefix}(w) \models \psi\overline{\mathcal{S}}\psi').$$

Therefore, a formula $\overline{\circ}\psi$ is satisfied in a return state iff ψ was satisfied at the corresponding matching call state. It is satisfied in a non-return state, including an end state, iff $\circ\psi$ is satisfied in that state (that is, if and only if ψ was satisfied in the concrete (non-abstract) previous state).

Fig. 3 compares the $\circ$ and $\overline{\circ}$ operators. The arrows point, for each state, where the formula ψ in $\circ\psi$ (A) and in $\overline{\circ}\psi$ (B) holds. For most states, their abstract previous state is the concrete previous one; the only difference is on return states, because the abstract previous state of a return state is its call state.

Figure 4 compares $\psi\,\mathcal{S}\,\psi'$ and $\psi\,\overline{\mathcal{S}}\,\psi'$. Notice that the various call/return levels play no role in the satisfaction of $\psi\,\mathcal{S}\,\psi'$, but that they play a crucial role in the

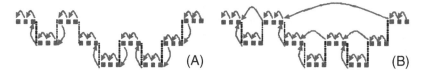

Fig. 3. Concrete (A) and abstract (B) "previous" states for $\circ$ and $\overline{\circ}$

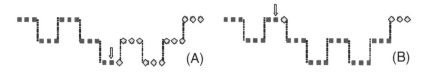

Fig. 4. $\psi \mathcal{S} \psi'$ (A) versus $\psi \overline{\mathcal{S}} \psi'$ (B). $\Downarrow$: where ψ' holds, $\diamond$: where ψ holds.

satisfaction of $\psi \overline{\mathcal{S}} \psi'$: for the latter, ψ' must hold on the same level or a higher level as the level of the current state. One can show the following expected property of abstract since:

Proposition 1. $\varphi_1 \overline{\mathcal{S}} \varphi_2$ *is semantically equivalent to* $\varphi_2 \vee \varphi_1 \wedge \overline{\circ}(\varphi_1 \overline{\mathcal{S}} \varphi_2)$.

One should not get tricked and assume that $w \models \overline{\circ}\varphi$ if and only if $\overline{w} \models \circ\varphi$, or that $w \models \varphi_1 \overline{\mathcal{S}} \varphi_2$ if and only if $\overline{w} \models \varphi_1 \mathcal{S} \varphi_2$! The reason is that subformulae φ, φ_1 or φ_2 may contain concrete temporal operators whose semantics still involve the entire execution trace, not only the abstract one. Some examples in this category are shown in Section 3. Nevertheless, the following holds:

Proposition 2. *For a* PTCARET *trace* w *and formula* φ *containing no concrete temporal operators* $\circ$ *and* $\mathcal{S}$, $w \models \varphi$ *iff* $\overline{w} \models \hat{\varphi}$, *where* $\hat{\varphi}$ *is the* PTLTL *formula replacing each abstract temporal operator in* φ *by its concrete variant.*

3   PTCARET **Derived Operators and Examples**

Besides the usual derived Boolean operators and past time temporal operators "eventually in the past", "always in the past", as well as "start", "stop", and "interval" operators like in [9], which can all be also defined abstract variants, we can define several other interesting, PTCARET-specific derived operators. In the rest of the paper we use the standard notation for the derived Boolean operators, e.g., "$\rightarrow$", "$\vee$", etc., with their usual precedences, and assume that "$\circ$" binds as tight as "$\neg$" while "$\mathcal{S}$" binds tighter than the binary Boolean operators.

At beginning. Suppose that one would like a particular property, say ψ, to hold at the beginning of the execution of the current function. We can define the derived temporal operator $@_b$, say "at beginning", as follows:

$$@_b\psi \stackrel{\text{def}}{=} (\text{begin} \rightarrow \psi) \wedge (\neg\text{begin} \rightarrow \circ(\text{begin} \rightarrow \psi) \overline{\mathcal{S}} \text{begin}).$$

Note that the concrete "previously" operator is used inside the argument of the "abstract since" operator. The above is correct because the last begin state seen by the "abstract since" is indeed the beginning of the current function or procedure. One should not get tricked and try to define the above as:

$$@_b\psi \overset{\text{def}}{=} (\text{begin} \to \psi) \wedge (\neg\text{begin} \to (\text{begin} \to \psi)\,\overline{\mathcal{S}}\,\text{call}).$$

That is because the current function may have called and returned from several other functions, and the "abstract since" can still see all the call/return states. The above would vacuously hold in such a case.

At call. Suppose now that one wants ψ to hold at the state when the current function was called. For the same reason as above, one cannot simply replace begin by call in the definition of $@_b$ above. However, one can define the derived temporal operator $@_c$, say "at call", in terms of "at beginning" simply as follows:

$$@_c\psi \overset{\text{def}}{=} @_b\circ\psi.$$

In Fig. 5 (A), supposing that the current state is the one pointed to by the arrow, ψ should hold in the diamond state for $@_b\psi$ and in the circle state for $@_c\psi$.

Stack since on beginnings. The "abstract since" can be used to write properties in which the terminated function executions are irrelevant. There may be cases in which one wants to write properties referring exclusively to the execution stack of a program, ignoring any other states. For example, one may want to say that ψ held on the stack since property ψ' held. As usual, one may be interested in properties ψ and ψ' to hold either at call time, or at execution beginning time. Let us first define a "stack since on beginnings" derived operator:

$$\psi\,\overline{\mathcal{S}}_b\psi' \overset{\text{def}}{=} (\text{begin} \to \psi)\,\overline{\mathcal{S}}\,(\text{begin} \wedge \psi').$$

Stack since on calls. To define a "stack since on calls" one cannot simply replace begin by call in the above. Instead, one can define it as follows:

$$\varphi_1\,\overline{\mathcal{S}}_c\varphi_2 \overset{\text{def}}{=} (\text{call} \to \varphi_1)\,\overline{\mathcal{S}}\,(\text{begin} \wedge \circ\varphi_2).$$

In Fig. 5 (B), if the current state is the one pointed by the arrow, the begin stack consists of the diamonds and the call stack consists of the circles.

With the stack since derived temporal operators above, one can further define other derived operators, such as "stack eventually in the past on calls" (say $\overline{\diamondsuit_c}$), "stack always in the past on beginnings" (say $\overline{\square_b}$), etc.

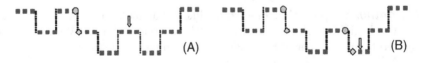

Fig. 5. Derived operators. $\Downarrow$: current state, $\diamond$: states for $@_b$, $\mathcal{S}_b$; $\circ$: states for $@_c$, $\mathcal{S}_c$

Let us next further illustrate the strength of PTCARET by specifying some concrete properties that would be hard or impossible to specify in PTLTL.

Suppose that in a particular context, function f must be called only directly by function g. Assuming $call\_f$ and $call\_g$ are predicates that hold when f and g are called, respectively, we can specify this property in PTCARET as follows:

$$call\_f \rightarrow @_c\, call\_g.$$

Suppose now that f can be called only directly or indirectly by g: a call to g must be on the stack whenever f is called. We can specify that as follows:

$$call\_f \rightarrow \overline{\diamondsuit_c}\, call\_g.$$

A common safety property in many systems is that resources acquired during a function execution must be released before the function ends. Assuming that *acquire* and *release* are predicates that hold when the resource of interest is acquired or released, respectively, we can specify this property as follows:

$$\mathsf{end} \rightarrow (\neg acquire\,\overline{\mathcal{S}}\,\mathsf{begin} \vee \neg(\neg release\,\overline{\mathcal{S}}\,acquire)).$$

A more complex example is discussed in Section 4.3.

4   A Monitor Synthesis Algorithm for PTCARET

As discussed in [12] for PTLTL, thanks to the recursive nature of the satisfaction relation on the standard PTLTL temporal operators (see Definition 2), the monitor generated from a PTCARET formula needs only one global bit per standard (non-abstract) temporal operator. This bit maintains the satisfaction status of the subformula corresponding to that standard temporal operator; when a new state is observed, the satisfaction status of that subformula is recalculated according to the recursive semantics in Definition 2 and the bit is updated. In order for this to work, one needs to have already updated or have an easy way to calculate the status of the subformulae.

The situation is more complex for the abstract temporal operators, as one needs to store enough information about the past so that one is able to update the status of abstract operators' satisfaction regardless of how the future evolves. The main complication comes from the fact that one needs to "freeze" the satisfaction status of the subformulae corresponding to abstract temporal operators whenever a begin state is observed, and then "unfreeze" it when the corresponding end state is observed, thus recovering the information that was available right when the function call took place. Fortunately, that can be obtained by using a stack to push/pop the satisfaction status of the abstract temporal subformulae.

More precisely, a stack bit is needed per abstract temporal operator in the PTCARET formula, maintaining the satisfaction status of the subformula corresponding to that abstract operator. When a new state is observed, the satisfaction status of that subformula is recalculated according to the recursive semantics in Definition 5 and the stack bit updated; if the newly observed state is a begin, then the status of the stack bits is pushed on the stack *before* the actual monitor state update; if the newly observed state is an end, then the status of the stack bits is popped from the stack *after* the monitor state update.

4.1   The Target Language

To state and prove the correctness of any program generation algorithm, one needs to have a formal semantics of the target language. This section gives a formal syntax and semantics to the simple and generic language in which we synthesize monitors. One can very easily translate this language into standard languages, such as C, C++, C#, Java, or even into native machine code. For each PTCARET formula φ, we are going to generate (in Section 4.2) a monitor $\mathcal{M}_\varphi$ as a statement in a language $\mathcal{L}_\varphi$. The only difference between the languages $\mathcal{L}_\varphi$ is the set of variables that one can assign values to; the rest of the language constructs are the same for all φ. The language $\mathcal{L}_\varphi$ has the following simple syntax (note that $\mathcal{L}_{\varphi_1} \subseteq \mathcal{L}_{\varphi_2}$ whenever φ_1 is a subformula of φ_2):

$$
\begin{aligned}
Var ::= {}& \alpha_\phi \text{ (one for each subformula } \phi \text{ of } \varphi \text{ rooted in } \circ \text{ or } \mathcal{S}\,) \\
& |\ \ \beta_\phi \text{ (one for each subformula } \phi \text{ of } \varphi \text{ rooted in } \overline{\circ} \text{ or } \overline{\mathcal{S}}\,) \\
Exp ::= {}& true \mid A \mid Var \mid \neg\ Exp \mid Exp \wedge Exp \\
Stm ::= {}& Var := Exp \mid \textsf{if begin then push} \mid \textsf{if end then pop} \mid \textsf{output}(Exp) \mid Stm\ Stm
\end{aligned}
$$

Therefore, programs in $\mathcal{L}_\varphi$ can use predicates in A (the atomic predicate set of PTCARET) as ordinary (Boolean) expressions, together with Boolean variables α_ϕ and β_ϕ, one per standard and abstract temporal operator in φ, respectively, and together with Boolean constructs such as complement and conjunction. Statements can be composed using juxtaposition, and can be: α_ϕ or β_ϕ variable assignment, output of a Boolean expression, or conditional push/pop, the latter pushing or popping, by convention, precisely the bit vector β. We assume a (rather conventional) denotational semantics for $\mathcal{L}_\varphi$ as follows:

Definition 7. *If φ has k_1 standard temporal operators and k_2 abstract temporal operators, then let MonState$_\varphi$ (we think of $\mathcal{L}_\varphi$ programs as monitors) be the state space of $\mathcal{L}_\varphi$, that is, the domain $Bool^{k_1} \times Bool^{k_2} \times Stack \times Output$, where Bool is the set $\{true, false\}$, Stack is the domain $(Bool^{k_2})^*$ of stacks, or lists, over bit vectors of size k_2, and Output is the domain $Bool^*$ of bit lists. Let the functions*

$$
\begin{aligned}
[\![\_]\!] : Exp &\to MonState_\varphi \to ProgState \to Bool \\
[\![\_]\!] : Stm &\to MonState_\varphi \to ProgState \to MonState_\varphi
\end{aligned}
$$

be defined as follows:

$\llbracket true \rrbracket(\alpha, \beta, \sigma, \omega)(s) = true, \quad \llbracket a \rrbracket(\alpha, \beta, \sigma, \omega)(s) = s(a),$

$\llbracket \alpha_\phi \rrbracket(\alpha, \beta, \sigma, \omega)(s) = \alpha(i), \ \ where \ i \leq k_1 \ is \ the \ \alpha\text{-}index \ corresponding \ to \ \phi,$

$\llbracket \beta_\phi \rrbracket(\alpha, \beta, \sigma, \omega)(s) = \beta(j), \ \ where \ j \leq k_2 \ is \ the \ \beta\text{-}index \ corresponding \ to \ \phi,$

$\llbracket b_1 \wedge b_2 \rrbracket(\alpha, \beta, \sigma, \omega)(s) = \llbracket b_1 \rrbracket(\alpha, \beta, \sigma, \omega)(s) \ and \ \llbracket b_2 \rrbracket(\alpha, \beta, \sigma, \omega)(s),$

$\llbracket \alpha_\phi := b \rrbracket(\alpha, \beta, \sigma, \omega)(s) = (\alpha[\alpha(i) \leftarrow \llbracket b \rrbracket(\alpha, \beta, \sigma, \omega)(s)], \beta, \sigma, \omega),$

$\llbracket \beta_\phi := b \rrbracket(\alpha, \beta, \sigma, \omega)(s) = (\alpha, \beta[\beta(j) \leftarrow \llbracket b \rrbracket(\alpha, \beta, \sigma, \omega)(s)], \sigma, \omega),$

$\llbracket if \ begin \ then \ push \rrbracket(\alpha, \beta, \sigma, \omega)(s) = \begin{cases} (\alpha, \beta, \beta \cdot \sigma, \omega) \ if \ s(begin), \\ (\alpha, \beta, \sigma, \omega) \ otherwise, \end{cases}$

$\llbracket if \ end \ then \ pop \rrbracket(\alpha, \beta, \sigma, \omega)(s) = \begin{cases} (\alpha, \beta', \sigma', \omega) \ if \ s(end) \ and \ \sigma = \beta' \cdot \sigma', \\ (\alpha, \beta, \sigma, \omega) \ otherwise, \end{cases}$

$\llbracket output(b) \rrbracket(\alpha, \beta, \sigma, \omega)(s) = (\alpha, \beta, \sigma, \omega \cdot \llbracket b \rrbracket(\alpha, \beta, \sigma, \omega)),$

$\llbracket stm \ stm' \rrbracket(\alpha, \beta, \sigma, \omega)(s) = \llbracket stm' \rrbracket(\llbracket stm \rrbracket(\alpha, \beta, \sigma, \omega)(s)).$

We can now associate a function $\llbracket \mathcal{M}_\varphi \rrbracket : MonState_\varphi \to ProgState \to MonState_\varphi$ to each program $\mathcal{M}_\varphi$ in $\mathcal{L}_\varphi$. For a monitor state $(\alpha, \beta, \sigma, \omega) \in MonState_\varphi$ and a program state $s \in ProgState$, $\llbracket \mathcal{M}_\varphi \rrbracket(\alpha, \beta, \sigma, \omega)(s) = (\alpha', \beta', \sigma', \omega')$ if and only if the monitor $\mathcal{M}_\varphi$ executed in state $(\alpha, \beta, \sigma, \omega)$ when program state s is observed, produces monitor state $(\alpha', \beta', \sigma', \omega')$.

Definition 8. *By abuse of notation, we also let* $\llbracket \mathcal{M}_\varphi \rrbracket : ProgState^* \to MonState_\varphi$ *be the function (false^{k_1} is the vector of k_1 false bits, and ϵ is the empty list):*

$$\begin{cases} \llbracket \mathcal{M}_\varphi \rrbracket(\epsilon) = (false^{k_1}, false^{k_2}, \epsilon, \epsilon) \quad - \ the \ \text{``initial''} \ monitor \ state \ - \\ \llbracket \mathcal{M}_\varphi \rrbracket(ws) = \llbracket \mathcal{M}_\varphi \rrbracket(\llbracket \mathcal{M}_\varphi \rrbracket(w))(s) \end{cases}$$

4.2 The Monitor Synthesis Algorithm

We next present the actual monitor synthesis algorithm at a high-level. We refrain from giving detailed pseudocode as in [9], because different applications may choose different implementation paradigms. For example, our implementation of the PTCARET logic plugin in the context of the context of the MOP system [6,7], discussed in Section 4.3, uses term rewriting techniques. The monitoring code for a PTCARET formula φ can be split into three pieces: code to be executed before the monitor outputs the satisfaction status of the formula, the outputting code, and code to be executed after the output. Let $Code^\varphi_{before}$ denote the former and let $Code^\varphi_{after}$ denote the latter.

$Code^\varphi_{before}$ is concerned with updating the status of the "since" operators in a bottom-up fashion, while $Code^\varphi_{after}$ with updating the status of the "previously" operators. Indeed, in order to output the satisfaction status of φ, one needs to know the status of all the "since" operators, which may depend upon values in the current state as well as upon values of nested "since" operators, so the inner "since" operators need to be processed before the outer ones. On the other hand, one need not know the particular details (values of atomic predicates) of the current state in order to know the status of the "previously" operators;

INPUT: A PTCARET formula φ
OUTPUT: Code that monitors φ

Step 1 Allocate a bit α_ϕ, initially *false*, for each subformula ϕ of φ rooted in a standard temporal operator. The intuition for this bit is as follows:
  – if $\phi = \circ\psi$ then α_ϕ says if ψ (no typo!) was satisfied at the previous state;
  – if $\phi = \psi \, \mathcal{S} \, \psi'$ then α_ϕ says if ϕ was satisfied at the previous state.
Step 2 Allocate a bit β_ϕ, initially *false*, for each subformula ϕ of φ rooted in an abstract temporal operator. The intuition for this bit is as follows:
  – if $\phi = \overline{\circ}\psi$ then β_ϕ says if ψ was satisfied at the abstract previous state;
  – if $\phi = \psi \, \overline{\mathcal{S}} \, \psi'$, β_ϕ says if ϕ was satisfied at the abstract previous state.
Step 3 Initialize $Code^\varphi_{before}$ and $Code^\varphi_{after}$ as follows:
  – $Code^\varphi_{before}$ to the code "if begin then push", and
  – $Code^\varphi_{after}$ to the code "if end then pop".
Notation: For subformulae ϕ of φ, let $\overline{\phi}$ be the Boolean expression replacing in ϕ each temporal-operator-rooted subformula ψ which is not a subformula of another temporal-operator-rooted subformula of ϕ, by either α_ψ when ψ is rooted in a standard temporal operator, or by β_ψ when ψ is rooted in an abstract operator. For example, $a \wedge \circ b \overline{\mathcal{S}} c \wedge \circ(d \, \mathcal{S} \, \overline{\circ}e)$ is $a \wedge \beta_{\circ b \overline{\mathcal{S}} c} \wedge \alpha_{\circ(d \, \mathcal{S} \, \overline{\circ}e)}$.
Step 4 Following a depth-first-search (DFS) traversal of φ, for each subformula ϕ of φ rooted in a temporal operator do:
  – if $\phi = \circ\psi$ then $Code^\varphi_{after} \leftarrow (\alpha_\phi := \overline{\psi}) \; Code^\varphi_{after}$
  – if $\phi = \overline{\circ}\psi$ then $Code^\varphi_{after} \leftarrow (\beta_\phi := \overline{\psi}) \; Code^\varphi_{after}$
  – if $\phi = \psi \, \mathcal{S} \, \psi'$ then $Code^\varphi_{before} \leftarrow Code^\varphi_{before} \; (\alpha_\phi := \overline{\psi'} \vee \overline{\psi} \wedge \alpha_\phi)$
  – if $\phi = \psi \, \overline{\mathcal{S}} \, \psi'$ then $Code^\varphi_{before} \leftarrow Code^\varphi_{before} \; (\beta_\phi := \overline{\psi'} \vee \overline{\psi} \wedge \beta_\phi)$
Step 5 Output monitor $\mathcal{M}_\varphi$ as the code "$Code^\varphi_{before}$ output($\overline{\varphi}$) $Code^\varphi_{after}$"

Fig. 6. The monitor synthesis algorithm for PTCARET

all one needs to make sure of is that the status of the "previously" operators has been updated at the appropriate previous state (or states in the case of "abstract previously"), after the monitor output. Interestingly, note that, unlike the "since" operators, the "previously" operators need to be processed in a top-down fashion, that is, the outer ones need to be processed before the inner ones.

Note that the monitors $\mathcal{M}_\varphi$ generated in Figure 6 are well-defined, in the sense that each time a generated Boolean expression $\overline{\psi}$ is executed, all the α and β bits that are needed have been calculated. That is because the code is generated following a DFS traversal of the original PTCARET formula. $\mathcal{M}_\varphi$ is run at each newly generated event, or program state, and outputs either *true* or *false*. Note that each $\mathcal{M}_\varphi$ has the form "(if begin then push) C^φ_1 output(O^φ) C^φ_2 (if end then pop)", for some potential statements C^φ_1 and C^φ_2, and for some Boolean expression O^φ. To simplify notation, we introduce the following:

Definition 9. *Let $\langle C_1^\varphi, O^\varphi, C_2^\varphi \rangle$ be a shorthand for (we use $\emptyset$ for C_1^φ or C_2^φ when they do not exist): "(if begin then push) C_1^φ output(O^φ) C_2^φ (if end then pop)".*

The following result structurally relates monitors generated for formulae φ to monitors generated for its subformulae. One can use this proposition as an equivalent, recursive way to synthesize monitors for PTCARET:

Proposition 3. *If $\mathcal{M}_\psi = \langle C_1^\psi, O^\psi, C_2^\psi \rangle$ and $\mathcal{M}_{\psi'} = \langle C_1^{\psi'}, O^{\psi'}, C_2^{\psi'} \rangle$ then:*

- $\mathcal{M}_{true} = \langle \emptyset, true, \emptyset \rangle$
- $\mathcal{M}_a = \langle \emptyset, a, \emptyset \rangle$
- $\mathcal{M}_{\neg\psi} = \langle C_1^\psi, \neg O^\psi, C_2^\psi \rangle$
- $\mathcal{M}_{\psi \wedge \psi'} = \langle C_1^\psi\, C_1^{\psi'},\ O^\psi \wedge O^{\psi'},\ C_2^{\psi'}\, C_2^\psi \rangle$
- $\mathcal{M}_{\odot\psi} = \langle C_1^\psi,\ \alpha_{\odot\psi},\ (\alpha_{\odot\psi} := \overline{\psi})\, C_2^\psi \rangle$
- $\mathcal{M}_{\psi \mathcal{S} \psi'} = \langle C_1^\psi\, C_1^{\psi'}\, (\alpha_{\psi \mathcal{S} \psi'} := \overline{\psi'} \vee \overline{\psi} \wedge \alpha_{\psi \mathcal{S} \psi'}),\ \alpha_{\psi \mathcal{S} \psi'},\ C_2^{\psi'}\, C_2^\psi \rangle$
- $\mathcal{M}_{\overline{\odot}\psi} = \langle C_1^\psi,\ \beta_{\overline{\odot}\psi},\ (\beta_{\overline{\odot}\psi} := \overline{\psi})\, C_2^\psi \rangle$
- $\mathcal{M}_{\psi \overline{\mathcal{S}} \psi'} = \langle C_1^\psi\, C_1^{\psi'}\, (\beta_{\psi \overline{\mathcal{S}} \psi'} := \overline{\psi'} \vee \overline{\psi} \wedge \beta_{\psi \overline{\mathcal{S}} \psi'}),\ \beta_{\psi \overline{\mathcal{S}} \psi'},\ C_2^{\psi'}\, C_2^\psi \rangle$

To prove the correctness of our monitor synthesis algorithm, we need to show that after observing any sequence of program states w, a synthesized monitor $\mathcal{M}_\varphi$ outputs the same result as the satisfaction status of $w \models \varphi$. Therefore, we need to define "the output of the monitor $\mathcal{M}_\varphi$ after observing w":

Definition 10. *Let $(\!|\mathcal{M}_\varphi|\!) : ProgState^+ \to Bool$ be defined for each (non-empty) $w \in ProgState^+$ as $(\!|\mathcal{M}_\varphi|\!)(w) = b$ iff $[\![\mathcal{M}_\varphi]\!](w) = (\alpha, \beta, \sigma, w \cdot b)$. For uniformity, let us extend $(\!|\mathcal{M}_\varphi|\!)$ to a function $ProgState^* \to Bool$ (as in Definitions 2 and 5):*

- $(\!|\mathcal{M}_\varphi|\!)(\epsilon) = false$ *when* $\varphi = a, \odot\psi, \psi \mathcal{S} \psi', \overline{\odot}\psi, \psi \overline{\mathcal{S}} \psi'$;
- $(\!|\mathcal{M}_{\neg\psi}|\!)(\epsilon) = \neg(\!|\mathcal{M}_\psi|\!)(\epsilon)$;
- $(\!|\mathcal{M}_{\psi \wedge \psi'}|\!)(\epsilon) = (\!|\mathcal{M}_\psi|\!)(\epsilon) \wedge (\!|\mathcal{M}_{\psi'}|\!)(\epsilon)$.

Proposition 4. *The following hold for any $w \in ProgState^*$:*

- $(\!|\mathcal{M}_{true}|\!)(w)$ *is always true,*
- $(\!|\mathcal{M}_a|\!)(w)$ *iff $w \neq \epsilon$ and $a \in last(w)$,*
- $(\!|\mathcal{M}_{\neg\psi}|\!)(w)$ *iff not $(\!|\mathcal{M}_\psi|\!)(w)$,*
- $(\!|\mathcal{M}_{\psi \wedge \psi'}|\!)(w)$ *iff $(\!|\mathcal{M}_\psi|\!)(w)$ and $(\!|\mathcal{M}_{\psi'}|\!)(w)$,*
- $(\!|\mathcal{M}_{\odot\psi}|\!)(w)$ *iff $w \neq \epsilon$ and $(\!|\mathcal{M}_\psi|\!)(prefix(w))$,*
- $(\!|\mathcal{M}_{\psi \mathcal{S} \psi'}|\!)(w)$ *iff $w \neq \epsilon$ and $((\!|\mathcal{M}_{\psi'}|\!)(w)$ or $(\!|\mathcal{M}_\psi|\!)(w)$ and $(\!|\mathcal{M}_{\psi \mathcal{S} \psi'}|\!)(prefix(w)))$,*
- $(\!|\mathcal{M}_{\overline{\odot}\psi}|\!)(w)$ *iff $w \neq \epsilon$ and $(\!|\mathcal{M}_\psi|\!)(\overline{prefix(w)})$,*
- $(\!|\mathcal{M}_{\psi \overline{\mathcal{S}} \psi'}|\!)(w)$ *iff $w \neq \epsilon$ and $((\!|\mathcal{M}_{\psi'}|\!)(w)$ or $(\!|\mathcal{M}_\psi|\!)(w)$ and $(\!|\mathcal{M}_{\psi \overline{\mathcal{S}} \psi'}|\!)(\overline{prefix(w)}))$.*

Proof. The non-trivial ones are those for temporal operators. We only discuss $\overline{\mathcal{S}}$, because the others follow the same idea and are simpler. The monitors for $\psi \overline{\mathcal{S}} \psi'$, ψ, and ψ', respectively, following the notations in Proposition 3 are:

	$\mathcal{M}_{\psi \overline{S} \psi'}$	$\mathcal{M}_\psi$	$\mathcal{M}_{\psi'}$
1.	if begin then push	if begin then push	if begin then push
2.	C_1^ψ $C_1^{\psi'}$	C_1^ψ	$C_2^{\psi'}$
3.	$\beta_{\psi S \psi'} := \overline{\psi'} \vee \overline{\psi} \wedge \beta_{\psi S \psi'}$		
4.	output($\beta_{\psi S \psi'}$)	output($\overline{\psi}$)	output($\overline{\psi'}$)
5.	$C_2^{\psi'}$ C_2^ψ	C_2^ψ	$C_2^{\psi'}$
6.	if end then pop	if end then pop	if end then pop

Note that the property holds vacuously if $w = \epsilon$. Assume now that $w = w's$, for some $s \in ProgState$. An interesting and useful property of the generated monitors is that their semantics is very modular, and that pushing or popping β does not affect the modular semantics. For example, note that C_1^ψ in $\mathcal{M}_{\psi S \psi'}$ uses no variables defined in $C_1^{\psi'}$ or in $C_2^{\psi'}$, and the bit $\beta_{\psi S \psi'}$ is only defined in line 3. and used in lines 3. and 4. This modularity guarantees that, if we were to output $\overline{\psi}$ or $\overline{\psi'}$ at line 3. or 4. in $\mathcal{M}_{\psi S \psi'}$, then its output after processing w would be nothing but $(\!(\mathcal{M}_\psi)\!)(w)$ or $(\!(\mathcal{M}_{\psi'})\!)(w)$, respectively. That means that the $\overline{\psi}$ and $\overline{\psi'}$ in the expression assigned to $\beta_{\psi S \psi'}$ at line 4. when processing the last state in w are $(\!(\mathcal{M}_\psi)\!)(w)$ and $(\!(\mathcal{M}_{\psi'})\!)(w)$, respectively. We claim that $\beta_{\psi S \psi'}$ in the assigned expression at line 4. is $(\!(\mathcal{M}_{\psi S \psi'})\!)(\overline{prefix(w)})$. There are two cases to analyze. (1) if s is not a return state, then $\beta_{\psi S \psi'}$ was assigned at line 3. in the previous execution of the monitor, when processing the last state in w', so it is nothing but $(\!(\mathcal{M}_{\psi S \psi'})\!)(prefix(w))$; and (2) if s is a return state, then it means that the last state in w' was an end state, so the vector β was popped from the stack at the end of the previous step. The only thing left to note is that our push on begins and pop or ends correctly match begin and end states; this follows from the fact that we assume traces complete and well-formed (Definition 4).

Theorem 1. *The monitor synthesis algorithm in Figure 6 is correct, that is, for any* PTCARET *formula φ and for any $w \in ProgState^*$, $(\!(\mathcal{M}_\varphi)\!)(w)$ iff $w \models \varphi$.*

Proof. Straightforward, by induction on both the structure of φ and the length of w, noticing that there is a one-to-one correspondence between the definition of satisfaction in Definitions 2 and 5, and the properties in Proposition 4.

4.3   Implementation as Logic Plugin, Optimizations, Example

MOP [6,7] is a configurable runtime verification framework, in which specification requirements formalisms can be added modularly, by means of *logic plugins*. A logic plugin essentially encapsulates a monitor synthesis algorithm for a formalism that one can then use to specify properties of programs. The current JavaMOP tool has logic plugins for future time LTL, past time LTL, Allen algebra, extended regular expressions, JML, JASS. JavaMOP takes a Java application to be monitored and specifications using any of the included formalisms together with validation and/or violation handlers (saying what to do if property validated or violated, in particular nothing), and then waves them together in a runtime verified application by first generating monitors for all the properties using their corresponding logic plugins, and then generating and compiling an AspectJ extension of the original program (runtime monitors are "aspects"). To maintain a reduced runtime overhead (shown on large benchmarks to be, on average, below 10%), MOP piggybacks monitor states onto object states.

The PTCARET ***MOP logic plugin.*** We implemented the PTCARET monitor synthesis algorithm in Section 4.2 as an MOP logic plugin. Our implementation can be found and experimented with online at [3]. Large-scale experiments are still to be performed; we are currently engineering the MOP system to allow monitor states to piggyback not only object states, but also the program stack. In short, our implementation uses *term rewriting* and the Maude system [8], and follows the monitor synthesis algorithm in Figure 6 and its "equivalent", recursive formulation in Proposition 3. Implementations in other languages are obviously also possible; however, term rewriting proved to be an elegant means to synthesize monitors from logical formulae in several other contexts (the other MOP plugins, as well as in JPaX [13]), and so seems to be here.

Our implementation starts by defining the Boolean expressions as an algebraic specification using Maude's mixfix notation (equivalent to context-free grammars); derived Boolean operators are also defined, together with several simplification rules ($\neg true = false$, etc.). Boolean expressions are imported both in the target language module and in the PTCARET module. Both the target language and the PTCARET modules are defined as algebraic signatures, enriched with structural equalities which turn into simplification rules when executed; this way, for example, each PTCARET derived operator is defined with one equation capturing its definition. Several other derived operators are defined in addition to those discussed in Section 3. The monitor generation module imports both the target language and the PTCARET modules, and adds two equations per temporal logic operator; e.g., the equations below process the "abstract since":

```
eq form(F1 Sa F2) = [form(F1), form(F2)] -> Sa .
eq k([exp(B1),exp(B2)] -> Sa -> K) code(I,C1,C2) nextBeta(N)
= k(exp(beta[N]) -> K) code(I beta[N] := false,
                          C1 beta[N] := B2 or B1 and beta[N], C2) nextBeta(N + 1) .
```

First equation says that subformulae should be processed first (DFS traversal). The second equation combines the codes generated from the subformulae as shown in Proposition 3, appending the assignment for the corresponding bit to C1. Note that C1 here accumulates the "code before" of both subformulae; in terms of Proposition 3, it is "$C_1^\psi\ C_1^{\psi'}$". I accumulates the monitor initialization code. Finally the optimizations below are implemented also as rewrite rules.

Optimizations. Term-rewriting-based code-generation algorithms can be easily extended with optimizations, because these can be captured as rewrite rules. We discuss some of the optimizations enabled in our implementation. First, we perform Boolean simplifications when calculating $\overline{\psi}$ to reduce runtime overhead ($\neg\neg\psi = \psi$, $true \wedge \psi = true$, etc.). Another immediate optimization is the following. The generated code originally has the form (see Fig. 6) "(if begin then push)

C (if end then pop)", for some code C. However, since a program state can only contain at most one of the special predicates, this can be optimized into (syntax of target language needs to be slightly extended):

if begin then (push; C[begin $\leftarrow$ *true*, end $\leftarrow$ *false*, call $\leftarrow$ *false*, return $\leftarrow$ *false*]; exit)
if end then (C[begin $\leftarrow$ *false*, end $\leftarrow$ *true*, call $\leftarrow$ *false*, return $\leftarrow$ *false*]; pop; exit)
C[begin $\leftarrow$ *false*, end $\leftarrow$ *false*];

After the substitutions above, further Boolean simplifications may be triggered. Also, some assignments may become redundant, such as, for example, "beta[3] := beta[3]"; rules to eliminate such assignments are also given. A further optimization on the generated code is possible, but we have not implemented it yet: some subformulae can repeat in different parts of the original formula; the current implementation generates monitoring code for each repeating instance, which is redundant and can be reduced using a smarter optimization algorithm.

Example. We here show the monitor generated by our implementation for a more complex PTCARET specification. Suppose that a program carries out a critical multi-phase task and the following safety properties must hold when execution enters the second phase:

1. Execution entered the first phase within the same procedure;
2. Resource acquired within same procedure since first phase must be released;
3. Caller of current procedure must have had approval for the second phase;
4. Task is executed directly or indirectly by the procedure *safe_exec*.

These can be captured as the following PTCARET formula:

$$enter\_phase\_2 \rightarrow (\neg(\neg enter\_phase\_1 \,\overline{S}\, begin)$$
$$\wedge(\neg acquire\,\overline{S}\, enter\_phase\_1 \vee \neg(\neg release\,\overline{S}\, acquire))$$
$$\wedge @_c(has\_phase\_2\_pass)$$
$$\wedge \overline{\diamondsuit}_b(safe\_exec)$$

Our implementation generates the following monitor for this specification:

```
if begin then {push(beta);
    beta[0] := safe_exec or beta[0]; beta[1] := enter_ph1 or not acquire and beta[1];
    beta[2] := acquire or not release and beta[2]; beta[3] := true; beta[4] := true;
    output(not enter_ph2 or not beta[4] and alpha[0] and beta[0] and (not beta[2] or beta[1]));
    alpha[3] := true; alpha[2] := alpha[1]; alpha[1] := has_ph2_pass; alpha[0] := has_ph2_pass;
    exit}
if end then {
    beta[1] := enter_ph1 or not acquire and beta[1]; beta[2] := acquire or not release and beta[2];
    beta[3] := beta[3] and (not alpha[3] or alpha[2]); beta[4] := not enter_ph1 and beta[4];
    output(not enter_ph2 or not beta[4] and beta[0] and beta[3] and (not beta[2] or beta[1]));
    alpha[3] := false; alpha[2] := alpha[1]; alpha[1] := has_ph2_pass; alpha[0] := has_ph2_pass;
    pop(beta); exit}
beta[1] := enter_ph1 or not acquire and beta[1]; beta[2] := acquire or not release and beta[2];
beta[3] := beta[3] and (not alpha[3] or alpha[2]); beta[4] := not enter_ph1 and beta[4];
output(not enter_ph2 or not beta[4] and beta[0] and beta[3] and (not beta[2] or beta[1]));
alpha[3] := false; alpha[2] := alpha[1]; alpha[1] := has_ph2_pass; alpha[0] := has_ph2_pass
```

The formula contains derived operators, e.g., $@_c$, which are first expanded. The monitoring code uses four α bits and five β bits (the expanded formula contains four concrete temporal operators and five abstract ones). For example,

$\overline{\diamondsuit}_b(\textit{safe\_exec})$ is expanded into $(\textsf{begin} \rightarrow \textsf{true})\,\overline{\mathcal{S}}\,(\textsf{begin} \wedge \textit{safe\_exec})$, which is then simplified to $\textsf{true}\,\overline{\mathcal{S}}\,(\textsf{begin} \wedge \textit{safe\_exec})$, equivalent to $\overline{\diamondsuit}(\textsf{begin} \wedge \textit{safe\_exec})$. beta[0] in the generated code is used to check this operation; it only needs to be updated at the begin state, where it becomes true if $\textit{safe\_exec}$ holds.

5   Conclusion and Future Work

We presented the logic PTCARET and a monitor synthesis algorithm for it. PTCARET includes abstract variants of past temporal operators. It can express safety properties about procedural programs which cannot be expressed using conventional PTLTL. The generated monitors contain both a local state and a stack. The local state is encoded on as many bits as concrete temporal operators the original formula had, while the stack pushes/pops bit vectors of size the number of abstract temporal operators the original formula had. An optimized implementation of the monitor synthesis algorithm has been organized as an MOP logic plugin, and is available to download from [3]. There is room for further optimizations of the generated code. An extensive evaluation of the effectiveness of PTCARET runtime verification on large programs needs to be conducted. On the theoretical side, it would be interesting to explore the relationship between our monitors generated for PTCARET and the nested word automata in [5]; [5] gives an operational monitoring language for nested words based on BLAST's specification language. In contrast, our language is declarative and an operational encoding synthesized automatically.

References

1. Allan, C., Avgustinov, P., Christensen, A.S., Hendren, L., Kuzins, S., Lhotak, O., de Moor, O., Sereni, D., Sittampalam, G., Tibble, J.: Adding trace matching with free variables to AspectJ. In: OOPSLA 2005 (2005)
2. Alur, R., Etessami, K., Madhusudan, P.: A temporal logic of nested calls and returns. In: Jensen, K., Podelski, A. (eds.) TACAS 2004. LNCS, vol. 2988, pp. 467–481. Springer, Heidelberg (2004)
3. F.S.L.: at UIUC. ptCaRet MOP Logic Plugin,
   http://fsl.cs.uiuc.edu/index.php/Special:JavaMOPPTCARETOnline
4. Avgustinov, P., Tibble, J., de Moor, O.: Making Trace Monitors Feasible. In: OOPSLA 2007 (2007)
5. Chaudhuri, S., Alur, R.: Instrumenting C programs with nested word monitors. In: Bošnački, D., Edelkamp, S. (eds.) SPIN 2007. LNCS, vol. 4595, pp. 279–283. Springer, Heidelberg (2007)
6. Chen, F., Roşu, G.: Towards Monitoring-Oriented Programming: A Paradigm Combining Specif. and Implementation. In: RV 2003. ENTCS, vol. 89(2) (2003)
7. Chen, F., Roşu, G.: MOP: An Efficient and Generic Runtime Verification Framework. In: OOPSLA 2007 (2007)
8. Clavel, M., Durán, F., Eker, S., Lincoln, P., Martí-Oliet, N., Meseguer, J., Talcott, C.: Maude Manual, http://maude.cs.uiuc.edu

9. Havelund, K., Roşu, G.: Efficient monitoring of safety properties. Software Tools and Technology Transfer 6(2), 158–173 (2004); In: Katoen, J.-P., Stevens, P. (eds.) TACAS 2002. LNCS, vol. 2280, Springer, Heidelberg (2002)

10. Lamport, L.: Proving the correctness of multiprocess programs. IEEE Trans. Software Eng. 3(2), 125–143 (1977)

11. Manna, Z., Pnueli, A.: Temporal verification of reactive systems: safety. Springer-Verlag New York, Inc., New York (1995)

12. Roşu, G.: On Safety Properties and Their Monitoring. Technical Report UIUCDCS-R-2007-2850, Dept. of Comp. Sci. Univ. of Illinois at Urbana-Champaign (2007)

13. Roşu, G., Havelund, K.: Rewriting-based techniques for runtime verification. Automated Software Engineering 12(2), 151–197 (2005)

Forays into Sequential Composition and Concatenation in EAGLE

Joachim Baran and Howard Barringer

The University of Manchester, School of Computer Science, Oxford Road,
Manchester, M13 9PL, United Kingdom
{joachim.baran,howard.barringer}@cs.manchester.ac.uk

Abstract. The run-time verification logic EAGLE is equipped with two
forms of binary cut operator, sequential composition (;) and concatenation (·). Essentially, a concatenation formula $F_1 \cdot F_2$ holds on a trace
if that trace can be cut into two non-overlapping traces such that F_1
holds on the first and F_2 on the second. Sequential composition differs
from concatenation in that the two traces must overlap by one state.
Both cut operators are non-deterministic in the sense that the cutting
point is not uniquely defined. In this paper we establish that sequential
composition and concatenation are equally expressive. We then extend
EAGLE with deterministic variants of sequential composition and concatenation. These variants impose a restriction on either the left or right
operand so that the cut point defines either the shortest or longest possible satisfiable cut trace. Whilst it is possible to define such deterministic operators recursively within EAGLE, such definitions based on the
non-deterministic cut operators impose a complexity penalty. By aug-
menting EAGLE's evaluation calculus for the deterministic variants, we
establish that the asymptotic time and space complexity of on-line monitoring for the variants with deterministic restrictions applied to the left
operand is no worse than the asymptotic time and space complexity of
the sub-formulæ.

1 Introduction

Although common temporal logics like propositional temporal logic, extended
temporal logic and the modal μ-calculus are quite expressive [Wol83, Koz83],
they define no operator analog to the most common principle in imperative
programming: sequential composition. Sequential composition allows one to glue
two traces together, where the last state of the first trace overlaps with the first
state of the second trace. A sequential composition formula is then satisfied at
the start of a trace, if the trace can be cut into two sub-traces, overlapping as
above, on which both its operands hold respectively.

Concatenation defines the cut of the trace such that there is no overlapping
part, so the two traces butted together form the original trace. Even though

M. Leucker (Ed.): RV 2008, LNCS 5289, pp. 69–85, 2008.

sequential composition and concatenation seem to be closely related, this has
not been formally investigated yet.[1]

In this paper the runtime verification logic EAGLE is examined [BGHS04b].
EAGLE is a temporal fixed-point logic on finite traces. EAGLE is able to perform
efficient on-line monitoring without storing the execution trace [BGHS04b]. In
EAGLE, both sequential composition and concatenation are part of the logics
language. We show that sequential composition can be expressed in terms of
concatenation and vice-versa. We then extend EAGLE with deterministic variants
of concatenation and sequential composition. These variants impose a restriction
on either the left or right operand so that the cut point defines either the shortest
or longest possible satisfiable cut trace. We augment EAGLE's evaluation calculus
by the new operators and establish that the asymptotic space complexity of on-
line monitoring for the variants with restrictions applied to the left operand is no
worse than the asymptotic space complexity of the sub-formulæ. Two examples
now follow to provide motivation for the deterministic cut operators.

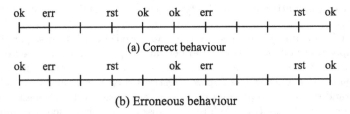

Fig. 1. Traces of a fail-safe system (Example 1)

Example 1. Consider a fail-safe system that in the occurrence of an error eventually resets itself and enters a predefined "good" system state in that way. In
Figure 1(a), an acceptable observation trace is depicted, where "ok" denotes that
the system is in a good state, "err" denotes the occurrence of an error and "rst"
denotes a reset of the system. We allow that a reset can occur with a finite delay
after an error has occured. We can formulate this behaviour by the following
specification:

$$\textbf{max ErrHandler}(\textbf{Form } F) = \lceil F \rceil \cdot (\lfloor err \wedge \text{Eventually}(rst) \rfloor \cdot \text{ErrHandler}(F))$$
$$\textbf{mon } \text{FailSafe} = \text{ErrHandler}(\text{Always}(ok))$$

The formulæ $\lceil F_1 \rceil \cdot F_2$ and $\lfloor F_1 \rfloor \cdot F_2$ are constraint variants of the concatenation
formula $F_1 \cdot F_2$, where the cut has to be placed so that there is no longer or shorter
sub-trace satisfying F_1, respectively. For the specification above it means that a
trace without erroneous behaviour is completely labelled with "ok"s. If an error

---

[1] In [CHMP81], concatenation was defined in terms of sequential composition. This
cannot be done in EAGLE so easily, which is shown in the following. Instead of
referring to the operators as sequential composition and concatenation, Chandra *et
al.* referred to them as "chop" and "chomp" respectively.

occurs, i.e. a state labelled by "err", then the good behaviour resumes after a reset, i.e. "rst".

While this specification can also be written without formulæ of the form $\lceil F_1 \rceil \cdot F_2$ and $\lfloor F_1 \rfloor \cdot F_2$, specification without these the new operators are not necessarily as succinct as specification that make use of $\lceil F_1 \rceil \cdot F_2$ and $\lfloor F_1 \rfloor \cdot F_2$, and furthermore, will incur a significant monitoring cost penalty for the compositional recodings.

Example 2. We introduce a *conditional concatenation operator*, $\lfloor F_1 \rfloor \overset{\rightarrow}{\cdot} F_2$, based on the operator $\lfloor F_1 \rfloor \cdot F_2$ which we used in the previous example. Let $\lfloor F_1 \rfloor \overset{\rightarrow}{\cdot} F_2$ be the syntactic abbreviation for $\neg(\lfloor F_1 \rfloor \cdot \mathbf{True}) \vee (\lfloor F_1 \rfloor \cdot F_2)$. Informally, $\lfloor F_1 \rfloor \overset{\rightarrow}{\cdot} F_2$ can be interpreted as "whenever F_1 matched, do F_2 afterwards".

Consider a nested locking pattern, where we wish to detect when a thread t takes a lock l_1 and does not release it until t has taken a different lock l_2, after which we verify another property φ. Using the newly defined operator, we can formulate the corresponding specification as

$$Always(\lfloor lock(t, l_1) \wedge Until(\neg release(t, l_1), lock(t, l_2) \wedge l_1 \neq l_2) \rfloor \overset{\rightarrow}{\cdot} \varphi$$

The latter specification is not an EAGLE monitoring formula, since data parametrisation in EAGLE is bound to evaluating the current state. However, we can formulate a semantically equivalent monitoring formula in EAGLE:

$$\mathbf{mon}\ NestedLck = Always(isLock() \rightarrow Nested(getThread(), getLock()))$$

with the rule definition

$$\mathbf{max}\ Nested(int\ t, int\ l) = \lfloor Until(\neg release(t, l), isLock() \wedge getLock() \neq l) \rfloor \overset{\rightarrow}{\cdot} \varphi$$

Since EAGLE is implemented in Java, we rely on the methods isLock(), getLock(), getThread() and release() with the obvious semantics and we use integers as handles for threads and locks. It should be noted that getLock() returns the last lock obtained by the current thread, so that its return value when called in the monitoring formula NestedLck and its return value when called in the rule Nested(...) eventually differ.

The shortest trace-length restriction in the concatenation formula of the rule definition Nested(...) ensures that we match the first occurrence of a newly obtained lock, i.e. the rule parameter l and the return value of getLock() differ, where it is also ensured that the previous lock is not released yet.

The paper is structured as follows. A formal definition of EAGLE is given in Section 2. In Section 3 it is proven that sequential composition and concatenation are definable in terms of each other. In Section 4 EAGLE is extended by deterministic cut operators, where it is shown that those operators are definable in unextended EAGLE. In Section 5 EAGLE's calculus is extended by the deterministic cut operators and it is proven that deterministic cut operators enable more efficient on-line monitoring. Section 6 concludes our work.

2   Preliminaries

EAGLE is a temporal logic based on recursively defined temporal predicates
(rules) with four primitive temporal operators, $\bigcirc$, $\odot$, $\cdot$, $;$. Formally:

Definition 1. *Specifications in* EAGLE *are formed by a pair* $\langle D, O \rangle$, *where* D
is the declaration part and O *the observer part. Rule definitions* R *define named
parametrised rules* N. *Monitors* M *specify the requirements.*

$$D ::= R^* \qquad\qquad\qquad\qquad O ::= M^*$$
$$R ::= \{\mathbf{min} \mid \mathbf{max}\}\; N(T_1\; x_1, \ldots, T_n\; x_n) = F \qquad M ::= \mathbf{mon}\; N = F$$
$$T ::= \mathbf{Form} \mid primitive\; type$$
$$F ::= \mathbf{False} \mid \mathbf{True} \mid x_i \mid expression \mid \neg F \mid F_1 \vee F_2 \mid \bigcirc F \mid \odot F \mid$$
$$F_1 \cdot F_2 \mid F_1\;;\; F_2 \mid N(F_1, \ldots, F_n)$$

In the following, we use standard operators of propositional logic that are defined
by De Morgan's laws.

Formulæ are evaluated over discrete finite traces of observation states. A se-
quence of states $s_1, s_2, \ldots, s_n$ constitutes a trace σ of length $|\sigma| = n$. In order to
keep track of the positions on the trace, states will be enumerated incrementally
starting with one. $\sigma^{[i,j]}$ denotes then the sub-trace $s_i, s_{i+1}, \ldots, s_j$ of a trace σ.
For sub-traces, the numbering of states will again begin from one. We write $\sigma(i)$
to denote the i-th state of the trace. The empty trace, i.e. the trace of length 0,
is abbreviated as ε.

Definition 2. *For trace* $\sigma = s_1 s_2 \ldots s_{|\sigma|}$, *the satisfiability relation* $\sigma, i \models_D F$,
with $0 \leq i \leq |\sigma| + 1$, *is defined as*

$$\sigma, i \models_D expression \;\; \text{iff}\;\; 1 \leq i \leq |\sigma| \text{ and } evaluate(expression)(\sigma(i)) == true$$
$$\sigma, i \models_D \bigcirc F \;\; \text{iff}\;\; i \leq |\sigma| \text{ and } \sigma, i+1 \models_D F$$
$$\sigma, i \models_D \odot F \;\; \text{iff}\;\; 1 \leq i \text{ and } |\sigma| \geq 1 \text{ and } \sigma, i-1 \models_D F$$
$$\sigma, i \models_D F_1 \cdot F_2 \;\; \text{iff}\;\; \exists j. i \leq j \leq |\sigma| + 1 \text{ and}$$
$$\sigma^{[1,j-1]}, i \models_D F_1 \text{ and } \sigma^{[j,|\sigma|]}, 1 \models_D F_2$$
$$\sigma, i \models_D F_1\;;\; F_2 \;\; \text{iff}\;\; \exists j. i < j \leq |\sigma| + 1 \text{ and}$$
$$\sigma^{[1,j-1]}, i \models_D F_1 \text{ and } \sigma^{[j-1,|\sigma|]}, 1 \models_D F_2$$

$$\sigma, i \models_D N(F_1, \ldots, F_n) \;\; \text{iff} \;\; \begin{cases} \text{if } 1 \leq i \leq |\sigma| \text{ then} \\ \quad \sigma, i \models_D F[F_1/x_1, \ldots, F_n/x_n], where \\ \quad (N(T_1\; x_1, \ldots, T_n\; x_n) = F) \in D \\ \text{if } i = 0 \text{ or } i = |\sigma| + 1 \text{ then} \\ \quad \text{if } (\mathbf{max}\; N(T_1\; x_1, \ldots, T_n\; x_n) = F) \in D \text{ then} \\ \quad\quad \sigma, i \models_D \mathbf{True}, \\ \quad \text{if } (\mathbf{min}\; N(T_1\; x_1, \ldots, T_n\; x_n) = F) \in D \text{ then} \\ \quad\quad \sigma, i \models_D \mathbf{False} \end{cases}$$

and the propositional constants and operators are defined in the obvious way.

If the set of declarations D follows from the context, then $\models$ is used instead of $\models_D$. In formulæ where an expression can be chosen arbitrarily, i.e. it is treated as a propositional variable, the evaluation is simplified to $evaluate(p)(\sigma(i)) ==$ $true$, where p denotes a propositional variable and p is **True** at $\sigma(i)$.

Remark: It should be noted that at trace boundaries, i.e. the absent states at index 0 and $|\sigma| + 1$, only the logical constant **True** and maximal defined rules evaluate to true, while all other formulæ including tautologies evaluate to **False**. Once the trace has been left, i.e. a step has been made onto the boundary of the trace, it is possible to step back into the trace, but stepping beyond the boundary (stepping to indices -1 and $|\sigma| + 2$) evaluates to **False**.

A specification $\langle D, O \rangle$ is satisfied by a trace σ if all monitoring formulæ of the specification are satisfied on σ. Each monitoring formula is evaluated from position one, regardless of the trace length. A trace is said to model a specification, if the specification is satisfied by the trace. The latter we denote by $\sigma \models \langle D, O \rangle$.

Definition 3. *A given trace σ satisfies a specification $\langle D, O \rangle$ if all monitoring formulæ hold on the trace from position one, i.e. $\sigma \models \langle D, O \rangle$ iff $\forall (\mathbf{mon}\ N = F) \in O.\ \sigma, 1 \models_D F$*

In the remainder of the paper, the rule **max** Limit$()$ = **False** is assumed to be part of every specification. It evaluates to **True** on the boundaries of a trace, i.e. when the current state is either 0 or $|\sigma| + 1$, otherwise it is **False**.

3 Interdefinability of Sequential Composition and Concatenation

Interdefinability of operators, i.e. expressibility of an operator in terms of another operator due to syntactical transformations, simplify definitions, proofs and implementations of a logic. A proof or implementation has only to focus on one of the operators then, where the obtained results can be carried forward to other operators.

For the logic EAGLE, we show that sequential composition and concatenation are equally expressive. Hence, sequential composition can be syntactically formulated in terms of concatenation and vice-versa. In Section 3.1 below we define sequential composition recursively in terms of concatenation. The other direction, however, is not so straightforward: Section 3.2 outlines our elimination procedure and argues its correctness.

3.1 Sequential Composition in Terms of Concatenation

A sequential composition formula F_1 ; F_2 can be expressed in terms of concatenation by simulation of the former operator's semantics using a fixed-point rule definition. We define and add the new rule **min** SequentialComposition(**Form** F_1, **Form** F_2) to every specification. The sequential composition operator can then be removed from arbitrary formulæ, by substituting each sub-formula of the form F_1 ; F_2 by an application of the rule SequentialComposition(F_1, F_2) ,where the rule is given as:

$$\textbf{min } \text{SequentialComposition}(\textbf{Form } F_1, \textbf{Form } F_2) =$$
$$(((F_1 \wedge \bigcirc \text{Limit}()) \cdot \textbf{True}) \wedge (\text{Limit}() \cdot (F_2 \wedge \odot \text{Limit}())))\ \vee$$
$$\bigcirc \text{SequentialComposition}(\odot F_1, F_2)$$

We defined the rule SequentialComposition(F_1, F_2) as a minimal fixed-point, so that it will not be satisfied on the empty trace or the boundaries of a trace. This behaviour coincides with the semantics of the sequential composition operator. For non-empty traces, the first application of the rule body splits the trace, so that F_1 is evaluated on a sub-trace with its boundary in the next state and F_2 is evaluated on a sub-trace with its boundary in the previous state. Hence, the evaluation of F_1 and F_2 overlaps at the index at which the rule is evaluated. Additionally, the rule body contains a recursion $\bigcirc$SequentialComposition$(\odot F_1, F_2)$ that repeats the just described splitting of the trace, but now the sub-trace boundary for F_1 is shifted one index to the right, and likewise, the evaluation of F_2 begins one index later. The recursion finally terminates when the boundary of the trace is reached, on which SequentialComposition(F_1, F_2) was first invoked.

Theorem 1.[2] *For every formula F of* EAGLE, *we can give a semantically equivalent formula F' of* EAGLE, *where F' contains no sequential composition subformula.*

This result can be carried forward to any arbitrary EAGLE-specification, where one subsequently replaces occurrences of sequential composition formulæ – from innermost sub-formulæ to outermost sub-formulæ.

3.2   Concatenation in Terms of Sequential Composition

Concatenation can be expressed in terms of sequential composition as well. However, due to the semantics of the concatenation operator, there is no single substitution mechanism for substituting all occurrences of concatenation sub-formulæ by equivalent sequential composition sub-formulæ. For concatenation, one or even both operands can hold on the empty trace, while sequential composition requires that its operands hold on sub-traces of non-zero length. Therefore a substitution of a concatenation sub-formula by an equivalent sequential composition formula has to take into account that one or both of the concatenation's sub-formulæ might hold on the empty trace. Depending on which of the two operands of concatenation sub-formulæ can hold on the empty trace, different sequential composition formulæ have to be substituted.

In the following, it will be proven that for a given EAGLE formula, it can be determined if it holds on the empty trace (Lemma 1). From this particular result it follows immediately that concatenation is expressible in terms of sequential

---

[2] We omit most proofs in this paper due to page number restrictions. The full proofs were included for the review of the paper and can be obtained from the authors.

composition, such that for each combination of concatenation sub-formulæ which may or may not hold on the empty trace, a suitable sequential composition formula can be substituted (Theorem 2).

We show that it is sufficient to inspect an EAGLE-formula syntactically, in order to verify whether it would be satisfied on the empty trace or not. More importantly, rule applications do not have to be substituted by their rule bodies at any point, which would otherwise lead to undecidability of the problem. The latter is due to the possible encoding of a Turing-machine or equivalent device in EAGLE.[3]

Lemma 1. *For an arbitrary formula in* EAGLE, *it is decidable whether it is satisfiable on the empty trace.*

Proof. For an arbitrary formula we can inductively determine whether it holds on the empty trace or not.

Base cases: The formulæ **False**, *expression*, $\bigcirc F$, $\odot F$, $F_1 \,;\, F_2$ and $N(\ldots)$, with $(\mathbf{min}\ N(T_1\ x_1, \ldots, T_n\ x_n) = F) \in D$, are not satisfied on the empty trace, whereas **True**, and $N(\ldots)$, with $(\mathbf{max}\ N(T_1\ x_1, \ldots, T_n\ x_n) = F) \in D$, are satisfied on the empty trace.

Inductive step: The formulæ $F_1 \wedge F_2$ and $F_1 \cdot F_2$ are satisfied on the empty trace, iff F_1 and F_2 are satisfied on the empty trace. $\neg F$ is satisfied on the empty trace, when F is not satisfied on the empty trace. $\square$

We give a translation from any formula $F_1 \cdot F_2$ to an equivalent concatenation-free formula, which is parametrised by which of the operands F_1 and F_2 are satisfiable on the empty trace. An arbitrary formula $F_1 \cdot F_2$ is substituted by

$$
\begin{aligned}
\psi & \text{ iff } \varepsilon, 1 \models \neg F_1 \wedge \neg F_2, \\
\psi \vee F_1 & \text{ iff } \varepsilon, 1 \models \neg F_1 \wedge F_2, \\
\psi \vee (\odot \text{Limit}() \wedge F_2) & \text{ iff } \varepsilon, 1 \models F_1 \wedge \neg F_2, \\
\psi \vee F_1 \vee (\odot \text{Limit}() \wedge F_2) \vee \text{Limit}() & \text{ iff } \varepsilon, 1 \models F_1 \wedge F_2,
\end{aligned}
$$

where $\psi \equiv (F_1 \,;\, (\bigcirc^2 \text{Limit}() \,;\, F_2)) \vee \odot(\bigcirc(F_1 \wedge \text{Limit}())) \,;\, (\bigcirc^2 \text{Limit}() \,;\, F_2))$.

Theorem 2. *For every formula F of* EAGLE, *we can give a semantically equivalent formula F' of* EAGLE, *where F' contains no concatenation sub-formula.*

Again, this result can be carried forward to any arbitrary EAGLE-specification, where one subsequently replaces occurrences of concatenation formulæ – from innermost sub-formulæ to outermost sub-formulæ.

4   Deterministic Cut Operators

Both sequential composition and concatenation allow a trace to be split non-deterministically, i.e. due to the semantics of the operators, several cut positions

---

[3] It is in fact straightforward to implement a Minsky machine in EAGLE, which is Turing complete [Min61].

may satisfy a formula F_1 ; F_2 or $F_1 \cdot F_2$ on a given trace. The designer of a monitoring specification may however desire a unique position of the cut, i.e. a deterministic choice of where a trace is being cut.

In the following, mixfix operators are introduced which allow us to express deterministic cuts in specifications. These operators extend sequential composition and concatenation by additionally verifying that there is no shorter, respectively longer, sub-trace on which the sub-formula holds. It is shown that all deterministic cut operators can be formulated in unextended EAGLE. Even though the operators do not increase EAGLE's expressiveness, we show in Section 5 that the new operators enable more efficient on-line monitoring.

4.1   Syntax and Semantics of Deterministic Cut Operators

EAGLE with deterministic cut operators extends the syntax of Definition 1. For brevity just the new BNF production F is given. The other productions are left unchanged.

Definition 4. EAGLE$_{[]}$ *denotes an extension of* EAGLE *with additional mixfix operators, where the production F of Definition 1 is replaced by*

$$F ::= \textbf{False} \,|\, \textbf{True} \,|\, x_i \,|\, expression \,|\, \neg F \,|\, F_1 \vee F_2 \,|\, \bigcirc F \,|\, \odot F \,|$$
$$F_1 \circ F_2 \;|\; \lfloor F_1 \rfloor \circ F_2 \;|\; \lceil F_1 \rceil \circ F_2 \;|\; F_1 \circ \lfloor F_1 \rfloor \;|\; F_1 \circ \lceil F_1 \rceil \;|\; N(F_1, \ldots, F_n)$$
$$\circ ::= \; ; \;|\; \cdot$$

In conjunction with a concatenation or sequential composition operator, we write $\lfloor F \rfloor$ and $\lceil F \rceil$ to denote that F is only satisfied on its respectively shortest and longest sub-trace of all the sub-traces that satisfy the unrestricted F. In the following, we will then refer to $\lfloor F \rfloor$ and $\lceil F \rceil$ as the minimally and maximally trace length restricting formulæ, respectively. As with the definition of EAGLE$_{[]}$'s syntax, only the extensions to EAGLE's semantics is given.

Definition 5. *On traces* $\sigma = s_1 s_2 \ldots s_{|\sigma|}$ *the satisfiability relation* $\sigma, i \models_D F$, *with* $0 \leq i \leq |\sigma| + 1$, *is extended by*

$\sigma, i \models_D \lfloor F_1 \rfloor \cdot F_2$ iff $\exists j. i \leq j \leq |\sigma| + 1$ and $\sigma^{[1,j-1]}, i \models_D F_1$ and
$\qquad \sigma^{[j,|\sigma|]}, 1 \models_D F_2$ and $\neg \exists k. i - 1 \leq k < j - 1$ and $\sigma^{[1,k]}, i \models F_1$

$\sigma, i \models_D \lceil F_1 \rceil \cdot F_2$ iff $\exists j. i \leq j \leq |\sigma| + 1$ and $\sigma^{[1,j-1]}, i \models_D F_1$ and
$\qquad \sigma^{[j,|\sigma|]}, 1 \models_D F_2$ and $\neg \exists k. j \leq k \leq |\sigma|$ and $\sigma^{[1,k]}, i \models F_1$

$\sigma, i \models_D F_1 \cdot \lfloor F_2 \rfloor$ iff $\exists j. i \leq j \leq |\sigma| + 1$ and $\sigma^{[1,j-1]}, i \models_D F_1$ and
$\qquad \sigma^{[j,|\sigma|]}, 1 \models_D F_2$ and $\neg \exists k. j < k \leq |\sigma| + 1$ and $\sigma^{[k,|\sigma|]}, 1 \models F_2$

$\sigma, i \models_D F_1 \cdot \lceil F_2 \rceil$ iff $\exists j. i \leq j \leq |\sigma| + 1$ and $\sigma^{[1,j-1]}, i \models_D F_1$ and
$\qquad \sigma^{[j,|\sigma|]}, 1 \models_D F_2$ and $\neg \exists k. 1 \leq k < j$ and $\sigma^{[k,|\sigma|]}, 1 \models F_2$

$\sigma, i \models_D \lfloor F_1 \rfloor ; F_2$ iff $\exists j. i < j \leq |\sigma| + 1$ and $\sigma^{[1,j-1]}, i \models_D F_1$ and
$\qquad \sigma^{[j-1,|\sigma|]}, 1 \models_D F_2$ and $\neg \exists k. i \leq k < j - 1$ and $\sigma^{[1,k]}, i \models F_1$

$$\sigma, i \models_D \lceil F_1 \rceil \,;\, F_2 \text{ iff } \exists j. \, i < j \leq |\sigma| + 1 \text{ and } \sigma^{[1,j-1]}, i \models_D F_1 \text{ and}$$
$$\sigma^{[j-1,|\sigma|]}, 1 \models_D F_2 \text{ and } \neg\exists k. j \leq k \leq |\sigma| \text{ and } \sigma^{[1,k]}, i \models F_1$$

$$\sigma, i \models_D F_1 \,;\, \lfloor F_2 \rfloor \text{ iff } \exists j. \, i < j \leq |\sigma| + 1 \text{ and } \sigma^{[1,j-1]}, i \models_D F_1 \text{ and}$$
$$\sigma^{[j-1,|\sigma|]}, 1 \models_D F_2 \text{ and } \neg\exists k. j \leq k \leq |\sigma| \text{ and } \sigma^{[k,|\sigma|]}, 1 \models F_2$$

$$\sigma, i \models_D F_1 \,;\, \lceil F_2 \rceil \text{ iff } \exists j. \, i < j \leq |\sigma| + 1 \text{ and } \sigma^{[1,j-1]}, i \models_D F_1 \text{ and}$$
$$\sigma^{[j-1,|\sigma|]}, 1 \models_D F_2 \text{ and } \neg\exists k. 1 \leq k < j - 1 \text{ and } \sigma^{[k,|\sigma|]}, 1 \models F_2$$

We depict three applications of the deterministic cut operators in Figure 2 below, where we show the evaluation of $\sigma, 1 \models \text{Eventually(err)} \,;\, \lceil \text{rst} \rceil$, $\sigma, 1 \models \varphi$ and $\sigma, 1 \models \psi$ on an example trace σ as shown below:

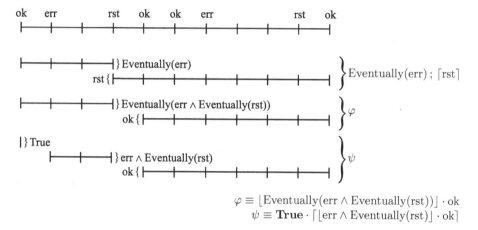

$$\varphi \equiv \lfloor \text{Eventually(err} \wedge \text{Eventually(rst))} \rfloor \cdot \text{ok}$$
$$\psi \equiv \textbf{True} \cdot \lceil \lfloor \text{err} \wedge \text{Eventually(rst)} \rfloor \cdot \text{ok} \rceil$$

Fig. 2. Examples of deterministic cut operator applications

Remark: It should be noted that while $\sigma, 1 \models \text{Eventually(err)} \,;\, \lceil \text{rst} \rceil$ is satisfied on the example trace, we have $\sigma, 1 \not\models \text{Eventually(err)} \,;\, \lceil \text{ok} \rceil$. The longest subtrace on which "ok" is satisfied is the whole trace, but for that cut the left-hand formula Eventually(err) is not true.

4.2   Definability of Deterministic Cut Operators in EAGLE

It is not apparent whether the mixfix variants of sequential composition and concatenation can also be defined in EAGLE. In the following it will be shown that EAGLE$_{[]}$ is not more expressive than EAGLE. The translation of the maximal mixfix operators into EAGLE is given first, followed by the translation for the minimal mixfix operators.

For the maximal mixfix-operators, we will use the rules[4]

---

[4] NonMtMxLT spells out as **NonEmptyMaximalLeftTrace**, etc.

min NonMtMxLT(**Form** F_1, **Form** F_2) =
$\quad$ $(((F_1 \wedge \bigcirc \text{Limit}()) \cdot F_2) \rightarrow \neg((F_1 \wedge \text{Eventually}(\bigcirc^2\text{Limit}())) \cdot \textbf{True})) \vee$
$\quad$ $\bigcirc\text{NonMtMxLT}(\odot F_1, F_2,),$

min NonMtMxRT(**Form** F_1, **Form** F_2) =
$\quad$ $((F_1 \cdot (F_2 \wedge \bigcirc\text{Limit}())) \rightarrow \neg(\textbf{True} \cdot (F_2 \wedge \text{Eventually}(\bigcirc^2\text{Limit}())))) \vee$
$\quad$ $\bigcirc\text{NonMtMxRT}(F_1, \odot F_2),$

min NonMtMxOvrlpngLT(**Form** F_1, **Form** F_2) =
$\quad$ $(((F_1 \wedge \bigcirc\text{Limit}()) ; F_2) \rightarrow \neg((F_1 \wedge \text{Eventually}(\bigcirc^2\text{Limit}())) ; \textbf{True})) \vee$
$\quad$ $\bigcirc\text{NonMtMxOvrlpngLT}(\odot F_1, F_2,),$

min NonMtMxOvrlpngRT(**Form** F_1, **Form** F_2) =
$\quad$ $((F_1 ; (F_2 \wedge \bigcirc\text{Limit}())) \rightarrow \neg(\textbf{True} ; (F_2 \wedge \text{Eventually}(\bigcirc^2\text{Limit}())))) \vee$
$\quad$ $\bigcirc\text{NonMtMxOvrlpngRT}(F_1, \odot F_2),$

in order to denote the semantics of $\lceil F_1 \rceil \cdot F_2$, $F_1 \cdot \lceil F_2 \rceil$, $\lceil F_1 \rceil ; F_2$ and $F_1 ; \lceil F_2 \rceil$ on non-empty traces, respectively. Since $\lceil F_1 \rceil \cdot F_2$ and $F_1 \cdot \lceil F_2 \rceil$ could be satisfiable on the empty trace, their corresponding rules in the respective translations have to be accompanied by a formula that explicitly handles the formulæ holding on the empty trace.

We outline the semantics of NonMtMxLT(F_1, F_2) only, since the semantics of the remaining rules can be explained similarly. When NonMtMxLT(F_1, F_2) is substituted for $\lceil F_1 \rceil \cdot F_2$, the first invocation of its rule body will cause a cut of the form $(((F_1 \wedge \bigcirc\text{Limit}()) \cdot F_2) \rightarrow \neg((F_1 \wedge \text{Eventually}(\bigcirc^2\text{Limit}())) \cdot \textbf{True}))$. The sub-formula $(F_1 \wedge \bigcirc\text{Limit}()) \cdot F_2$ denotes that the cut is enforced so that the right boundary of the left-subtrace follows immediately the current index at which the rule body is evaluated at. Then, the implication following the formula $\neg((F_1 \wedge \text{Eventually}(\bigcirc^2\text{Limit}())) \cdot \textbf{True}))$ assures that F_1 is not satisfied on any sub-trace for which the cut is made further to the right. Alternatively, the rule body enters a recursion due to the disjunctive formula $\bigcirc\text{NonMtMxLT}(\odot F_1, F_2)$. With each recursion, the cut is moved one index further to the right, where the recursion terminates as soon as the boundary of the trace under inspection is reached.

With these rule definitions, the maximal mixfix operators can be expressed in EAGLE as

$$\lceil F_1 \rceil \cdot F_2 \equiv (((F_1 \wedge \text{Limit}()) \cdot F_2) \rightarrow \neg((F_1 \wedge \neg\text{Limit}()) \cdot \textbf{True})) \vee$$
$$\text{NonMtMxLT}(F_1, F_2)$$
$$F_1 \cdot \lceil F_2 \rceil \equiv ((F_1 \cdot (F_2 \wedge \text{Limit}())) \rightarrow \neg(\textbf{True} \cdot (F_2 \wedge \neg\text{Limit}()))) \vee$$
$$\text{NonMtMxRT}(F_1, F_2)$$
$$\lceil F_1 \rceil ; F_2 \equiv \text{NonMtMxOvrlpngLT}(F_1, F_2)$$
$$F_1 ; \lceil F_2 \rceil \equiv \text{NonMtMxOvrlpngRT}(F_1, F_2)$$

Theorem 3. *For each of the formulæ* $\lceil F_1 \rceil \cdot F_2$, $F_1 \cdot \lceil F_2 \rceil$, $\lceil F_1 \rceil ; F_2$ *and* $F_1 ; \lceil F_2 \rceil$ *of* EAGLE$_{[]}$ *there exists a semantically equivalent formula in* EAGLE.

For the minimal mixfix-operators, the translations are much simpler. Here, we only need an additional rule

$$\textbf{min ShorterNonEmptyTrace}(\textbf{Form } F) =$$
$$((F \wedge \bigcirc\text{Limit}()) \cdot \bigcirc\textbf{True}) \vee \bigcirc\text{ShorterNonEmptyTrace}(\odot F)$$

which is satisfied when there is a shorter non-empty sub-trace of the current trace under inspection on which F is satisfied. In the actual translation, it is then sufficient to verify whether the restricted sub-formula cannot be satisfied on a shorter sub-trace. For example, $\lfloor F_1 \rfloor \cdot F_2$ becomes $(F_1 \wedge \neg\text{ShorterNonEmptyTrace}(F_1)) \cdot F_2$, which reflects the semantics of $\lfloor F_1 \rfloor \cdot F_2$ under the assumption that F_1 is not satisfied on the empty trace. Since for mixfix concatenation formulæ it is the case that the trace length restricted formula can also be satisfied on the empty trace, we have to add a formula to the translations which explicitly addresses this.

When also considering the minimal mixfix operators' semantics on the empty trace, we get the following translations into EAGLE:

$$\lfloor F_1 \rfloor \cdot F_2 \equiv ((F_1 \wedge \text{Limit}()) \cdot F_2) \vee$$
$$(((F_1 \wedge \neg\text{ShorterNonEmptyTrace}(F_1)) \cdot F_2) \rightarrow \neg(F_1 \wedge \text{Limit}() \cdot \textbf{True}))$$
$$F_1 \cdot \lfloor F_2 \rfloor \equiv (F_1 \cdot (F_2 \wedge \text{Limit}())) \vee$$
$$((F_1 \cdot (F_2 \wedge \neg\text{ShorterNonEmptyTrace}(F_2))) \rightarrow \neg(\textbf{True} \cdot (F_2 \wedge \text{Limit}())))$$
$$\lfloor F_1 \rfloor \, ; \, F_2 \equiv (F_1 \wedge \neg\text{ShorterNonEmptyTrace}(F_1)) \, ; \, F_2$$
$$F_1 \, ; \, \lfloor F_2 \rfloor \equiv F_1 \, ; \, (F_2 \wedge \neg\text{ShorterNonEmptyTrace}(F_2))$$

Theorem 4. *For each of the formulæ* $\lfloor F_1 \rfloor \cdot F_2$, $F_1 \cdot \lfloor F_2 \rfloor$, $\lfloor F_1 \rfloor \, ; \, F_2$ *and* $F_1 \, ; \, \lfloor F_2 \rfloor$ *of* EAGLE$_{[]}$ *there exists a semantically equivalent formula in* EAGLE.

5   On-Line Monitoring of Deterministic Cut Operators

In [BGHS04b], a calculus for EAGLE was presented that defines directly an on-line monitoring algorithm in which observation states are consumed on a step-by-step basis in tandem with a partial evaluation of the monitoring formula. Here, EAGLE's calculus is extended by rules that encode the semantics of the mixfix operators of EAGLE$_{[]}$. For the calculus of EAGLE$_{[]}$, we establish that the asymptotic space complexity of on-line monitoring for the variants with restrictions applied to the left operand is no worse than the asymptotic space complexity of the sub-formulæ. For the operators with restrictions applied to the right operand, we show that the space complexity coincides with the corresponding non-deterministic operators.

The extended calculus allows us an efficient evaluation, which can not be achieved by substituting appearances of mixfix operators by their semantically equivalent EAGLE-formulæ. For example, in the extended calculus the evaluation of $F_1 \, ; \, \lfloor F_2 \rfloor$ takes $|\sigma|$ applications of $eval\langle\!\langle \ldots \rangle\!\rangle$, while the semantically equivalent EAGLE-formula $F_1 \, ; \, (F_2 \wedge \neg\text{ShorterNonEmptyTrace}(F_2))$ takes already $|\sigma|^2$ applications of $eval\langle\!\langle \ldots \rangle\!\rangle$ due to evaluation of the sequential composition operator in the formula, plus the evaluation steps for the rule ShorterNonEmptyTrace(F_2).

5.1   EAGLE's On-Line Monitoring Algorithm

The evaluation calculus presented in [BGHS04b] used four functions. First, a formula is initialised using $init\langle\!\langle \ldots \rangle\!\rangle$, which substitutes rules by their rule bodies. Second, $eval\langle\!\langle \ldots \rangle\!\rangle$ evaluates the resulting formula in the current state, where $update\langle\!\langle \ldots \rangle\!\rangle$ takes care of $\odot$-operators so that a history of states does not need to be stored. Third, $value\langle\!\langle \ldots \rangle\!\rangle$ determines the truth value of the verification at the boundaries of the trace.

In the following, $\rho b.F(b)$ is a closed term which denotes a fixed-point, such that $\rho b.F(b) = F(\rho b.F(b))$, where b represents the recursion variable. Furthermore, named operators are introduced. The named operators are indeed functions of some type $\mathbf{Form} \times \ldots \times \mathbf{Form} \to \mathbf{Form}$ such that it is possible to rewrite a formula during evaluation.

Rules are assumed to have their parameters ordered by their type in the form $N(\mathbf{Form}\ F_1, \ldots, \mathbf{Form}\ F_m, primitive\ type\ x_1, \ldots, primitive\ type\ x_n) = F$. W.l.o.g. all definitions can be rewritten into this form by simply reordering the rule's arguments. The arguments are then written as two vectors $\vec{F}$ and $\vec{P}$ with types $\overrightarrow{\mathbf{Form}}$ and $\vec{T}$ respectively. Similar to the rewriting of $\bigcirc$, each rule N is rewritten as $\overline{N} : \mathbf{Form} \times \vec{T} \to \mathbf{Form}$ during initialisation, where the first argument denotes a recursive application of the rule body of N.

Definition 6. *A monitoring formula F holds on a trace $\sigma = s_1 s_2 \ldots s_{|\sigma|}$, iff the formula $value\langle\!\langle eval\langle\!\langle \ldots eval\langle\!\langle eval\langle\!\langle init\langle\!\langle F, \mathtt{null}, \mathtt{null} \rangle\!\rangle, s_1 \rangle\!\rangle, s_2 \rangle\!\rangle \ldots, s_{|\sigma|} \rangle\!\rangle \rangle\!\rangle$ evaluates to* **True**, *where* $\mathtt{null}$ *denotes a special element that is not equivalent to any other formula of* EAGLE. *Instances of vector types $\overrightarrow{\mathbf{Form}}$ and $\vec{T}$ are denoted by $\langle F_1, \ldots, F_n \rangle$ and $\langle p, \ldots, r \rangle$ respectively. For both vector types, $\vec{\emptyset}$ denotes the empty vector. The rules for the temporal operators and temporal predicates are:*

$$init\langle\!\langle \bigcirc F, Z, b' \rangle\!\rangle = \underline{\mathrm{Next}}(init\langle\!\langle F, Z, b' \rangle\!\rangle)$$

$$init\langle\!\langle \odot F, Z, b' \rangle\!\rangle = \underline{\mathrm{Previous}}(\alpha, value\langle\!\langle \alpha \rangle\!\rangle), \text{ where } \alpha = init\langle\!\langle F, Z, b' \rangle\!\rangle$$

$$init\langle\!\langle F_1 \circ F_2, Z, b' \rangle\!\rangle = init\langle\!\langle F_1, Z, b' \rangle\!\rangle \circ init\langle\!\langle F_2, Z, b' \rangle\!\rangle, \text{ where } \circ \in \{\cdot, ; \}$$

$$init\langle\!\langle N(\vec{F}, \vec{P}), N(\vec{F}, \vec{P}'), b' \rangle\!\rangle = \overline{N}(b', \vec{P})$$

$$init\langle\!\langle N(\vec{F}, \vec{P}), Z, b' \rangle\!\rangle = \overline{N}(\rho b.init\langle\!\langle F[\hat{F}/\vec{F}], N(\vec{F}, \vec{P}), b \rangle\!\rangle, \vec{P}), \text{ where}$$
$$\hat{F} = init\langle\!\langle \vec{F}, Z, b' \rangle\!\rangle \text{ and } Z \not\equiv \overline{N}(\vec{F}, \ldots)$$

$$value\langle\!\langle \underline{\mathrm{Next}}(F) \rangle\!\rangle = \begin{cases} F & \text{if at the beginning of the trace} \\ \mathbf{False} & \text{if at the end of the trace or } |\sigma| = 0 \end{cases}$$

$$value\langle\!\langle \underline{\mathrm{Previous}}(F, \hat{F}) \rangle\!\rangle = \begin{cases} \mathbf{False} & \text{if at the beg. of the trace or } |\sigma| = 0 \\ value\langle\!\langle F \rangle\!\rangle & \text{if at the end of the trace} \end{cases}$$

$$value\langle\!\langle F_1 \cdot F_2 \rangle\!\rangle = value\langle\!\langle F_1 \rangle\!\rangle \wedge value\langle\!\langle F_2 \rangle\!\rangle$$

$$value\langle\!\langle F_1 ; F_2 \rangle\!\rangle = \mathbf{False}$$

$$value\langle\!\langle \overline{N}(\vec{F}, \vec{P}) \rangle\!\rangle = \begin{cases} \mathbf{True} & \text{if } (\mathbf{max}\ N(\ldots)) \in R, \\ \mathbf{False} & \text{otherwise} \end{cases}$$

$$eval\langle\!\langle\underline{\text{Next}}(F), s\rangle\!\rangle = update\langle\!\langle F, s, \texttt{null}, \texttt{null}\rangle\!\rangle$$
$$eval\langle\!\langle\underline{\text{Previous}}(F, \hat{F}), s\rangle\!\rangle = eval\langle\!\langle \hat{F}, s\rangle\!\rangle$$
$$eval\langle\!\langle F_1 \cdot F_2, s\rangle\!\rangle = \underline{\text{if }} value\langle\!\langle F_1\rangle\!\rangle = \textbf{True} \underline{\text{ then }} (\alpha \cdot F_2) \vee eval\langle\!\langle F_2, s\rangle\!\rangle$$
$$\underline{\text{else }} \alpha \cdot F_2, \text{ where } \alpha = eval\langle\!\langle F_1, s\rangle\!\rangle$$
$$eval\langle\!\langle F_1 \,;\, F_2, s\rangle\!\rangle = \underline{\text{if }} value\langle\!\langle \alpha\rangle\!\rangle = \textbf{True} \underline{\text{ then }} (\alpha \,;\, F_2) \vee eval\langle\!\langle F_2, s\rangle\!\rangle$$
$$\underline{\text{else }} \alpha \,;\, F_2, \text{ where } \alpha = eval\langle\!\langle F_1, s\rangle\!\rangle$$
$$eval\langle\!\langle \overline{N}(\rho b'.F(b'), \vec{P}), s\rangle\!\rangle = eval\langle\!\langle F(\rho b'.F(b'))[eval\langle\!\langle \vec{P}, s\rangle\!\rangle/\vec{p}], s\rangle\!\rangle$$

$$update\langle\!\langle\underline{\text{Next}}(F), s, Z, b'\rangle\!\rangle = \underline{\text{Next}}(update\langle\!\langle F, s, Z, b'\rangle\!\rangle)$$
$$update\langle\!\langle\underline{\text{Previous}}(F, \hat{F}), s, Z, b'\rangle\!\rangle = \underline{\text{Previous}}(update\langle\!\langle F, s, Z, b'\rangle\!\rangle, eval\langle\!\langle F, s\rangle\!\rangle)$$
$$update\langle\!\langle F_1 \circ F_2, s, Z, b'\rangle\!\rangle = update\langle\!\langle F_1, s, Z, b'\rangle\!\rangle \circ F_2, \text{ where } \circ \in \{\,;\,, \cdot\,\}$$
$$update\langle\!\langle\alpha, s, \alpha, b'\rangle\!\rangle = \overline{N}(b', \vec{P}), \text{ where } \alpha \equiv \overline{N}(\rho b.F(b), \vec{P})$$
$$update\langle\!\langle\alpha, s, \hat{F}, Z\rangle\!\rangle = \overline{N}(\rho b'.update\langle\!\langle F(\rho b'.F(b')), s, \alpha, \vec{P}\rangle\!\rangle, \vec{P}),$$
$$\text{where } \alpha \equiv \overline{N}(\rho b.F(b), \vec{P}) \text{ and } Z \not\equiv \overline{N}(\vec{F}, \dots)$$

The rules for propositional constants and operators are defined in the obvious way.

We provide a rather simple example that shows the evaluation of the temporal operators $\bigcirc$ and $\odot$. As example trace we have chosen a trace of length one, where in its only state the proposition p is true.
Evaluating $\bigcirc\odot p$ on $\langle\{p\}\rangle$:

1. $value\langle\!\langle eval\langle\!\langle init\langle\!\langle \bigcirc\odot p, \texttt{null}, \texttt{null}\rangle\!\rangle, s_1\rangle\!\rangle\rangle\!\rangle$
2. $value\langle\!\langle eval\langle\!\langle\underline{\text{Next}}(init\langle\!\langle \odot p, \texttt{null}, \texttt{null}\rangle\!\rangle), s_1\rangle\!\rangle\rangle\!\rangle$

For the next step, $init\langle\!\langle \odot p, \texttt{null}, \texttt{null}\rangle\!\rangle$ is rewritten to $\underline{\text{Previous}}(init\langle\!\langle p, \texttt{null}, \texttt{null}\rangle\!\rangle, value\langle\!\langle init\langle\!\langle p, \texttt{null}, \texttt{null}\rangle\!\rangle\rangle\!\rangle)$. The first parameter of $\underline{\text{Previous}}(\dots)$ stores the formula that would be evaluated after the $\odot$-operator. In the second parameter, the past is stored, which is referring to the left boundary of the trace now.

3. $value\langle\!\langle eval\langle\!\langle$
   $\underline{\text{Next}}(\underline{\text{Previous}}(init\langle\!\langle p, \texttt{null}, \texttt{null}\rangle\!\rangle, value\langle\!\langle init\langle\!\langle p, \texttt{null}, \texttt{null}\rangle\!\rangle\rangle\!\rangle)), s_1\rangle\!\rangle\rangle\!\rangle$
4. $value\langle\!\langle eval\langle\!\langle\underline{\text{Next}}(\underline{\text{Previous}}(p, value\langle\!\langle p\rangle\!\rangle)), s_1\rangle\!\rangle\rangle\!\rangle$
5. $value\langle\!\langle eval\langle\!\langle\underline{\text{Next}}(\underline{\text{Previous}}(p, \textbf{False})), s_1\rangle\!\rangle\rangle\!\rangle$
6. $value\langle\!\langle update\langle\!\langle\underline{\text{Previous}}(p, \textbf{False}), s_1, \texttt{null}, \texttt{null}\rangle\!\rangle\rangle\!\rangle$

When $\underline{\text{Next}}(\dots)$ is evaluated, it is rewritten to $update\langle\!\langle\dots\rangle\!\rangle$. The last two parameters of $update\langle\!\langle\dots\rangle\!\rangle$ are only used in conjunction with the evaluation of rules, so that they can be ignored in this example. $update\langle\!\langle\dots\rangle\!\rangle$ rewrites the arguments of appearances of $\underline{\text{Previous}}(\dots)$, since due to the next operator, previous states occur now as being shifted one state to the end of the trace. Hence, the first parameter of $\underline{\text{Previous}}(\dots)$, which was used to store the initialised parameter of the $\odot$-operator, is evaluated in this state and the result of this evaluation is placed in the second parameter.

7. $value\langle\!\langle\underline{\text{Previous}}(update\langle\!\langle p, s_1, \texttt{null}, \texttt{null}\rangle\!\rangle, eval\langle\!\langle p, s_1\rangle\!\rangle)\rangle\!\rangle$

$value\langle\!\langle\ldots\rangle\!\rangle$ is now referring to the right boundary of the trace. Hence, the second parameter of $\underline{\text{Previous}}(\ldots)$, which is storing the result of the last state, determines the outcome of $value\langle\!\langle\ldots\rangle\!\rangle$.

8. $value\langle\!\langle\underline{\text{Previous}}(p, \textbf{True})\rangle\!\rangle$
9. $value\langle\!\langle\textbf{True}\rangle\!\rangle$
10. **True**

5.2 EAGLE's Monitoring Algorithm Extended

The following ternary rules $\underline{\text{LMxConcat}}(\ldots)$, $\underline{\text{RMnConcat}}(\ldots)$, $\underline{\text{RMxConcat}}(\ldots)$, $\underline{\text{LMxSeqComp}}(\ldots)$, and $\underline{\text{RMnSeqComp}}(\ldots)$, $\underline{\text{RMxSeqComp}}(\ldots)$, with self-explanatory correspondences to their respective mixfix operators, are used during evaluation to sort out the shortest/longest sub-traces by updating the third argument depending on whether the first two arguments allow a cut to be made or not.

Definition 7. (Extension of Definition 6) EAGLE's calculus is extended by mix-fix variants of sequential composition, such that

$$init\langle\!\langle\lfloor F_1\rfloor \circ F_2, Z, b'\rangle\!\rangle = \lfloor init\langle\!\langle F_1, Z, b'\rangle\!\rangle\rfloor \circ init\langle\!\langle F_2, Z, b'\rangle\!\rangle$$
$$init\langle\!\langle\lceil F_1\rceil \circ F_2, Z, b'\rangle\!\rangle = \varphi(init\langle\!\langle F_1, Z, b'\rangle\!\rangle, init\langle\!\langle F_2, Z, b'\rangle\!\rangle, \texttt{null})$$
$$init\langle\!\langle F_1 \circ \lfloor F_2\rfloor, Z, b'\rangle\!\rangle = \varphi(init\langle\!\langle F_1, Z, b'\rangle\!\rangle, init\langle\!\langle F_2, Z, b'\rangle\!\rangle, \texttt{null})$$
$$init\langle\!\langle F_1 \circ \lceil F_2\rceil, Z, b'\rangle\!\rangle = \varphi(init\langle\!\langle F_1, Z, b'\rangle\!\rangle, init\langle\!\langle F_2, Z, b'\rangle\!\rangle, \underline{\text{List}}(\textbf{False}, \textbf{False}, \texttt{null}))$$

$$value\langle\!\langle\texttt{null}\rangle\!\rangle = \textbf{False}$$
$$value\langle\!\langle\underline{\text{List}}(F_1, F_2, F_3)\rangle\!\rangle = \underline{\text{if }} value\langle\!\langle F_2\rangle\!\rangle = \textbf{True } \underline{\text{then }} F_1$$
$$\underline{\text{else }} value\langle\!\langle F_3\rangle\!\rangle$$
$$value\langle\!\langle\lfloor F_1\rfloor \cdot F_2\rangle\!\rangle = value\langle\!\langle F_1\rangle\!\rangle \wedge value\langle\!\langle F_2\rangle\!\rangle$$
$$value\langle\!\langle\underline{\text{LMxConcat}}(F_1, F_2, F_3)\rangle\!\rangle = \underline{\text{if }} value\langle\!\langle F_1\rangle\!\rangle = \textbf{True } \underline{\text{then }} value\langle\!\langle F_2\rangle\!\rangle$$
$$\underline{\text{else }} value\langle\!\langle F_3\rangle\!\rangle$$
$$value\langle\!\langle\underline{\text{RMnConcat}}(F_1, F_2, F_3)\rangle\!\rangle = \underline{\text{if }} value\langle\!\langle F_2\rangle\!\rangle = \textbf{True } \underline{\text{then }} value\langle\!\langle F_1\rangle\!\rangle$$
$$\underline{\text{else }} value\langle\!\langle F_3\rangle\!\rangle$$
$$value\langle\!\langle\underline{\text{RMxConcat}}(F_1, F_2, F_3)\rangle\!\rangle = value\langle\!\langle\underline{\text{Append}}(F_3, \underline{\text{List}}(value\langle\!\langle F_1\rangle\!\rangle, F_2, \texttt{null}))\rangle\!\rangle$$
$$value\langle\!\langle\lfloor F_1\rfloor ; F_2\rangle\!\rangle = \textbf{False}$$
$$value\langle\!\langle\underline{\text{LMxSeqComp}}(F_1, F_2, F_3)\rangle\!\rangle = value\langle\!\langle\underline{\text{RMnSeqComp}}(F_1, F_2, F_3)\rangle\!\rangle =$$
$$value\langle\!\langle\underline{\text{RMxSeqComp}}(F_1, F_2, F_3)\rangle\!\rangle = value\langle\!\langle F_3\rangle\!\rangle$$

$$eval\langle\!\langle\texttt{null}, s\rangle\!\rangle = \texttt{null}$$
$$eval\langle\!\langle\underline{\text{List}}(F_1, F_2, F_3), s\rangle\!\rangle = \underline{\text{List}}(F_1, \beta, \gamma)$$
$$eval\langle\!\langle\lfloor F_1\rfloor \cdot F_2, s\rangle\!\rangle = \underline{\text{if }} value\langle\!\langle F_1\rangle\!\rangle = \textbf{True } \underline{\text{then }} \beta$$
$$\underline{\text{else }} \lfloor\alpha\rfloor \cdot F_2$$

$$eval\langle\!\langle \underline{\text{LMxConcat}(F_1, F_2, F_3)}, s\rangle\!\rangle = \text{if } value\langle\!\langle F_1\rangle\!\rangle = \textbf{True } \underline{\text{then}}$$
$$\underline{\text{LMxConcat}}(\alpha, F_2, \beta)$$
$$\underline{\text{else LMxConcat}}(\alpha, F_2, \gamma)$$
$$eval\langle\!\langle \underline{\text{RMnConcat}(F_1, F_2, F_3)}, s\rangle\!\rangle =$$
$$\underline{\text{RMnConcat}}(\alpha, F_2, eval\langle\!\langle \underline{\text{List}}(value\langle\!\langle F_1\rangle\!\rangle, F_2, F_3), s\rangle\!\rangle)$$
$$eval\langle\!\langle \underline{\text{RMxConcat}(F_1, F_2, F_3)}, s\rangle\!\rangle =$$
$$\underline{\text{RMxConcat}}(\alpha, F_2, eval\langle\!\langle \text{Append}(F_3, \underline{\text{List}}(value\langle\!\langle F_1\rangle\!\rangle, F_2, \texttt{null})), s\rangle\!\rangle)$$
$$eval\langle\!\langle \lfloor F_1 \rfloor \, ; \, F_2, s\rangle\!\rangle = \text{if } value\langle\!\langle \alpha\rangle\!\rangle = \textbf{True } \underline{\text{then}} \, \beta$$
$$\underline{\text{else}} \, \lfloor \alpha \rfloor \, ; \, F_2$$
$$eval\langle\!\langle \underline{\text{LMxSeqComp}(F_1, F_2, F_3)}, s\rangle\!\rangle = \text{if } value\langle\!\langle \alpha\rangle\!\rangle = \textbf{True } \underline{\text{then}}$$
$$\underline{\text{LMxSeqComp}}(\alpha, F_2, \beta)$$
$$\underline{\text{else LMxSeqComp}}(\alpha, F_2, \gamma)$$
$$eval\langle\!\langle \underline{\text{RMnSeqComp}(F_1, F_2, F_3)}, s\rangle\!\rangle =$$
$$\underline{\text{RMnSeqComp}}(\alpha, F_2, eval\langle\!\langle \underline{\text{List}}(value\langle\!\langle \alpha\rangle\!\rangle, F_2, F_3), s\rangle\!\rangle)$$
$$eval\langle\!\langle \underline{\text{RMxSeqComp}(F_1, F_2, F_3)}, s\rangle\!\rangle =$$
$$\underline{\text{RMxSeqComp}}(\alpha, F_2, eval\langle\!\langle \text{Append}(F_3, \underline{\text{List}}(value\langle\!\langle \alpha\rangle\!\rangle, F_2, \texttt{null})), s\rangle\!\rangle)$$
$$update\langle\!\langle \lfloor F_1 \rfloor \circ F_2, s, Z, b'\rangle\!\rangle = \lfloor update\langle\!\langle F_1, s, Z, b'\rangle\!\rangle \rfloor \circ F_2$$
$$update\langle\!\langle \varphi(F_1, F_2, F_3), s, Z, b'\rangle\!\rangle =$$
$$\varphi(update\langle\!\langle F_1, s, Z, b'\rangle\!\rangle, F_2, F_3)$$

where $\alpha \equiv eval\langle\!\langle F_1, s\rangle\!\rangle$, $\beta \equiv eval\langle\!\langle F_2, s\rangle\!\rangle$, $\gamma \equiv eval\langle\!\langle F_3, s\rangle\!\rangle$, $\circ \in \{\, ; \, , \cdot \}$, *and* φ *denotes the rule* LMxSeqComp, RMnSeqComp, RMxSeqComp, LMxConcat, RMnConcat, RMxConcat, *which is apparent from the context.*

Theorem 5. *The semantics of* EAGLE$_{[]}$ *'s calculus (Definition 7) coincide with the semantics of the corresponding logic (Definition 5).*

5.3   On-Line Monitoring Complexity

We now consider the time and space requirements of the evaluation of concatenation, sequential composition and the mixfix operators. In [BGHS04a], we showed that the time and space complexity of the future LTL fragment of EA-GLE is independent of the length of the monitoring trace. We first show below that the evaluation of a non-deterministic cut operator $F_1 \circ F_2$, $\circ \in \{\, ; \, , \cdot \}$, whose operands are free of cut formula may require $O(|\sigma|^2)$ number of calls to evaluate F_2 (Theorem 6). However, for the mixfix operators with restrictions on the left, the complexity is reduced to being independent of the trace length again (Theorem 7).

Consider an arbitrary formula $F_1 \cdot F_2$. The state evaluation rule for concatenation is given by

$$eval\langle\!\langle F_1 \cdot F_2, s\rangle\!\rangle = \text{if } value\langle\!\langle F_1\rangle\!\rangle = \textbf{True } \underline{\text{then}} \, (eval\langle\!\langle F_1, s\rangle\!\rangle \cdot F_2) \vee eval\langle\!\langle F_2, s\rangle\!\rangle$$
$$\underline{\text{else}} \, eval\langle\!\langle F_1, s\rangle\!\rangle \cdot F_2$$

In the worst case scenario of evaluating concatenation, a non-deterministic cut is made at each state of a trace. This can be enforced by the formula $\textbf{True} \cdot F_2$. On an arbitrary trace σ, $\textbf{True} \cdot F_2$ is evaluated as

$$value \langle\!\langle eval \langle\!\langle \ldots eval \langle\!\langle eval \langle\!\langle init \langle\!\langle \textbf{True} \cdot F_2, \texttt{null}, \texttt{null} \rangle\!\rangle, s_1 \rangle\!\rangle, s_2 \rangle\!\rangle \ldots, s_{|\sigma|} \rangle\!\rangle \rangle\!\rangle$$

By straightforward applications of rules of EAGLE$_{[]}$'s calculus, the evaluation can be unfolded as

$$value \langle\!\langle \bigvee_{n=1}^{|\sigma|} eval \langle\!\langle \ldots eval \langle\!\langle eval \langle\!\langle init \langle\!\langle F_2, \texttt{null}, \texttt{null} \rangle\!\rangle, s_n \rangle\!\rangle, s_{n+1} \rangle\!\rangle \ldots, s_{|\sigma|} \rangle\!\rangle \rangle\!\rangle$$

Relative to the evaluation of F_2, the formula requires $(|\sigma|^2 + |\sigma|)/2$ applications of $eval \langle\!\langle \ldots \rangle\!\rangle$. This argumentation can be carried forward to sequential composition as well, and additionally, to all mixfix operators with restrictions on the right operand.

Theorem 6. *For a given trace σ, the operators $F_1 \cdot F_2$, $F_1 \,;\, F_2$, $F_1 \cdot \lfloor F_2 \rfloor$, $F_1 \cdot \lceil F_2 \rceil$, $F_1 \,;\, \lfloor F_2 \rfloor$ and $F_1 \,;\, \lceil F_2 \rceil$ require up to $O(|\sigma|^2)$ applications of $eval \langle\!\langle \ldots \rangle\!\rangle$ in addition to the applications required to evaluate F_1 and F_2.*

When we consider a mixfix formula with deterministic restrictions on the left operand, e.g. $\lfloor F_1 \rfloor \cdot F_2$, then we can show that we only need linear-space for its evaluation – relative to the space required to evaluate the operands. By taking the state-evaluation rule for $\lfloor F_1 \rfloor \cdot F_2$, i.e.

$$eval \langle\!\langle \lfloor F_1 \rfloor \cdot F_2, s \rangle\!\rangle = \text{if } value \langle\!\langle F_1 \rangle\!\rangle = \textbf{True } \underline{\text{then }} eval \langle\!\langle F_2, s \rangle\!\rangle$$
$$\underline{\text{else}} \lfloor eval \langle\!\langle F_1, s \rangle\!\rangle \rfloor \cdot F_2$$

one can immediately see that the non-deterministic choice of concatenation (i.e. $(eval \langle\!\langle F_1, s \rangle\!\rangle \cdot F_2) \vee eval \langle\!\langle F_2, s \rangle\!\rangle$) is replaced by a single application of $eval \langle\!\langle \ldots \rangle\!\rangle$. We can carry this forward to all mixfix operators with restrictions on the left operand, so that we obtain the following result:

Theorem 7. *For a given trace σ, the left mixfix operators $\lfloor F_1 \rfloor \cdot F_2$, $\lceil F_1 \rceil \cdot F_2$, $\lfloor F_1 \rfloor \,;\, F_2$ and $\lceil F_1 \rceil \,;\, F_2$ require only $O(|\sigma|)$ applications of $eval \langle\!\langle \ldots \rangle\!\rangle$ in addition to the applications required to evaluate F_1 and F_2.*

6   Conclusion

For the runtime verification logic EAGLE, we have shown that concatenation and sequential composition are equally expressive. Furthermore, mixfix operators were introduced, which limit the possible number of cuts of sequential composition and concatenation. The new operators restrict the lengths of the sequential composition/concatenation sub-traces, such that the corresponding sub-formula is satisfied on a sub-trace of minimal or maximal length. Since the cut is then uniquely defined on the trace, the mixfix variants of sequential composition and concatenation are deterministic counterparts of their corresponding non-mixfix operators. We further showed that the semantics of the mixfix operators are already definable in unextended EAGLE. For all mixfix operators, semantically equivalent mixfix operator free formulæ were presented. We then extended EAGLE's on-line monitoring calculus with rules for the new operators, where we could show that right-hand side restricted mixfix operators evaluate as efficiently as their non-deterministic counterparts, and left-hand side restricted mixfix operators can be evaluated more efficiently.

Acknowledgements

Joachim Baran thanks the EPSRC and the School of Computer Science for the research training awards enabling this work to be undertaken.

References

[BGHS04a]   Barringer, H., Goldberg, A., Havelund, K., Sen, K.: Program monitoring with LTL in EAGLE. In: 18th International Parallel and Distributed Processing Symposium, IPDPS 2004. IEEE Computer Society, Los Alamitos (2004)

[BGHS04b]   Barringer, H., Goldberg, A., Havelund, K., Sen, K.: Rule-based runtime verification. In: Steffen, B., Levi, G. (eds.) VMCAI 2004. LNCS, vol. 2937, pp. 44–57. Springer, Heidelberg (2004)

[CHMP81]   Chandra, A., Halpern, J., Meyer, A., Parikh, R.: Equations between regular terms and an application to process logic. In: STOC 1981: Proceedings of the 13th Annual ACM Symposium on Theory of Computing, pp. 384–390. ACM Press, New York (1981)

[Koz83]   Kozen, D.: Results on the propositional μ-calculus. Theoretical Computer Science 27, 333–354 (1983)

[Min61]   Minsky, M.L.: Recursive unsolvability of Post's problem of "tag" and other topics in theory of Turing machines. The Annals of Mathematics 74(3), 437–455 (1961)

[Wol83]   Wolper, P.: Temporal logic can be more expressive. Information and Control 56(1–2), 72–99 (1983)

Checking Traces for Regulatory Conformance[*]

Nikhil Dinesh, Aravind Joshi, Insup Lee, and Oleg Sokolsky

Department of Computer Science,
University of Pennsylvania,
Philadelphia, PA 19104-6389, USA
{nikhild,joshi,lee,sokolsky}@seas.upenn.edu

Abstract. We consider the problem of checking whether the operations of an organization conform to a body of regulation. The immediate motivation comes from the analysis of the U.S. Food and Drug Administration regulations that apply to bloodbanks - organizations that collect, process, store, and use donations of blood and blood components. Statements in such regulations convey constraints on operations or sequences of operations that are performed by an organization. It is natural to express these constraints in a temporal logic.

There are two important features of regulatory texts that need to be accommodated by a representation in logic. First, the constraints conveyed by regulation can be obligatory (required) or permitted (optional). Second, statements in regulation refer to others for conditions or exceptions. An organization conforms to a body of regulation if and only if it satisfies all the obligations. However, permissions provide exceptions to obligations, indirectly affecting conformance.

In this paper, we extend linear temporal logic to distinguish between obligations and permissions, and to allow statements to refer to others. While the resulting logic allows for a direct representation of regulation, evaluating references between statements has high complexity. We discuss an empirically motivated assumption that lets us replace references with tests of lower complexity, leading to efficient trace-checking algorithms in practice.

1 Introduction

Regulations, laws and policies that affect many aspects of our lives are represented predominantly as documents in natural language. Mechanically checking compliance with these regulations and policies is an area of growing importance [1,2,3].

In this paper, we will consider one such regulation, the Food and Drug Administration's Code of Federal Regulations (FDA CFR) [4] that governs the operations of U.S. bloodbanks. The CFR is developed by experts in the field of medicine, and regulates the tests that need to be performed on donations of blood before they are used.

Bloodbanks are organizations that perform collection, testing, storage, and distribution of blood donations and are required to conform to the regulation (CFR). The operations of a bloodbank are logged in a database that keeps track of donations that are collected by the bloodbank, tests that are performed on them and, ultimately, the

---

[*] This research was supported in part by NSF CCF-0429948, NSF-CNS-0610297, ARO W911NF-05-1-0158, and ONR MURI N00014-04-1-0735.

M. Leucker (Ed.): RV 2008, LNCS 5289, pp. 86–103, 2008.

way each donation is used. Our goal is to check in an efficient manner that the operations as recorded in the database are compliant with the CFR, and to raise an alarm if a non-compliant action is detected. To achieve this goal, we first need to settle on an approach to formalize regulatory documents, and then consider the feasibility of checking database logs with respect to the formalized regulations.

As we illustrate with examples in Section 2, the basic structure of regulatory statements is to declare that a certain action can take place when certain conditions apply. At a first glance, it seems that such statements can be encoded as logical clauses, where a set of preconditions imply a postcondition. However, there are two complications that need to be addressed. First, regulations convey permissions and obligations, which have to be reflected in the formal description and handled accordingly during the checking. Second, a common phenomenon in regulatory texts is for sentences to function as conditions or exceptions to others. This function of sentences makes them dependent on others for their interpretation, and makes the translation to logic difficult. We call this the problem of *references to other laws*, and it is the central focus of this paper.

In Section 2, we argue that a logic to represent regulation should provide mechanisms for statements to refer to others, and to make inferences from the sentences referred to. We then turn to formalization of regulatory documents and regulated operations. In Section 3.1, we define an abstract model for representing the operations of an organization, followed in Section 3.2 by a predicate-based linear temporal logic to express normative statements in regulation. Formal definitions of conformance are given. We then extend the logic to allow sentences to refer to others, in Section 3.3.

Section 4 describes the checking process. We adapt the methodology of the rule-based formalism Eagle [5] to handle references. In order to check statements with references, we need to compute a fixed point, propagating information between references from one statement to another until we get a consistent evaluation. The evaluation of references has high complexity. We identify a condition, motivated by a case study of the CFR, under which references can be replaced by tests of lower complexity. We also discuss a prototype checking tool.

Section 5 concludes with a discussion of future research directions and a survey of related work.

2 Motivation

In this section, we consider a representative sample of the CFR and argue that a logic to represent regulation should provide a mechanism for sentences to refer to others.

Example. Below we present shortened versions of sentences from the CFR Section 610.40, which we will use as a running example throughout the paper.

(1) Except as specified in (2), every donation of blood or blood component must be tested for evidence of infection due to Hepatitis B.

(2) You are not required to test donations of source plasma for evidence of infection due to Hepatitis B.

Statement (1) conveys an obligation to test donations of blood or blood component for Hepatitis B, and (2) conveys a permission not to test a donation of source plasma (a blood component) for Hepatitis B. To assess an organization's conformance to (1) and (2), it suffices to check whether "all non-source plasma donations are tested for Hepatitis B". In other words, (1) and (2) imply the following obligation:

(3)   Every non-source plasma donation must be tested for evidence of infection due to Hepatitis B.

There are a variety of logics in which one can capture the interpretation of (3), as needed for conformance. For example, in first-order logic, one can write $\forall x : (d(x) \land \neg sp(x)) \Rightarrow test(x)$, where $d(x)$ is true iff x is a donation, $sp(x)$ is true iff x is a source plasma donation, and $test(x)$ is true iff x is tested for Hepatitis B. Thus, to represent (1) and (2) formally, we inferred that they implied (3) and (3) could be represented more directly in a logic.

Now suppose we have a sentence that refers to (1):

(4)   To test for Hepatitis B, you must use a screening test kit.

The reference is more indirect here, but the interpretation is: "if (1) requires a test, then the test must be performed using a screening test kit". A bloodbank is not prevented from using a different kind of test for source plasma donations. (4) can be represented by first producing (3), and then inferring that (3) and (4) imply the following:

(5)   Every non-source plasma donation must be tested for evidence of infection due to Hepatitis B using a screening test kit.

It is easy to represent the interpretation of (5) directly in a logic. However, (5) has a complex relationship to the sentences from which it was derived, i.e., (1), (2) and (4). The derivation takes the form of a tree:

We argue that constructing a single derived obligation from multiple statements should be avoided. On the one hand, the derived obligation can become very complex. The full version of statement (1) in the CFR contains six exceptions, and these exceptions in turn have statements that qualify them further. A statement can be used as an exception to multiple other statements, and it is easy to see that the derived obligation can be exponentially larger than the original set of statements. We advocate an approach that allows us to introduce references into the syntax of the logic, and resolve references during evaluation.

3   Formalization of Regulatory Documents

In this section, we extend linear temporal logic (LTL) to distinguish between obligations and permissions, and allow references between statements. We begin, in Section 3.1, by representing a bloodbank as a run or trace. Section 3.2 extends LTL to distinguish between obligations and permissions, leading to definitions of conformance. We then extend the logic to allow sentences to refer to others (Section 3.3).

3.1   Model for Regulated Operations

Given the need to demonstrate conformance to the regulation in case of an audit, regulated organizations such as bloodbanks keep track of their operations in a database, for example donor information and the tests they perform. Such a system can be thought of abstractly as a relational structure evolving over time. At each point in time (state), there are a set of objects (such as donations and donors) and relations between the objects (such as an association between a donor and her donations). The state changes by the creation, removal or modification of objects. We represent this as a run.

Definition 1 (A Run of a System). *Given a set O (of objects) and countable sets $\Phi_1, ..., \Phi_n$ (where Φ_j is a set of predicate names of arity j), a run of a system $R(O, \Phi_1, ..., \Phi_n)$, abbreviated as R, is a tuple $(r, \pi_1, ..., \pi_n)$ where:*

- *$r : N \rightarrow S$ is a sequence of states. N is the set of natural numbers, and S is a set of states.*
- *$\pi_j : \Phi_j \times S \rightarrow 2^{O^j}$ is a truth assignment to predicates of arity j. Given $p \in \Phi_j$, we will say that $p(o_1, ..., o_j)$ is true at state s iff $(o_1, ..., o_j) \in \pi_j(p, s)$.*

Given a run R and a time $i \in N$, the pair (R, i) is called a point (statements in linear temporal logic are evaluated at points). Given the predicate names $(\Phi_1, ..., \Phi_n)$, the corresponding space of runs is denoted by $\mathcal{R}(\Phi_1, ..., \Phi_n)$, abbreviated as $\mathcal{R}$.

Table 1. A run of a bloodbank

Time	Objects	Predicates
1	o_1	$d(o_1), sp(o_1), \neg test(o_1)$
2	o_1	$d(o_1), sp(o_1), \neg test(o_1)$
	o_2	$d(o_2), \neg sp(o_2), \neg test(o_2)$
3	o_1	$d(o_1), sp(o_1), test(o_1)$
	o_2	$d(o_2), \neg sp(o_2), \neg test(o_2)$

Table 1 shows a possible run of a bloodbank. First, an object o_1 is entered into the system. o_1 is a donation of source plasma ($d(o_1)$ and $sp(o_1)$ are true). When a donation is added, its test predicate is initially false. Then, an object o_2 is added, which is a donation but not of source plasma. In the third step, the object o_1 is tested.

3.2   Logic for Regulatory Conformace

Predicate-based Linear Temporal Logic (PredLTL). The logic that we define in this section is a restricted fragment of first-order modal logic. The restriction is that we allow formulas with free variables, but no quantification over objects. Formulas will be interpreted using the universal generalization rule, i.e., over all assignments to free variables. The restrictions are similar in spirit to logic programs, which have been observed to be sufficiently expressive for the generic statements in regulation [6,7].

Definition 2 (Syntax). *Given sets $\Phi_1, ..., \Phi_n$ (of predicate names) and a set of variables X, the language $L(\Phi_1, ..., \Phi_n, X)$, abbreviated as L, is the smallest set such that:*

- *$p(y_1, ..., y_j) \in L$ where $p \in \Phi_j$ and $(y_1, ..., y_j) \in X^j$.*
- *If $\varphi \in L$, then $\neg\varphi \in L$ and $\Box\varphi \in L$. If $\varphi, \psi \in L$, then $\varphi \wedge \psi \in L$.*

Disjunction $\varphi \vee \psi = \neg(\neg\varphi \wedge \neg\psi)$ and implication $\varphi \Rightarrow \psi = \neg\varphi \vee \psi$ are derived connectives. The temporal operator is understood in the usual way: $\Box\varphi$ (φ holds and will always hold (globally)). $\Diamond\varphi$ (φ will eventually hold) is defined as $\neg\Box\neg\varphi$.

We now extend the syntax to express normative statements in a body of regulation, by distinguishing between obligations and permissions.

Definition 3 (Syntax of Regulation). *Given a finite set of identifiers ID, a body of regulation Reg is a set of statements such that for each $id \in ID$, there exist $\varphi, \psi \in L$ such that either: $id.\mathbf{o}: \varphi \rightsquigarrow \psi \in Reg$, or $id.\mathbf{p}: \varphi \rightsquigarrow \psi \in Reg$*

$id.\mathbf{o}: \varphi \rightsquigarrow \psi$ ($id.\mathbf{p}: \varphi \rightsquigarrow \psi$) is read as: "it is obligated (permitted) that the precondition φ leads to the postcondition ψ".

Definition 4 (Semantics). *Given a run $R = (r, \pi_1, ..., \pi_n)$, $\varphi \in L$, and a variable assignment $v : X \rightarrow O$, the relation $(R, i, v) \models \varphi$ is defined inductively as follows:*

- *$(R, i, v) \models p(y_1, ..., y_j)$ iff $(v(o_1), ..., v(o_j)) \in \pi_j(p, r(i))$.*
- *The semantics of conjunction and negation is defined in the usual way.*
- *$(R, i, v) \models \Box\varphi$ iff for all $k \geq i : (R, k, v) \models \varphi$.*

We extend the semantic relation to regulatory statments. We take $\models$ to stand for "conforms to":

- *$(R, i, v) \models id.\mathbf{o}: \varphi \rightsquigarrow \psi$ iff $(R, i, v) \models \varphi \Rightarrow \psi$ ($\Rightarrow$ is implication)*
- *$(R, i, v) \models id.\mathbf{p}: \varphi \rightsquigarrow \psi$. Runs vacuously conform to permissions. Permissions will become relevant when references from obligations are present (Section 3.3).*

Consider again our example from Section 2. We use three predicates defined as follows. $d(x)$ is true iff x is a donation. $sp(x)$ is true iff x consists of source plama. $test(x)$ is true iff x is tested for Hepatitis B.

Statement (3) is represented as: $3.\mathbf{o}: d(x) \wedge \neg sp(x) \rightsquigarrow \Diamond test(x)$. Statement (2) can be represented as: $2.\mathbf{p}: d(y) \wedge sp(y) \rightsquigarrow \neg\Diamond test(y)$. However, statement (1) cannot be represented directly.

The deontic concepts of obligation and permission are treated as properties of sentences. Only obligations matter for conformance. If a non-source plasma donation is not tested, there is a problem. On the other hand, a bloodbank may choose to test a donation of source plasma or not. In assessing conformance, the function of a permission is to serve as an exception to an obligation, and in this indirect manner it becomes relevant. We will give a semantics to this function of permissions in Section 3.3. Such a treatment of permissions has its basis in the legal theory of Ross [8].

In the formulation here, obligations and permissions are top-level operators and cannot be negated. This restriction can be removed in several ways, e.g., using a many-valued interpretation. However, we avoid this to simplify presentation. A more crucial restriction is that iterated deontic constructs cannot be expressed directly, i.e., sentences of the form "required to allow x" or "allowed to require x.". One has to decide what top-level obligations or permissions are implied by these constructs. To our knowledge, handling iterated constructs is an open problem in deontic logic [9].

Conformance of a run R is defined using the notion of validity. φ is valid at the point (R, i), $(R, i) \models \varphi$, iff for all variable assignments v: $(R, i, v) \models \varphi$. φ is valid in R, $R \models \varphi$ iff for all i : $(R, i) \models \varphi$.

Definition 5 (Run Conformance). *Given a body of regulation Reg and a run R representing the operations of an organization, we say that R conforms to the regulation iff for all obligations id.$\mathbf{o}$: $\varphi \leadsto \psi \in$ Reg we have $R \models$id.$\mathbf{o}$: $\varphi \leadsto \psi$.*

The definition of conformance is given in terms of obligations. We now extend the logic to allow sentences to refer to others making permissions relevant to conformance.

3.3 References to Other Laws

In this section, we describe the logical machinery we use to express and handle references to laws. We give an example-driven account here, followed by a formal account in the context of a runtime checking algorithm in Section 4.1.

We extend the syntax with *an inference predicate* $\mathrm{by}_{\mathrm{Id}}(\varphi)$, where Id is a set of identifiers. $\mathrm{by}_{\mathrm{Id}}(\varphi)$ is read as "by the laws in Id φ holds". There are two restrictions: (a) φ is a statement in PredLTL (Definition 2) and (b) the predicate $\mathrm{by}_{\mathrm{Id}}(\varphi)$ can appear only in preconditions of laws. These restrictions are similar to those that apply to justifications in default logic [11]. In the examples that we discuss, the set Id has a single element, i.e., a statement refers to a single other law. In general, laws refer to sets of statements, e.g., "except as specified in this section".

Consider again our example statements (1) and (2), which can now be represented as follows:

- 1.$\mathbf{o}$: $d(x) \wedge \neg\mathrm{by}_{\{2\}}(\varphi(x)) \leadsto \Diamond test(x)$, and
- 2.$\mathbf{p}$: $d(y) \wedge sp(y) \leadsto \neg\Diamond test(y)$

In the formula above, the subformula $\mathrm{by}_{\{2\}}(\varphi(x))$ is understood as "by the law (2) the formula $\varphi(x)$ holds". It remains to define the formula $\varphi(x)$. Intuitively, this should be the negation of the postcondition of (1). In other words, if $\neg\Diamond test(x)$ follows from (2), then the postcondition of (1) need not hold.[1]

1.$\mathbf{o}$: $d(x) \wedge \neg\mathrm{by}_{\{2\}}(\neg\Diamond test(x)) \leadsto \Diamond test(x)$

We interpret $\mathrm{by}_{\{2\}}(\neg\Diamond test(x))$, by letting formulas have output. In other words, when the precondition of an obligation or permission is true at a point, the point is *annotated* with the postcondition. Given a point (R, i) and a variable assignment v, first we consider the formula 2.$\mathbf{p}$: $d(y) \wedge sp(y) \leadsto \neg\Diamond test(y)$. We evaluate this as follows:

---

[1] When $\mathrm{by}_{\mathrm{Id}}(\varphi)$ appears in the precondition of a law, φ need not be the negation of the postcondition. An example is statement (4) in Section 2, which can be represented as:
4.$\mathbf{o}$: $\mathrm{by}_{\{1\}}(\Diamond test(z)) \leadsto \Diamond scr(z)$, where $scr(z)$ is true iff z is tested using a screening test.

- If $(R, i, v) \models d(y) \wedge sp(y)$, (R, i) is *annotated* with 2: $\neg \Diamond test(v(y))$. Observe that the annotation happens regardless of whether $(R, i, v) \models \neg \Diamond test(y)$ and the variable is replaced with the object assigned to it.
- Otherwise, there is no annotation.

Given a variable assignment v and a PredLTL formula φ, $v(\varphi)$ is the formula obtained by replacing all variables x by an identifier for the object $v(x)$. Note that $v(\varphi)$ is equivalent to a propositional LTL formula, as the variables have been replaced by constant symbols. We now define annotations:

Definition 6 (Annotation). *Given a run R, a set of identifiers ID, a variable assignment v, and a body of regulation Reg, an annotation is a statement id: $v(\psi)$ such that $id \in ID$ and id.$\mathbf{x}$: $\varphi \rightsquigarrow \psi \in Reg$ (which is either an obligation or a permission). The set of annotations is denoted by $A(R, ID, Reg)$, abbreviated A.*

Definition 7 (Annotation Function). *Given a run R, an annotation function $\alpha : N \rightarrow 2^A$ assigns a set of annotations to each point. Given a set of identifiers ID and $Id \subseteq ID$, we use $\alpha.Id(i)$ to denote the set of annotations id: $\psi \in \alpha(i)$ such that $id \in Id$.*

Table 2. A run and its annotations

Time	Objects	Predicates	Annotations
1	o_1	$d(o_1)$, $sp(o_1)$, $\neg test(o_1)$	2: $\neg \Diamond test(o_1)$
2	o_1	$d(o_1)$, $sp(o_1)$, $\neg test(o_1)$	2: $\neg \Diamond test(o_1)$
	o_2	$d(o_2)$, $\neg sp(o_2)$, $\neg test(o_2)$	1: $\Diamond test(o_2)$
3	o_1	$d(o_1)$, $sp(o_1)$, $test(o_1)$	2: $\neg \Diamond test(o_1)$
	o_2	$d(o_2)$, $\neg sp(o_2)$, $\neg test(o_2)$	1: $\Diamond test(o_2)$

Table 2 shows a run of a bloodbank augmented with annotations. As we discussed in Section 3.1, o_1 is a donation of source plasma which is tested at time 3 and o_2 is a non-source plasma donation which has not been tested. Unless the run is extended to test o_2 as well, it does not conform with the regulation according to Definition 5.

Since the precondition of statement (2) is true for the assignment of y to o_1, we have the annotation 2: $\neg \Diamond test(o_1)$ at all points. However, since o_2 is not a donation of source plasma, there is no correponding annotation.

Now consider the formula $by_{\{2\}}(\neg \Diamond test(x))$. This is evaluated as follows:

- Evaluate 2.$\mathbf{p}$: $d(y) \wedge sp(y) \rightsquigarrow \neg \Diamond test(y)$ at (R, i) w.r.t. all variable assignments.
- Let ψ_2 be the conjunction of the annotations produced by the formula for (2), i.e., $\psi_2 = \bigwedge \varphi$ for all $\varphi \in \alpha.\{2\}(i)$.
- $(R, i, v) \models by_{\{2\}}(\neg \Diamond test(x))$ iff $\models \psi_2 \Rightarrow \neg \Diamond test(v(x))$.

Notice that the last step requires a validity check, but it is a validity check in (propositional) LTL. Validity in LTL is coNP-complete when the only modality is *globally*, and PSPACE-complete with the *until* modality [12]. In Section 4, we discuss cases where the size of the validity tests grows large, and we explore a restriction that lets us avoid validity tests during checking.

Returning to the run in Table 2, the states are annotated with 2: $\neg\Diamond test(o_1)$ and $\models \neg\Diamond test(o_1) \Rightarrow \neg\Diamond test(o_1)$, since $\varphi \Rightarrow \varphi$ is a propositional tautology. So $(R, i, v) \models$ by$_{\{2\}}(\neg\Diamond test(x))$ when $v(x) = o_1$.

We can evaluate 1.o: $d(x) \wedge \neg$by$_{\{2\}}(\neg\Diamond test(x)) \rightsquigarrow \Diamond test(x)$ similarly by annotating states with $\Diamond test(x)$ if the precondition holds. In Table 2, this results in an annotation of 1: $\Diamond test(o_2)$ on the appropriate states. If o_2 is never tested, the run will be declared non-conforming (by Definition 5), but the annotation will remain. This lets a law which depends on (1) draw the correct inference.

The semantic evaluation outlined above works only when the references are acyclic, since an order of evaluation needs to be defined. To handle cycles, we move to a three-valued logic where the third (middle) value stands for undetermined. Initially, all statements are undetermined, and there are no annotations. At each step we assign truth values and annotations, using truth values and annotations from the previous step, until we reach a fixed point. In a companion paper [10], which focusses on the design of the logic, we prove that there is a least fixed point, which can be computed in an iterative fashion. In this paper, we use the existence of the least fixed point to derive a runtime checking algorithm.

4 Runtime Checking of Specifications with References

4.1 An Algorithm for Evaluating Specifications with References

We augment the evaluation procedure of the rule-based formalism Eagle [5] to handle references. In Eagle, formulas in LTL are evaluated by transforming them into other formulas, and discharging the remainder (if any) at trace end. The update calculus used in [5] provides a general treatment of past modalities and data dependencies. To simplify presentation, we will work directly with the formulas in the logic.

The key idea is to treat the predicate by$_{Id}(\varphi)$ as kind of eventuality. As we discussed in Section 3.3, to evaluate by$_{Id}(\varphi)$ at time i, we need to check the annotations obtained from the laws in Id at time i. If the preconditions of the laws in Id are temporal, we need to wait until they are evaluated before the annotations are obtained. So, we need to keep annotations for a time i until all subformulas by$_{Id}(\varphi)$ for time i have been evaluated. Given by$_{Id}(\varphi)$ and a time i, we attempt to evaluate it using the current set of annotations. If we cannot determine the truth value, by$_{Id}(\varphi)$ is transformed into by$_{Id}(\varphi, i)$ (read as "by$_{Id}(\varphi)$ is true at time i"), and evaluated at subsequent times.

Following [13], we use a three-valued logic with values from $\mathcal{B}^3 = \{\top, \bot, ?\}$, with the meaning true, false, and undetermined, respectively. For notational simplicity, we use truth values as terms in preconditions:

Definition 8 (Syntax of Preconditions). *Given sets $\Phi_1, ..., \Phi_n$ (of predicate names), a set of variables X, and a finite set of identifiers ID, the language $L'(\Phi_1, ..., \Phi_n, X, ID)$, abbreviated as L', is the smallest set such that:*

- *If $t \in \mathcal{B}^3$, then $t \in L'$. $p(y_1, ..., y_j) \in L'$, where $p \in \Phi_j$ and $(y_1, ..., y_j) \in X^j$.*
- *If $\varphi \in L'$, then $\neg\varphi \in L'$ and $\Box\varphi \in L'$. If $\varphi, \psi \in L'$, then $\varphi \wedge \psi \in L'$*
- *If $Id \subseteq ID$ and $\varphi \in L(\Phi_1, ..., \Phi_n, X)$ (Definition 2), then by$_{Id}(\varphi) \in L'$. In addition, for all natural numbers $i \in N$, by$_{Id}(\varphi, i) \in L'$*

The syntax of regulatory statements (Definition 3) is modified so that the preconditions of laws are statements from L'. The set L' together with a set of regulatory statements Reg is denoted by $L^+ = L' \cup Reg$. Given a set of objects O, $V(X, O)$ denotes the set of all variable assigments, i.e., functions $v : X \to O$.

We can now adapt the Eagle procedure of transforming formulas. The transformation function uses two annotation functions α and α' such that for all i, $\alpha(i) \subseteq \alpha'(i)$. $\alpha(i)$ is the set of annotations obtained from laws with true preconditions, while $\alpha'(i)$ is set of annotations from laws with true or undetermined preconditions. The truth of $\text{by}_{\text{Id}}(\varphi)$ is determined using α, and falsity is determined using α'.

Definition 9 (Transformation function). *Given a set of objects O and annotation functions α and α' such that $\alpha(i) \subseteq \alpha'(i)$ for all $i \in N$, the transformation function $\tau_{(\alpha,\alpha')} : L^+ \times S \times N \times V(X, O) \to L^+$ is defined as follows:*

- $\tau_{(\alpha,\alpha')}(t, s, i, v) = t$ *if* $t \in \mathcal{B}^3$.
- $\tau_{(\alpha,\alpha')}(p(y_1, ..., y_j), s, i, v) = \top$ *if* $(v(y_1), ..., v(y_j)) \in \pi_j(p, s)$.
  $\tau_{(\alpha,\alpha')}(p(y_1, ..., y_j), s, i, v) = \bot$ *otherwise.*
- $\tau_{(\alpha,\alpha')}(\varphi \wedge \psi, s, i, v) = \tau_{(\alpha,\alpha')}(\varphi, s, i, v) \wedge \tau_{(\alpha,\alpha')}(\psi, s, i, v)$.
  $\tau_{(\alpha,\alpha')}(\neg\varphi, s, i, v) = \neg\tau_{(\alpha,\alpha')}(\varphi, s, i, v)$
- $\tau_{(\alpha,\alpha')}(\Box\varphi, s, i, v) = \tau_{(\alpha,\alpha')}(\varphi, s, i, v) \wedge \Box\varphi$
- $\tau_{(\alpha,\alpha')}(\text{by}_{\text{Id}}(\varphi), s, i, v) = \tau_{(\alpha,\alpha')}(\text{by}_{\text{Id}}(\varphi, i), s, i, v)$

$$\tau_{(\alpha,\alpha')}(\text{by}_{\text{Id}}(\varphi, j), s, i, v) = \begin{cases} \top & \text{if } j \leq i \text{ and } \bigwedge \alpha.Id(j) \wedge v(\neg\varphi) \text{ is not satisfiable} \\ \bot & \text{if } j \leq i \text{ and } \bigwedge \alpha'.Id(j) \wedge v(\neg\varphi) \text{ is satisfiable} \\ \text{by}_{\text{Id}}(\varphi, j) & \text{otherwise} \end{cases}$$

- $\tau_{(\alpha,\alpha')}(id.\mathbf{o}: \varphi \rightsquigarrow \psi, s, i, v) = id.\mathbf{o}: \tau_{(\alpha,\alpha')}(\varphi, s, i, v) \rightsquigarrow \tau_{(\alpha,\alpha')}(\psi, s, i, v)$
  $\tau_{(\alpha,\alpha')}(id.\mathbf{p}: \varphi \rightsquigarrow \psi, s, i, v) = id.\mathbf{p}: \tau_{(\alpha,\alpha')}(\varphi, s, i, v) \rightsquigarrow \psi$

Note that the postcondition of permissions are not transformed, as their truth value is irrelevant. The only use of postconditions of permissions is to provide annotations. To update the annotation function, we need to know if a precondition has become true or false. We now define a function to map formulas to truth values:

Definition 10. *Given a set of objects O and annotation functions α and α' such that $\alpha(i) \subseteq \alpha'(i)$ for all $i \in N$, the function $\mathbf{value}_{(\alpha,\alpha')} : L^+ \times S \times N \times V(X, O) \to \mathcal{B}^3$ is defined as follows:*

- *Truth values, predicates, conjunction and negation are handled in the usual way.*
- $\mathbf{value}_{(\alpha,\alpha')}(\Box\varphi, s, i, v) = \top$ *if s is the final state.*
  $\mathbf{value}_{(\alpha,\alpha')}(\Box\varphi, s, i, v) = ?$ *otherwise.*
- $\mathbf{value}_{(\alpha,\alpha')}(\text{by}_{\text{Id}}(\varphi), s, i, v) = \mathbf{value}_{(\alpha,\alpha')}(\text{by}_{\text{Id}}(\varphi, i), s, i, v)$

$$\mathbf{value}_{(\alpha,\alpha')}(\text{by}_{\text{Id}}(\varphi, j), s, i, v) = \begin{cases} \top & \text{if } j \leq i \text{ and } \bigwedge \alpha.Id(j) \wedge v(\neg\varphi) \text{ is not satisfiable} \\ \bot & \text{if } j \leq i \text{ and } \bigwedge \alpha'.Id(j) \wedge v(\neg\varphi) \text{ is satisfiable} \\ ? & \text{otherwise} \end{cases}$$

- $\mathbf{value}_{(\alpha,\alpha')}(id.\mathbf{o}: \varphi \rightsquigarrow \psi, s, i, v) = \mathbf{value}_{(\alpha,\alpha')}(\varphi \Rightarrow \psi, s, i, v)$.
  $\mathbf{value}_{(\alpha,\alpha')}(id.\mathbf{p}: \varphi \rightsquigarrow \psi, s, i, v) = \top$

At the end of the trace, subformulas $\Box\varphi$ are replaced by $\top$, but subformulas $\mathrm{by}_{\mathrm{Id}}(\varphi, j)$ may still be undetermined. This is due to the fact that with circular references, we can create paradoxical statements – id.**o**: $\neg\mathrm{by}_{\{\mathrm{id}\}}(\varphi) \rightsquigarrow \varphi$. This statement requires φ to hold when it doesn't require φ, and is always undetermined.

Update$(Reg, \Phi, \alpha, \alpha', s, i)$:
Input: The regulation Reg, the set of formulas to be updated Φ, the annotation functions α
       and α', the state s and time i
Let $\alpha(i) = \alpha'(i) = \emptyset$;
for *all id.***x***: $\varphi \rightsquigarrow \psi \in Reg$ and assignments v* **do**
    Let $\phi = \tau_{(\alpha,\alpha')}(\mathrm{id}.\mathbf{x}: \varphi \rightsquigarrow \psi, s, i, v)$;
    $\Phi = \Phi \cup \{(\phi,\mathrm{id}: v(\psi), i, v)\}$, and $\alpha'(i) = \alpha'(i) \cup \{\mathrm{id}: v(\psi)\}$
end
repeat
    for *all* $(id.\mathbf{x}: \varphi \rightsquigarrow \psi, a, j, v) \in \Phi$ **do**
        If **value**$(\varphi, s, i, v) = \top$, then $\alpha(j) = \alpha(j) \cup \{a\}$;
        If **value**$(\varphi, s, i, v) = \bot$, then $\alpha'(j) = \alpha'(j) - \{a\}$
    end
    Let $\Phi' = \emptyset$;
    for *all* $(id.\mathbf{x}: \varphi \rightsquigarrow \psi, a, j, v) \in \Phi$ **do**
        Let $\phi = \tau_{(\alpha,\alpha')}(\mathrm{id}.\mathbf{x}: \varphi \rightsquigarrow \psi, s, i, v)$ and $\varphi' = \tau_{(\alpha,\alpha')}(\varphi, s, i, v)$;
        If **value**$(\phi, s, i, v) =?$ or **value**$(\varphi', s, i, v) =?$, then $\Phi' = \Phi' \cup \{(\phi, j)\}$;
        If **value**$(\phi, s, i, v) = \bot$, then raise alarm.
    end
    $\Phi = \Phi'$
until α and α' *do not change* ;

Algorithm 1. An algorithm for evaluating statements with references

We note that the function **value**$_{(\alpha,\alpha')}$ does not determine a formula to be true or false as early as possible. To decide if a formula is true as early as possible, we need to check whether all possible suffixes to the trace satisfy the formula, as in [13]. In other words, we need to decide if the transformed formula is valid. In [10], we show that with references one can encode formulas in first-order logic as regulations, and as a result, the validity problem is undecidable for L^+. The satisfiability tests used to evaluate the inference predicates are in propositional LTL, and are decidable.

Fixed points are defined at the level of a run. Suppose we are given a body of regulation Reg, a run R and annotation functions (α_1, α'_1). The result of evaluation gives us new annotations (α_2, α'_2) corresponding to laws that have true preconditions (α_2), and true or undetermined preconditions (α'_2). We will say that (α_1, α'_1) is a fixed point iff $(\alpha_1, \alpha'_1) = (\alpha_2, \alpha'_2)$.

The function **value**$_{(\alpha,\alpha')}$ is extended to runs. The definition remains identical except that for $\mathrm{by}_{\mathrm{Id}}(\varphi, j)$ we do not require that $j \leq i$ to determine truth or falsity, and for the temporal operator:

$$\mathbf{value}_{(\alpha,\alpha')}(\Box\varphi, R, i, v) = \begin{cases} \top \text{ if for all } j \geq i, \mathbf{value}_{(\alpha,\alpha')}(\varphi, R, i, v) = \top \\ \bot \text{ if there exists } j \geq i, \mathbf{value}_{(\alpha,\alpha')}(\varphi, R, i, v) = \bot \\ ? \text{ otherwise} \end{cases}$$

Definition 11 (Consistent Annotations). *Given a body of regulation Reg and a run R with a set of objects O, the pair of annotation functions (α, α') is consistent iff for all* $(id.\mathbf{x}: \varphi \rightsquigarrow \psi, i, v) \in Reg \times N \times V(X, O)$:

If id: $v(\psi) \in \alpha(i) \cap \alpha'(i)$, *then* $\mathbf{value}_{(\alpha, \alpha')}(\varphi, R, i, v) = \top$
If id: $v(\psi) \notin \alpha(i) \cup \alpha'(i)$, *then* $\mathbf{value}_{(\alpha, \alpha')}(\varphi, R, i, v) = \bot$
In addition, for all i, we require that $\alpha(i) \subseteq \alpha'(i)$.

Definition 12 (Fixed Point). *Given a body of regulation Reg and a run R with a set of objects O, the pair of consistent annotation functions (α, α') is a fixed point iff for all* $(id.\mathbf{x}: \varphi \rightsquigarrow \psi, i, v) \in Reg \times N \times V(X, O)$:

If $\mathbf{value}_{(\alpha, \alpha')}(\varphi, R, i, v) = \top$, *then id:* $v(\psi) \in \alpha(i) \cap \alpha'(i)$
If $\mathbf{value}_{(\alpha, \alpha')}(\varphi, R, i, v) = ?$, *then id:* $v(\psi) \in \alpha'(i) - \alpha(i)$
Otherwise, id: $v(\psi) \notin \alpha(i) \cup \alpha'(i)$

We say that $(\alpha_1, \alpha_1') \leq (\alpha_2, \alpha_2')$ if for all i, we have $\alpha_1(i) \subseteq \alpha_2(i)$. We now review some results that are proved in [10]. The partially ordered set of consistent annotations has a least fixed point and one or more maximal fixed points. Distinct fixed points arise if there are circular references. The converse is not necessarily true, i.e., there may be circular references and a unique fixed point. There is a smallest element in the set of consistent annotations (α_0, α_0') such that for all i, $\alpha_0(i) = \emptyset$ and $\alpha_0'(i)$ contains all annotations. The least fixed point can be obtained iteratively using (α_0, α_0').

Algorithm 1 describes the procedure for computing the least fixed point in a runtime setting. In addition to α and α', we maintain a set of tuples Φ, where each element is a transformed regulatory statement, the associated annotation, time and variable assignment. Given $(id.\mathbf{x}: \varphi \rightsquigarrow \psi, a, j, v) \in \Phi$, if φ is determined to be true, the annotation a is added to $\alpha(j)$. On the other hand, if φ is determined to be false a is removed from $\alpha'(j)$. For all $j \in N$, $\alpha(j)$ increases monotonically, and $\alpha'(j)$ decreases monotonically with each execution of the repeat loop, until a fixed point is reached.

4.2 Complexity Analysis by Example

The complexity of Algorithm 1 in each state of a run depends on two factors – the number of steps necessary to reach a fixed point, and the size of satisfiability problem instances that need to be handled in the evaluation of the predicate $\mathrm{by}_{\mathrm{Id}}(\varphi)$. We discuss examples that illustrate these two aspects, by encoding the graph reachability problem in different ways. In the first example, the number of steps taken to reach the fixed point grows with the number of objects. In the second example, the size of the satisfiability instances grows with the number of objects.

Both examples operate on the same model, where a state in the run contains a description of a graph. Objects o_1 and o_2 represent nodes, and the predicate $\delta(o_1, o_2)$ is true iff there is an edge between o_1 and o_2. In addition, $\delta^+(o_1, o_2)$ is true iff there is a path from o_1 to o_2. Suppose we wish to check whether δ^+ has been computed correctly.

Example 1. Consider a self-referential sentence:

id.**o**: $\delta(x, z) \vee (\delta(x, y) \wedge \mathrm{by}_{\{id\}}(\delta^+(y, z))) \rightsquigarrow \delta^+(x, z)$

The precondition of this sentence corresponds to the definition of a path. In other words, there is a path between x and z ($\delta^+(x, z)$), if there is an edge between x and y ($\delta(x, y)$), and a path between y and z (by$_{\{id\}}(\delta^+(y, z))$). Consider the sequence of annotations obtained in the least fixed point computation – $\alpha_0, ..., \alpha_f$. It is easy to see that id: $\delta^+(o, o') \in \alpha_j(i)$ iff there is a path of length at most j from o to o'. Given a graph with $|O|$ nodes, there is a path from o to o' iff there is a path of length at most $|O|$ from o to o'. As a result, the fixed point will be reached in at most $|O|$ steps. The worst-case number of steps needed to reach the fixed point is $\mathbf{O}(m \times |O|^k)$, where m is the size of the regulation, and k is the maximum number of variables appearing in a sentence.

Example 2. Consider now the following statements:

A.o: by$_{\{B,C\}}(\delta^+(x, y)) \rightsquigarrow \delta^+(x, y)$
B.o: $\delta(x, y) \rightsquigarrow \delta^+(x, y)$
C.o: $\top \rightsquigarrow (\delta^+(x, y) \wedge \delta^+(y, z)) \Rightarrow \delta^+(x, z)$

Note that A refers to C. The presence of implication in the postcondition of C is an important feature of this example. Let, for simplicity, the graph in the state be a chain. Since the precondition of C is always true, the first step of the fixed point computation yields an annotation that contains C: $(\delta^+(o, o') \wedge \delta^+(o', o'')) \Rightarrow \delta^+(o, o'') \in \alpha_1(i)$ for all o, o', o'' in the graph. The next step of the evaluation will yield the fixed point, but the size of the validity test performed in this step is $\mathbf{O}(|O|^3)$, as Algorithm 1 uses all the available annotations. The worst-case size of the validity instances is in $\mathbf{O}(m \times |O|^k)$, and the time complexity of a step in computing the fixed point is $\mathbf{O}(2^{m \times |O|^k})$.

Discussion. In both examples above, Algorithm 1 checks validity instances of size polynomial in $|O|$. However, there is a crucial difference in the maximum size of tests that are needed. In Example 1, by$_{\{id\}}(\delta^+(o, o'))$ is true iff id: $\delta^+(o, o') \in \alpha(i)$. In other words, at most one annotation is need to evaluate by$_{\{id\}}(\delta^+(o, o'))$. In Example 2, we do need validity tests of size $|O|$ to evaluate by$_{\{B,C\}}(\delta^+(o, o'))$. A case study of the CFR revealed that the references behaved like Example 1 in that a single annotation or copy of the referenced statement suffices to evaluate formulas by$_{Id}(\varphi)$. We call this *the single copy property*.

Definition 13 (Single Copy Property). *Given a body of regulation Reg,* by$_{Id}(\varphi, j)$ *has the single copy property iff for all runs R, and consistent annotations* (α, α'):

$$t = \begin{cases} \top \text{ if } \psi \wedge v(\neg\varphi) \text{ is not satisfiable for some } \psi \in \alpha.Id(j) \\ \bot \text{ if } \psi \wedge v(\neg\varphi) \text{ is satisfiable for all } \psi \in \alpha'.Id(j) \\ ? \text{ otherwise} \end{cases}$$

where, $t = \mathbf{value}_{(\alpha, \alpha')}(\text{by}_{Id}(\varphi, j), s, i, v)$

While the single copy property allows us to reduce the size of the satisfiability tests, we need to perform $\mathbf{O}(m \times |O|^k)$ tests for each inference predicate. The question arises as to whether satisfiability tests can be avoided during checking. We answer this question positively in the following section.

4.3 Pre-computing Satisfiability

Algorithm 1 evaluates by$_{Id}(\varphi)$ using satsfiabilty tests. The size of the satisfiability tests depends on $\alpha.Id(i)$, which in turn depends on the number of objects. If by$_{Id}(\varphi)$ has the single copy property, we can consider smaller satisfiability tests. In this section, we show that the single copy property gives us a way to assess satisfiability symbolically, and use tests of lower complexity during checking.

The strategy we use is as follows. Given a body of regulation, we perform a compilation step which involves: a) testing satisfiability, and b) replacing the predicates by$_{\mathrm{Id}}(\varphi)$ by equivalent formulas in another logic. We begin by discussing two examples, and then formalize the compilation step.

Example 1. Consider our regulatory sentences:

- 1.**o**: $d(x) \wedge \neg\mathrm{by}_{\{2\}}(\neg\Diamond test(x)) \rightsquigarrow \Diamond test(x)$, and
- 2.**p**: $d(y) \wedge sp(y) \rightsquigarrow \neg\Diamond test(y)$

Consider a state at which $o_1, o_2, ..., o_n$ are source plasma donations. This would result in $\neg\Diamond test(o_1), \neg\Diamond test(o_2), ..., \neg\Diamond test(o_n)$ being available as annotations. To evaluate by$_{\mathrm{Id}}(\neg\Diamond test(o_i))$, Algorithm 1 uses all the annotations in the satifiability test. However, in this case, it suffices to check if $\neg\Diamond test(o_i)$ is present as an annotation. The other annotations are irrelevant. To check if $\neg\Diamond test(o_i)$ is present as an annotation, it suffices to evaluate the precondition of the referenced law, i.e., whether $d(o_i) \wedge sp(o_i)$ is true (whether o_i is a donation of source plasma). Instead of evaluating by$_{\mathrm{Id}}(\phi)$ using satisfiability tests, we will check if the precondition of a referenced law is true.

Informally, the compilation step involves anwering the question *when does statement 2 provide an exception for statement 1*. Equivalently, when does $\neg\Diamond test(y)$ imply $\neg\Diamond test(x)$. The answer is only when $y = x$. We can then evaluate the precondition of 2 with y replaced by x, i.e., $d(x) \wedge sp(x)$. This lets us replace statement 1 with 1.**o**: $d(x) \wedge \neg(d(x) \wedge sp(x)) \rightsquigarrow \Diamond test(x)$, which is equivalent to 1.**o**: $d(x) \wedge \neg sp(x) \rightsquigarrow \Diamond test(x)$. Observe that this is the derived obligation implied by statements 1 and 2, i.e., every non-source plasma donation must be tested.

Example 2. The example above is simple in two ways: a) the number of variables in both statements are the same, and b) the references are acyclic. We discuss the general case in the context of the reachability example we saw in the previous section:

id.**o**: $\delta(x, z) \vee (\delta(x, y) \wedge \mathrm{by}_{\{\mathrm{id}\}}(\delta^+(y, z))) \rightsquigarrow \delta^+(x, z)$

We observe that the precondition is structurally similar to a procedure that checks if a path exists between two nodes x and z. That is, if $\delta(x, z)$ then $\delta^+(x, z)$ is true. Otherwise, if there exists y such that $\delta(x, y)$ and there is a path from y to z, then $\delta^+(x, z)$ is true, otherwise false.

We will produce a formula which mimics the procedure. There are two pieces of machinery used by the procedure that are not directly available in the logic: a) an existential quantifier over objects (there exists y), and b) a mechanism for recursion. To address this, let us consider a logic which extends PredLTL with existential quantifiers, and a function symbol P_{id} for $id \in ID$ (P stands for precondition). P_{id} takes as argument a substitution $\theta : X \to X$, which is a function from variables to variables. A substitution is represented a set of replacements x/y (read as "x is replaced by y"), such that each variable has at most one replacement. We replace the formula above with:

id.**o**: $\delta(x, z) \vee (\delta(x, y) \wedge \exists y_1 : \mathrm{P}_{\mathrm{id}}(\{x/y, y/y_1, z/z\})) \rightsquigarrow \delta^+(x, z)$

It remains to give this formula a semantics. Given a variable assignment v and a substitution θ, $\theta(v)$ denotes the variable assignment v' such that $v'(x) = v(\theta(y))$. Given a run R, time i and regulation Reg, the idea is to say that $(R, i, v) \models P_{id}(\theta)$ iff $(R, i, \theta(v)) \models \varphi$ where id.x: $\varphi \rightsquigarrow \psi \in Reg$. We now formalize the compilation procedure.

Compiling References into Precondition Tests: We begin by defining the syntax of compiled preconditions:

Definition 14 (Syntax of Compiled Preconditions). *Given sets $\Phi_1, ..., \Phi_n$ (of predicate names), a set of variables X, and a finite set of identifiers ID, the language $L'_C(\Phi_1, ..., \Phi_n, X, ID)$, abbreviated as L'_C, is the smallest set such that:*

- *If $t \in \mathcal{B}^3$, $t \in L'_C$. And, $p(y_1, ..., y_j) \in L'_C$ where $p \in \Phi_j$ and $(y_1, ..., y_j) \in X^j$.*
- *If $\varphi \in L'_C$, then $\neg\varphi \in L'_C$ and $\Box\varphi \in L'_C$. If $\varphi, \psi \in L'_C$, then $\varphi \wedge \psi \in L'_C$*
- *If $\varphi \in L'_C$, for all $y \in X$, we have $\exists y : \varphi \in L'_C$.*
- *For all $id \in Id$ and substitutions $\theta : X \to X$, we have $P_{id}(\theta) \in L'_C$. In addition, for all natural numbers $i \in N$, $P_{id}(\theta, i) \in L'_C$*

The syntax of regulatory statements (Definition 3) is modified so that the preconditions of laws are statements from L'_C. The set L'_C together with a set of regulatory statements Reg_C is denoted by $L^+_C = L'_C \cup Reg_C$. We remind the reader that L^+ and L' are the languages with the predicate by$_{Id}(\varphi)$.

The semantics of L^+_C is defined in a manner similar to L^+. Rather than using annotations (α, α'), we now evaluate statements w.r.t. two sets of assignment functions (γ, γ'). $\gamma(i, id)$ (resply., $\gamma'(i, id)$) is a set of variable assignments for which the precondition of the law with identifier id is true (resply., true or undetermined). As with annotations, we require that for all $i \in N$ and $id \in ID$, $\gamma(i, id) \subseteq \gamma'(i, id)$. Given an assignment v and a substitution θ, $\theta(v)$ denotes the assignment v' such that for all $y \in X$, we have $v'(y) = v(\theta(y))$. We can now adapt the **value** function:

$$\mathbf{value}_{(\gamma,\gamma')}(P_{id}(\theta, j), R, i, v) = \begin{cases} \top \text{ if } \theta(v) \in \gamma(j, id) \\ \bot \text{ if } \theta(v) \notin \gamma'(j, id) \\ ? \text{ otherwise} \end{cases}$$

The definitions of consistency and fixed points (Definitions 11 and 12) are easily adapted, and we leave the details to the reader.

We now describe the compilation procedure. Given $\varphi \in L^+$, we use $X(\varphi)$ to denote the set of variables appearing in φ, and $\theta(\varphi)$ to denote the formula obtained by performing the substitution θ on φ. Consider by$_{Id}(\varphi, j)$, which has the single copy property, and variables disjoint from all regulatory statements:

- Let $\mathcal{S}(\varphi, id) = \{ \theta|$ id.x: $\varphi \rightsquigarrow \psi \in Reg$, and $\theta(\psi \Rightarrow \varphi)$ is valid$\}$.
- For all $\theta \in \mathcal{S}(\varphi, id)$, let $\varphi_C(\theta, id) = \exists z_1, ..., z_m : P_{id}(\theta, j)$, where the existentially quantified variables are in one-to-one correspondence with those in $X(\phi) - X(\psi)$. More formally, $z_j \notin X(\phi) - X(\psi)$ and θ is a one-to-one function from $\{z_j | 1 \leq j \leq m\}$ to $X(\phi) - X(\psi)$.
- $\varphi_C(\text{by}_{Id}(\varphi, j), id) = \bigvee \{\varphi_C(\theta, id)|\theta \in \mathcal{S}(\varphi, id)\}$, and
- $\varphi_C(\text{by}_{Id}(\varphi, j)) = \bigvee \{\varphi_C(\text{by}_{Id}(\varphi, j), id)|id \in Id\}$

We note that the first step makes crucial use of the single copy property (SCP). In computing $\mathcal{S}(\varphi, id)$, it suffices to find substitutions such that $\theta(\psi \Rightarrow \varphi)$ is valid. If the SCP does not hold, then we need to check if multiple copies of postconditions provide the necessary implication (as in Example 2, Section 4.2). For example, we need to check if $\theta(\psi_1 \wedge ... \wedge \psi_n \Rightarrow \varphi)$, where $\psi_1, ..., \psi_n$ are copies of the postcondition of a law with the variables renamed. It can be shown that detecting whether the SCP holds is undecidable. In future work, we plan to investigate restrictions on postconditions that make SCP-detection decidable.

To prove the correctness of the compilation procedure, we use a notion of correspondence between annotations and assignments. Let us assume as given a body of regulation Reg (in L^+), a run R and consistent annotations (α, α'). Rather than producing a regulation in L_C^+, we prove correctness by evaluating formulas in L_C' against Reg. We construct $(\gamma_\alpha, \gamma_{\alpha'}')$ such that for all $i \in N$ and $id \in ID$, $v \in \gamma_\alpha(i, id)$ iff id: $v(\psi) \in \alpha(i)$, and $v \in \gamma_{\alpha'}'(i, id)$ iff id: $v(\psi) \in \alpha'(i)$. We can now show the following:

Lemma 1. *Given a body of regulation Reg, a run R, consistent annotations (α, α'), and $by_{Id}(\varphi, j)$ which has the single copy property, for all $i \in N$ and assignments v:*

$$\mathbf{value}_{(\alpha, \alpha')}(by_{Id}(\varphi, j), R, i, v) = \mathbf{value}_{(\gamma_\alpha, \gamma_{\alpha'}')}(\varphi_C(by_{Id}(\theta, j)), R, i, v)$$

Proof. The proof follows straightforwardly from the construction of $\varphi_C(by_{Id}(\theta, j))$ and the single copy property. We sketch one of the cases.

Suppose $\mathbf{value}_{(\alpha, \alpha')}(by_{Id}(\varphi, j), R, i, v) = \top$. There exists id: $v'(\psi) \in \alpha(i)$ such that $v'(\psi) \wedge v(\neg\varphi)$ is not satisfiable, or equivalently $v'(\psi) \Rightarrow v(\varphi)$ is valid. It follows that there exists a substitution θ such that $\theta(\psi \Rightarrow \varphi)$ is valid. By definition $v' \in \gamma_\alpha(i)$, and hence, $\mathbf{value}_{(\gamma_\alpha, \gamma_{\alpha'}')}(P_{id}(\theta, j), R, i, v') = \top$. We can then argue using the construction that $\mathbf{value}_{(\gamma_\alpha, \gamma_{\alpha'}')}(\exists z_1, ..., z_m : P_{id}(\theta, j), R, i, v) = \top$, and as a result, $\mathbf{value}_{(\gamma_\alpha, \gamma_{\alpha'}')}(\varphi_C(by_{Id}(\theta, j)), R, i, v) = \top$. The other cases are handled similarly. $\square$

Given Reg in which all subformulas $by_{Id}(\varphi)$ have the single copy property, we can now produce the regulation Reg_C in L_C^+ with all occurences of $by_{Id}(\varphi)$ replaced by $\varphi_C(by_{Id}(\varphi))$. It follows from Lemma 1 that if (α, α') is a fixed point w.r.t. Reg, then $(\gamma_\alpha, \gamma_{\alpha'}')$ is a fixed point w.r.t. Reg_C. In addition, the truth values assigned to regulatory statements are identical.

The complexity of evaluation depends on the number of disjuncts in $\varphi_C(by_{Id}(\varphi))$, which in turn depends on the size of the set: $\mathcal{S}(\varphi, id)$. $|\mathcal{S}(\varphi, id)| \leq (2k)^{2k}$, where k is the maximum number of variables in a regulatory statement. $(2k)^{2k}$ is a bound on the number of equivalence classes, i.e., we have $2k$ variables (k in φ and k in ψ) and at most one equivalence class for each variable. Hence, the size of $\varphi_C(by_{Id}(\varphi))$ is $\mathbf{O}(m \times (2k)^{2k})$, where m is the number of regulatory statements. Each quantified precondition test can be evaluated in $\mathbf{O}(|O|^k)$ time, where O is the set of objects. As a result, the time complexity for evaluating $\varphi_C(by_{Id}(\varphi))$ is $\mathbf{O}(m \times (2k)^{2k} \times |O|^k)$. We now describe an evaluation of the system, using a prototype implementation which performs this compilation procedure.

4.4 Evaluation

We have developed a prototype implementation of the checker. We briefly describe two aspects of the implementation: (a) the interface between regulations and traces (schemas), and (b) the trace-checker.

Schemas form the interface between the regulation and trace. A schema is a set of class and type definitions. Classes can inherit from others, and have attributes which have atomic types, tuples or unions of types, pointers to other objects or sets of values.

Our current implementation of the trace-checker is static in the sense that the entire trace is stored on disk (in an NDBM database). The objects at each state belong to classes in a given schema. The regulation, which is type-checked against the same schema, is compiled using the techniques discussed in Section 4.3, and evaluated at each state. We do not have any special optimizations for speed. The objects are stored as strings, and reparsed every time they are loaded into memory. The checker evaluates each obligation w.r.t. all variable assignments, loading into memory a single variable assignment at a time.

We now describe a preliminary evaluation of the implementation. Our goal was to check if we could scale to traces with a large number of objects, rather than very long traces. We created a schema based on the CFR, capturing donors, donations of several types, and various tests. We then checked a number of synthetic (final) states for conformance. Given a schema, we generate a set of donors by choosing random values for atomic attributes. For each donor we generate a set of donations again choosing attribute values at random. Each donation is randomly tested as follows: with $p = 0.3$ it is tested for all diseases with negative results, with $p = 0.3$ it is test for diseases with a random result, and otherwise it is not tested.

On the regulatory side, we created logic formulas for a portion of the CFR 610.40. A total of 12 sentences, and a list of 6 disease names were used. Lists are frequent in regulation, and statements refer to particular list items. Of the 12 sentences, 7 were obligations and 5 were permissions. A total of 8 reference formulas ($\text{by}_{\text{Id}}(\varphi)$) were used, and of these 3 referred to list items. The compilation step of removing the references took 26 seconds with a total of 96 satisfiability tests. Each statement had at most 2 variables (one for donations and the other for disease names).

We evaluated performance of the checker against a number of states. The number of disease names was 8, and the number of donations varied. The time taken varied linearly with a number of donations. For states with 100, 1000, 5000, and 10000 donations the conformance check took 12s, 130s, 500s, and 1042s respectively. The performance suggests that the approach is practical for checking short traces. However, more incremental algorithms are needed to deploy such specifications in a runtime setting.

5   Discussion and Conclusions

We have described a logic for representing regulatory documents for the application of conformance checking. The logic allows statements to refer to others for conditions or exceptions. While references give us a way to represent regulation directly, the

evaluation of references during checking has high complexity. Algorithm 1 uses satisfiability tests of size polynomial in the number of objects. In Sections 4.2 and 4.3, we
described an emprically motivated assumption (*the single copy property*), which lets
us replace satifiablity tests with tests of lower complexity. The evaluation of our prototype implementation suggests that the approach is suitable for conformance audits of
medium-sized traces.

An important part of making this approach useful in practice is to provide support for
translating the regulatory documents into their formal representation. Such support has
to rely heavily on natural language processing techniques, which require substantial
extension of current state of the art. We are actively pursuing this line of research.
Preliminary results are reported in [14,15].

Related Work. The use of logic to represent and reason about regulation has been of
interest for several years. We begin by discussing the literature in relation to two issues:
a) the representation of obligation and permission, and b) references between laws. We
compare our work with other approaches to conformance checking, and place it in the
context of previous work on run-time checking of LTL.

The goal of deontic logic is a formalization of concepts such as obligation, permission and rights. There are many systems of deontic logic, but the most common
approach is to treat obligation and permission as modal operators [16,17]. The logic developed here focusses on the problem of references between laws, and we believe that
the representation of obligation and permission is an important but orthogonal issue.
In future work, we plan to add a modal treatment of obligation and permission to our
system.

The problem of references between laws has been observed in regulatory texts in
different domains [2,18]. More generally, the function of sentences as conditions or
exceptions to others has been studied in a variety of contexts. Alchourron and Makinson
[19] proposed a hierarchical structure for a legal discourse, to handle exceptions to
statements. This led to the development of input-output logic [20], which is closely
related to default logic [11]. Previous work on applying default logic has been mainly
in the context of computing extensions to a theory, in the manner of logic programs
[7,18,6]. We believe that the application of these ideas in conformance checking is
novel.

Conformance checking has been receiving increasing attention in recent years
[1,2,3,21]. [1] represents business contracts as SQL queries. [3,21] use a logic on a
UML description of a domain. While the approaches of [1,3,21] are similar in spirit to
ours, they do not provide a treatment of references. [2] discusses the problem of references in the context of privacy regulation, and the references are resolved manually.

Our work builds upon the well-established work on run-time checking of LTL and its
extensions. We have adapted the calculus of Eagle [5] to handle references. Rule-based
formalisms [5,22] are quite general, but the transformation of formulas at each state
can be expensive. Automata-based approaches [13] offer a more efficient alternative at
the price of generality. We are currently exploring ways to adapt the automata-based
approach to our setting.

References

1. Abrahams, A.: Developing and Executing Electronic Commerce Applications with Occurrences. PhD thesis, Univeristy of Cambridge (2002)
2. Breaux, T.D., Vail, M.W., Anton, A.I.: Towards regulatory compliance: Extracting rights and obligations to align requirements with regulations. In: Proceedings of the 14th IEEE International Requirements Engineering Conference (2006)
3. Giblin, C., Liu, A., Muller, S., Pfitzmann, B., Zhou, X.: Regulations Expressed as Logical Models (REALM). In: Moens, M.-F., Spyns, P. (eds.) Legal Knowledge and Information Systems (2005)
4. U.S. Food and Drug Administration: Code of Federal Regulations, http://www.gpoaccess.gov/cfr/index.html
5. Barringer, H., Goldberg, A., Havelund, K., Sen, K.: Rule-based runtime verification. In: Steffen, B., Levi, G. (eds.) VMCAI 2004. LNCS, vol. 2937, pp. 44–57. Springer, Heidelberg (2004)
6. McCarty, L.T.: A language for legal discourse - i. basic features. In: Proceedings of ICAIL (1989)
7. Sergot, M., Sadri, F., Kowalski, R., Kriwaczek, F., Hammond, P., Cory, H.: The british nationality act as a logic program. Communications of the ACM 29(5), 370–386 (1986)
8. Ross, A.: Directives and Norms. Routlege and Kegan Paul (1968)
9. Marcus, R.B.: Iterated deontic modalities. Mind 75(300) (1966)
10. Dinesh, N., Joshi, A., Lee, I., Sokolsky, O.: Reasoning about conditions and exceptions to laws in regulatory conformance checking (in submission, 2008), http://www.cis.upenn.edu/ nikhild/reasoning.pdf (2008)
11. Reiter, R.: A logic for default reasoning. In: Readings in nonmonotonic reasoning, pp. 68–93. Morgan Kaufmann Publishers Inc., San Francisco (1987)
12. Sistla, A.P., Clarke, E.M.: The complexity of propositional linear temporal logic. ACM 32, 733–749 (1985)
13. Bauer, A., Leucker, M., Schallhart, C.: Monitoring of real-time properties. In: Arun-Kumar, S., Garg, N. (eds.) FSTTCS 2006. LNCS, vol. 4337. Springer, Heidelberg (2006)
14. Dinesh, N., Joshi, A.K., Lee, I., Webber, B.: Extracting formal specifications from natural language regulatory documents. In: Proceedings of the Fifth International Workshop on Inference in Computational Semantics (2006)
15. Dinesh, N., Joshi, A., Lee, I., Sokolsky, O.: Logic-based regulatory conformance checking. In: Proceedings of the 14th Monterey Workshop (2007)
16. von Wright, G.H.: Deontic logic. Mind 60, 1–15 (1951)
17. Aqvist, L.: Deontic logic. In: Gabbay, D., Guenthner, F. (eds.) Handbook of Philosophical Logic, Extensions of Classical Logic, vol. II, pp. 605–614 (1984)
18. Bench-Capon, T.J., Robinson, G., Routen, T., Sergot, M.: Logic programming for large scale applications in law: A formalisation of supplementary benefit legislation. In: Proceedings of the 1st International Conference on AI and Law (1987)
19. Alchourron, C., Makinson, D.: Hierarchies of regulation and their logic. In: Hilpinen, R. (ed.) New Studies in Deontic Logic (1981)
20. Makinson, D., van der Torre, L.: Input/output logics. Journal of Philosophical Logic 29, 383–408 (2000)
21. Glasse, E., Engers, T.V., Jacobs, A.: Power: An integrated method for legislation and regulations from their design to their use in e-government services and law enforcement. In: Moens, M.-F. (ed.) Digitale Wetgeving, Digital Legislation, pp. 175–204 (2003)
22. Barringer, H., Rydeheard, D., Havelund, K.: Rule systems for run-time monitoring: From Eagle to RuleR. In: Sokolsky, O., Taşiran, S. (eds.) RV 2007. LNCS, vol. 4839, pp. 111–125. Springer, Heidelberg (2007)

Deadlocks: From Exhibiting to Healing*

Yarden Nir-Buchbinder, Rachel Tzoref, and Shmuel Ur

IBM Haifa Research Laboratory, Israel
{yarden,rachelt,ur}@il.ibm.com

Abstract. Deadlocks are possibly the best known bug pattern in computer systems in general; certainly they are the best known in concurrent programming. Numerous articles, some dating back more than 40 years, have been dedicated to the questions of how to design deadlock free programs, how to statically or dynamically detect possible deadlocks, how to avoid deadlocks at runtime, and how to resolve deadlocks once they happen. We start the paper with an investigation on how to exhibit potential deadlocks. Exhibiting deadlocks is very useful in testing, as verifying if a potential deadlock can actually happen is a time-consuming debugging activity. There was recently some very interesting research in this direction; however, we believe our approach is more practical, has no scaling issues, and in fact is already industry-ready.

The second contribution of our paper is in the area of healing multithreaded programs so they do not get into deadlocks. This is an entirely new approach, which is very different from the approaches in the literature that were meant for multi-process scenarios and are not suitable (and indeed not used) in multithreaded programming. While the basic ideas are fairly simple, the details here are very important as any mistake is liable to actually create new deadlocks. The paper describes the basic healing idea and its limitations, the pitfalls and how to overcome them, and experimental results.

1 Introduction

The increasing popularity of concurrent programming has brought the issue of concurrent defect analysis to the forefront. While the server side has been employing concurrency ubiquitously for some time, it is now becoming a requirement also for clients and stand-alone applications, as every CPU available these days is multicore, so if applications are to take advantage of it they should become concurrent. Hardware companies such as Intel invest a lot in educating programmers and testers on how to create concurrent software. Otherwise, the new many-cored processors will be of little use.

---

* This work is partially supported by the European Community under the Information Society Technologies (IST) programme of the 6th FP for RTD - project SHADOWS contract IST-035157. The authors are solely responsible for the content of this paper. It does not represent the opinion of the European Community, and the European Community is not responsible for any use that might be made of data appearing therein.

M. Leucker (Ed.): RV 2008, LNCS 5289, pp. 104–118, 2008.

Deadlock is possibly the best known concurrent bug pattern. There are many types of deadlocks and many definitions. For our purposes, a deadlock is when a number of processes or threads cannot proceed as each is waiting for a resource held by the others. The simplest, best known type of potential deadlock can be seen in Figure 1. The deadlock manifests when each of the two threads waits for a lock held by the other. Unlike sequential deterministic code, where if a test passed once it is expected to pass again (unless the code changes), this is not true in the concurrent realm. A deadlock as described above can exist in the code for a long time, and then manifest only when specific timing scenarios occur.

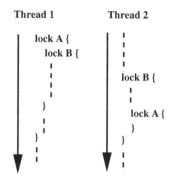

Fig. 1. A program with a potential deadlock

The problem of deadlocks and their avoidance has been around for a long time; the Baker Algorithm for deadlock avoidance was published by Dijkstra as early as 1965. For several decades, this work centered on *preventing* or *resolving* deadlocks between processes competing for resources. In this context, deadlock handling is seen as the burden of the operating system. See [4, 5, 6, 16, 19] for some algorithms for deadlock prevention or resolution. These solutions require processes to declare up-front which resources they need, or alternatively, work by killing one of the processes involved in the deadlock. Neither are applicable to the more modern problem of deadlocks in multithreaded programs synchronizing on mutual exclusion objects. In this domain, deadlocks are considered an internal problem of the program; i.e., a bug.

One useful programming technique to avoid deadlocks is *lock discipline* [2]: when several locks need to be taken together (nestedly), they must be taken in a predefined order, and this order is shared among all threads in the system [1]. There are quite a number of other guidelines related to additional bug patterns [11], such as avoiding lost-notify, and writing small synchronized blocks that avoid blocking operations.

An additional direction in deadlock research is *detection*. Deadlock detection is about statically [20] or dynamically [9] finding that a deadlock is possible in

---

[1] The term "lock discipline" has been used in the literature also in another context – in [17] it is defined as a programming policy that ensures the absence of data races.

the code. For example, if lock discipline violation is detected, even if no deadlock occurred, then the developer is informed that a deadlock is possible, similar in spirit to much of the work on race detection.

This paper is about two complementary techniques: exhibiting, first suggested by [8, 14], and healing. Exhibiting is about making the deadlocks more likely to manifest. The idea is to adjust the timing so that if a deadlock can happen, it will occur with a higher probability. This is very useful in testing, as unlike deadlock detection methods that may exhibit false positives, deadlock exhibiting shows only genuine deadlocks by causing them to happen. The algorithms we present are effective, efficient, and fairly easy to implement. Because we do not control the execution flow we have no guarantee of success. However, the overhead of our interventions is small.

Healing is about detecting potential deadlocks and then modifying the control flow with wrapper locks to ensure that lock cycles do not cause deadlocks. Unlike exhibiting, healing is very complicated. There are many wrong ways to do it and a mistake can cause deadlocks that did not exist in the first place. In the paper we explain the general idea and the many details that complicate the solution.

For both healing and exhibiting we show experimental results on two real-life Java examples. Both techniques worked successfully on these examples. The use case for exhibiting is very clear and we are starting now to try it out in industrial setting. Exhibiting techniques improve the efficiency of testing. For healing—the much harder of the two problems—the scenario in which it should be applied needs very careful attention. An example of such a scenario where healing may be applied is a programming environment where the code was written by people with little experience in concurrent programming (sometimes referred to as business programmers). In such a case the risks of adding our healing algorithm are outweighed by the benefits. We would like to stress that translating our work on healing to other programming languages and concurrency primitives should be done with care.

2   Background

The classical deadlock situation happens when a thread T_1 has taken lock L_1 and attempts to take (nestedly) L_2, while another thread T_2 has taken L_2 and attempts to take L_1. A well-known methodology to avoid deadlocks is lock discipline; when several locks need to be taken together (nestedly), they must be taken in a predefined order, and this order is shared among all threads in the system.

The order can be described as a directed graph, where the nodes are the locks in the system, and an edge exists from node A to B if and only if the system may take lock A and then lock B. If the system may take lock A, lock B inside it, and lock C inside that, there will be edges $A \rightarrow B$ and $B \rightarrow C$. If the graph contains no cycles, then this classical deadlock cannot happen. Conversely, if there are cycles, i.e., lock discipline is not kept, then there is a danger of deadlocks. Figure 1 illustrates a run of a program that violates lock discipline.

A cycle ($A \rightarrow B$, $B \rightarrow A$) may be safe, however, if it is guarded by a *gate lock* – if there is another lock D which is scoped outside all pairs of locking from the cycle, that is, if whenever A is taken inside B or vice versa, D is taken prior to taking the first lock of the pair, and held at least after the second one has been taken. This can obviously be generalized to cycles of more than two locks. Some concurrent algorithms call for this pattern. A cycle may also be deadlock-free for other reasons such as that only one part of the code may be executed, for example, a start-join relationship may prevent concurrent execution of the two orders. However, relying on such guarantees is considered bad programming practice because the cycle is prone to become a real deadlock as the code evolves.

As noted above, most of the related work so far has been on detecting potential deadlocks. Several works, such as the GoodLock algorithm ([14] augmented in [8]), and Microsoft's Driver Verifier [1], identify violations of lock discipline during test runtime. GoodLock monitors events of lock taking and releasing by the program under test. It knows at each time which thread is holding which lock, and so it creates a lock graph and searches for unguarded cycles. The work described in [3] is similar, except that at test runtime it only prints trace information about lock taking and releasing (lock ID and thread ID). The graph creation and analysis is done off-line. This has the advantage that the additional runtime cost at test time is negligible, and hence there is less intrusion to the program under test. The advantage of on-line analysis is that if a cycle is found, direct debugging is possible.

The three tools mentioned look within the scope of one process run. If a cycle in the graph is caused by lock sequences from two different runs, then these tools do not reveal it. A test suite is often composed of many small tests, each in a different process, each activating only a few and short paths, so these tools are less likely to reveal cycles than a tool that has a view of the entire test suite run. The ConTest tool's [10] lock discipline feature [12] tries to overcome this limitation by identifying locks across different runs. The challenge here is that lock ID in Java has no meaning outside the scope of a given run.

As in [3], ConTest traces information during test runtime, creates the graph, and analyzes it off-line. However, the information traced at test runtime includes, in addition to lock ID and thread ID, the source location of taking the lock. A different trace file is written for each test run (each Java process in the test suite). When the test suite has finished running, there is a set of traces, and the analyzer is run. It creates a partition of the code locations to the "same lock" relation, as follows:

1. Two locations l_1 and l_2 are the same-lock' if there exists a trace t in the set of traces and a runtime ID x such that both l_1 and l_2 appear in t associated with x at least once.
2. Same-lock is the transitive closure of same-lock'.

In effect, different lock operations are associated according to the disjunction of two conditions: that they involve the same lock object in some run (similarly to the previously mentioned tools), and that they were done in the same code location (this is unique to ConTest). We argued that from the programmer's point of view, this is the correct, as well as the natural, unit for defining lock discipline.

Then, a directed graph is created, where each node is an equivalence class of same-lock. An edge exists from $\mathcal{L}_1$ to $\mathcal{L}_2$ if and only if there is at least one trace entry where a member of L_2 was taken inside a member of L_1. The graph is searched for unguarded cycles, or more precisely, strongly-connected components (SCC; a maximal subset of the nodes such that a path exists between each two nodes in the subset). An SCC is guarded if and only if an equivalence class L_g (a gate lock) exists such that whenever two members of the component were taken together, it was under the scope of a lock from L_g. In addition, a warning is given for *mixtures*; when two different lock objects from the same equivalence class were taken together, this also represents a deadlock potential.

This summarizes the previous work on deadlock-potential detection. In addition, there has been work on deadlock exhibiting. ConTest's core functionality (as opposed to the enhancement described in this paper) uses "noise" – adding instructions of `yield`, `sleep`, and `wait` (with timeout) to raise the probability that concurrent bugs will occur. If a test *may* deadlock, then with ConTest the probability that it *will* deadlock increases, since more interleavings are exercised. However, ConTest does not target deadlocks in particular, and makes no use of lock graph data.

Two works by Havelund et. al. use the deadlock-potential warnings from an algorithm such as those described above to aid in exhibiting deadlocks. In [14], the warnings are used to narrow down the state space in a model checking aimed at finding actual deadlocks. While this reduction may be very effective in some scenarios (when the warning applies to a few, small threads), in many other scenarios the state space is still too big for practical purposes.

In the second work [8], the deadlock-potential data is used in a subsequent run of the program under test to try to guide it towards a deadlock. This guiding is intrusive, in that it introduces an extra control thread; the original program's threads request the controller's permission to proceed before taking locks. The deadlock exhibition aspect of our work is probably similar, although it uses a less intrusive approach in which there is no controller thread, and instead the original program's threads perform "noise" guided towards the deadlock[2].

3   Exhibiting Deadlocks Using Targeted Noise

As explained in Section 2, given the output of the lock discipline analysis in the form of a directed lock graph, each unguarded strongly connected component (SCC) in the graph represents one or more deadlock potentials, since there can be several cycles in the SCC, and several lock locations represented by a node. To check whether a deadlock potential can actually occur, we try to exhibit the deadlocks using noise targeted at the SCCs. The intuition is that if a deadlock actually exists, we will raise the probability of manifesting it. We emphasize

---

[2] The paper [8] is not explicit about how the locks are identified between the runs. In private communication, the authors indicated that this can be done according to variable names or program locations.

that since the locks are represented by program locations, there is no problem in using a lock graph generated in previous runs as input for a new run.

Our technique for exhibiting deadlocks works as follows: whenever a thread T is about to take a lock that appears in an unguarded SCC, if T already holds another lock from the same SCC, then noise is inserted to delay acquiring the lock. This technique is similar to the ideas presented in [8]. The difference is that [8] used a central controller that decides which thread can advance, whereas our technique only injects noise into the program and hence is simpler, less intrusive, and has no scalability issues. The downside is that we have less control over the execution of the program.

3.1   Experimental Results for Deadlock Exhibiting

We implemented the deadlock exhibiting technique for Java programs using Con-Test's listener architecture [15]. The listener architecture is a library that can be used to write tools that need to hook into given programs under test, for example, race detectors. ConTest Listeners provide an API for doing things when certain types of events happen in the program under test.

At initialization stage, the lock graph is constructed based on ConTest's lock discipline analysis output from previous runs. The events we listen to include entry and exit of synchronization blocks, where we keep an updated record of the locks from unguarded SCCs that each thread is holding or trying to take, and insert noise accordingly through noise API provided by ConTest. The type of noise is determined by ConTest runtime parameters. The noise API that ConTest provides ensures that the inserted noise does not affect the semantics of the program. For example, it prevents an injected call to `sleep` for a certain thread from occurring simultaneously with an interrupt of the thread. We also disable ConTest's own noise through its runtime parameters, to make sure that the only noise injected into the program is the one performed by the listener for exhibiting deadlocks.

All runs were performed on an IBM ThinkPad T60 with an Intel dual core CPU 1.83GHz and 2GB RAM.

NASA Ames K9 Rover Executive. The first example we ran on was the NASA Ames K9 Rover Executive, whose verification is presented in [13]. The NASA Ames K9 Rover is an experimental platform for autonomous wheeled vehicles called rovers, targeted for the exploration of a planetary surface such as Mars. The Rover Executive software prototype monitors the executions of actions, and performs responses and cleanup when execution fails. The Java version of the prototype contains 82 classes and consists of eight threads.

ConTest's lock discipline analysis detected one unguarded SCC, consisting of two nodes. Each node in the SCC represented four different program locations, and so our exhibiting technique can potentially inject noise in only eight locations in the program, out of the 31 locations where a lock is taken. To try exhibiting a deadlock, we first ran the Rover Executive 100 times without instrumentation and noise injection. No deadlock was exhibited. Next, we tried to exhibit a deadlock using ConTest's random noise. When using ConTest default parameters (that are not necessarily targeted at deadlocks), a deadlock was still never exhibited in 100 runs. Since we are trying to exhibit a deadlock caused by lock discipline violation, accesses to shared variables are probably irrelevant [7], and so we turned off the shared variables noise heuristic in ConTest. We set the noise type to `sleep`—our experience shows that this is an effective noise type for exhibiting deadlocks—and ran the Rover Executive with increasing noise strength. 100 runs were performed for each value for noise strength. Once more, a deadlock was never exhibited. We then ran with ConTest and our deadlock exhibiting technique, again using the `sleep` noise type and the strength values that were tried out with ConTest. A deadlock from the SCC was exhibited starting from 3 times out of 100 runs, to 35 out of 100 runs for the maximal strength tried.

We also tried out a simple heuristic where noise is injected whenever a thread tries to take a lock while already holding a lock, regardless of the lock graph information. The purpose is to compare the effectiveness of our technique with techniques that use noise targeted at deadlocks without lock discipline analysis. The same noise parameters and number of runs were used as for our deadlock exhibiting technique. The simple heuristic did not exhibit the deadlock.

The runtime overhead depends both on the frequency of noise injection and on the noise strength. The overhead of the book-keeping in our deadlock exhibiting technique is negligible. Of all the noise injection techniques we tried, our deadlock exhibiting technique uses the most targeted noise, and thus injects noise with the lowest frequency. In comparison, ConTest's random noise can be potentially injected at a call to any synchronization primitive, start and end of threads and accesses (read and write) of shared variables. The simple heuristic that ignores lock discipline is much more targeted than ConTest, as it injects noise only at lock acquisitions, but can still potentially inject noise with a much higher frequency than our deadlock exhibiting technique, depending on the number of nested locks taken throughout the run. For example, in the Rover Executive, our technique injects noise with an average frequency of 6.3 times per run, whereas the simple heuristic injects noise with an average frequency of 18.9 times per run. Note that the performance of our method is not directly affected by the number of threads, but rather by the number of locks participating in unguarded SCCs.

To conclude, of all the techniques we tried out, only our deadlock exhibiting technique using lock analysis was able to exhibit a deadlock. The results confirm that too much noise may mask the bug [7], and that our targeted noise based on runtime analysis is more effective than our targeted noise that considers only the bug pattern.

Java 1.4 Collection Library. The second example is the Java 1.4 collection library that was used as a case study in [18]. This is a thread-safe Collection framework implemented as part of the `java.util` package of the standard Java library provided by Sun Microsystems. ConTest lock discipline analysis discovered two unguarded mixtures in this implementation, using six different tests that were performed in [18], each consisting of two threads. The first mixture consists of three nodes and the second consists of six nodes.

For each test, we compared five different modes of runs, similarly to the runs that were performed for the first example. The first mode is a regular run with no instrumentation and noise injection. The second mode is with ConTest alone, using random noise and default parameters. The third mode is with ConTest and without shared variables noise. The fourth mode is with ConTest and the deadlock exhibiting technique on top of it. The fifth mode is with the simple heuristic that injects noise at nested lock acquisitions, regardless of lock discipline analysis. For all modes, the strength and type of noise were randomly set according to ConTest's default parameters. For each mode of run, we present the number of times a deadlock manifested out of 100 runs. The results are presented in Table 1.

Table 1. Deadlock exhibiting results for Java 1.4 collection library

Name	No noise	ConTest	No shared vars	With lock analysis	Without lock analysis
Vector	0/100	24/100	52/100	93/100	97/100
ArrayList	2/100	32/100	61/100	98/100	98/100
LinkedList	2/100	16/100	81/100	96/100	99/100
LinkedHashSet	96/100	100/100	100/100	100/100	100/100
TreeSet	93/100	97/100	100/100	100/100	98/100
HashSet	95/100	96/100	100/100	100/100	99/100

Upon analyzing the results, we observe the following: for the List tests, where deadlocks are hardly ever exhibited without noise, there is indeed a clear order of effectiveness of methods; noise targeted at the SCCs outperforms random noise that ignores shared variables, which outperforms random noise. For example, if we statistically compare noise targeted at SCCs with random noise that ignores shared variables, then assuming normal distribution, we get that at 95% confidence, the former method will succeed in finding the Vector bug in more than 88% of the runs, while the latter method will succeed in less than 61% of the runs. Similarly, the former method will succeed in finding the ArrayList bug in more than 95% of the runs, while the latter method will succeed in less than 70% of the runs. As for the LinkedList bug, the former method will succeed in finding it in more than 92% of the runs, while the latter method will succeed in less than 88% of the runs. As a result, we can conclude that at 90% confidence, noise targeted at SCCs is significantly better than random noise that ignores shared variables. Similar analysis can be done for the other methods.

The simple heuristic—injecting noise at nested lock acquisitions regardless of lock analysis—performs similarly to our deadlock exhibiting technique. The reason is that these tests are small and focus only on the problematic scenarios. As a result, the simple heuristic injected noise in the same locations as our technique. However, if the test is bigger and activates larger parts of the software where additional locks are acquired, then our technique is expected to outperform the simple heuristic, as demonstrated by the Rover Executive example.

For the Set tests, where deadlocks are easily exhibited without noise, all noise injection methods maintain the high rate of deadlock exhibiting, or even slightly improve it. The advantage of our method over other noise injection methods in such a case is in the low runtime overhead until reaching a deadlock, since its noise injection frequency is considerably lower than the other methods.

4   Healing Deadlocks

Given the lock graph as input, our healing technique works as follows: for each set of deadlock potentials, given in the form of an unguarded SCC in the lock graph, we generate a new wrapper lock that is acquired by a thread before any of the locks in the SCC are acquired, and is released by the thread when all locks in the SCC are not held by the thread anymore. Figure 2 illustrates our healing technique, activated on the program from Figure 1.

A limitation of the algorithm is that it currently supports only scoped locks: synchronized blocks (referred to as implicit locks), `java.util.concurrent.ReentrantLock` (referred to as explicit locks), and pthread mutexes in C. If semaphores, barriers, etc. are involved in the original program then our wrapper lock may lead to a deadlock. Such cases can easily be filtered out (for the purposes of avoiding a healing attempt), either statically (if the program uses them anywhere), or dynamically (if it uses them in the presence of scoped locks; if different threads use different mechanisms, it is OK). Note that a mixed usage of mechanisms probably merits a lock discipline warning in itself; it is very hard to reason about the correctness of such programming. Note also that scoped locks are probably the most common kind of locks, certainly in Java. Thus, for many programs this limitation does not apply.

A problem that rises from the proposed healing solution is that new deadlocks involving a wrapper lock can occur when the graph is incomplete. We refer to this

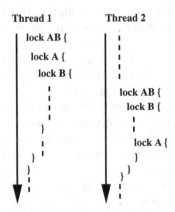

Fig. 2. The healed version of the program from Figure 1. *AB* is the added wrapper lock.

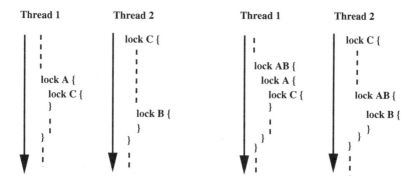

Fig. 3. A possible run of the program from Figure 1

Fig. 4. The incomplete input problem. The addition of wrapper lock AB causes a deadlock that did not exist in the original run.

problem as the *incomplete input problem*. The graph may be incomplete since it describes only lock acquiring patterns observed in previous runs rather than in all possible runs. *Statically* finding all SCCs is undecidable, since we cannot calculate all possible program executions. To illustrate the problem, consider the program from Figure 1. Suppose that lock analysis was performed according to runs of the form depicted in Figure 1, where locks A and B form an SCC. Thus, a wrapper lock AB is added as depicted in Figure 2. Now suppose that the run depicted in Figure 3 is a possible run of the program, i.e., a thread T_1 acquires lock A and then lock C, while a thread T_2 acquires C and then B. This means that locks A, B, and C are in the same SCC, but the healing algorithm is unaware of this fact, since the type of run where C is taken with A or B was never seen before. Note that the run in Figure 3 does not deadlock. However, if the healing algorithm is activated, as depicted in Figure 4, then the following occurs: thread T_1 needs to acquire AB, then A and then C, while thread T_2 needs to acquire C, then AB and then B, resulting in a deadlock.

An additional manifestation of the incomplete input problem is when the *same lock* relation is incomplete, i.e., there are two program locations which should be considered the same lock, but were not detected as such. This can similarly lead to a deadlock involving a wrapper lock.

Any attempt to continue healing once a new deadlock involving a wrapper lock has been detected, may result in inserting new deadlocks into the program, or alternatively cause race conditions. Therefore, we handle the incomplete input problem by aborting the healing of the involved SCCs (by canceling the wrapper lock and continuing the run without it), and updating the lock graph with the missing information. This both guarantees that the healing is safe, and that the observed deadlock does not occur in the future.

To implement the solution, at runtime we maintain the dynamic lock graph of the program (as opposed to the input lock graph built from lock discipline analysis), representing the current state of lock requests and acquisitions in the program, so that there is an edge from node A to B if and only if there is a thread holding lock object A while requesting or acquiring lock object B. Each thread, before requesting or releasing a lock (either an original lock or a wrapper lock), updates the graph. When a thread updates the graph before requesting a lock, it checks whether the resulting graph contains an SCC involving at least one wrapper lock. If so, the thread cancels the wrapper locks, effectively aborting the healing of the involved SCCs.

If a new SCC with no wrapper locks is detected in the dynamic lock graph, then this is an actual deadlock resulting from an SCC which was not part of the input lock graph. In this case we cannot avoid the deadlock; we print debugging information and update the SCCs of the input lock graph, so that in future runs this deadlock is healed.

How are the wrapper locks implemented in Java? since we need to take the wrapper lock in one method run (listener call) and release it in another, `java.util.concurrent.ReentrantLock` are a natural implementation for wrapper locks, but the following problem exists: as described before, sometimes a thread needs to notify other threads that are waiting for the wrapper lock to abort and not try to take it (premature release). This cannot be done straightforwardly with `ReentrantLock`s. Interrupts should not be used either, since they may interfere with the original program's interrupt semantics. The solution is to use `java.util.concurrent.Semaphore`. Usually it is given one permit, so it behaves like a `ReentrantLock`. `aquireUninterruptibly` is used, so that it cannot interfere with the original program's interrupts. When a thread wants to cancel the wrapper lock, it simply raises the number of permits to infinity.

Naively, one would think that while the wrapper lock is taken, there is no need to take the original locks. This fails because it can lead to a race in case of an incomplete graph. Moreover, even if the graph is complete, we need to consider the issue of the `wait` synchronization primitive. The semantics of `wait` attach it to a certain lock. This leads to the following question. Suppose locks A and B are in an SCC, a thread T_1 takes lock A and then B, and then waits on B, and a thread T_2 tries to take A. Now suppose that only the wrapper lock is taken. Should T_1 wait on the wrapper lock instead of waiting on B? If it does, then this can lead to a race condition, since T_2 can now proceed. If T1 does not wait on the wrapper lock, then the `wait` is effectively canceled, which can result in a different semantics for the program. Thus, the original locks must also be taken in addition to the wrapper lock.

Looking more into the `wait` primitive, we observe additional pitfalls. Suppose the thread still holds another lock from the same SCC as the lock it waits on. If the thread releases the wrapper lock, then the thread is holding a lock without its wrapper lock, which may lead to a deadlock involving the wrapper lock. If the thread does not release the wrapper lock, then another thread that is supposed to notify this thread will be blocked. Thus, we cancel the wrapper lock before the call to `wait`, and abort the healing of this SCC. Note that if a thread holds a lock while waiting on another lock, this is already hazardous. For example, if a thread acquires lock A and inside it lock B, and then waits on A, another thread (possibly running the same code!) may take lock A, and then deadlock on B.

If the thread holds no other locks from the same SCC as the lock it waits on, the thread releases the wrapper lock before the call to `wait`. When the thread returns from wait, it reacquires the lock. Thus, it first needs to reacquire the wrapper lock. There is a problem that in a typical implementation of the `wait` primitive (such as in Java and the pthread library for C), by the time the execution of the thread continues after `wait`, it has already reacquired the lock. For example, in Java there is no bytecode event related to reacquiring the lock when returning from wait. Therefore, using program instrumentation (either source level or binary), we cannot force the thread to reacquire the wrapper lock before it reacquires the original lock. Note that if the thread acquires the wrapper lock after it returns from `wait`, a deadlock can occur since we reversed the order of lock acquisitions.

Our solution is as follows: immediately after returning from wait, we temporarily release the original lock, acquire the wrapper lock, and reacquire the original lock. This requires acquiring and releasing of the original locks not through synchronized blocks, which we have implemented, as will be described in Section 4.1.

Without these complications, the implementation of the healing algorithm can be performed *statically*, by adding to the code acquires and releases of wrapper locks before those of the program locks appearing in SCCs. If the locks are represented by program locations, as in our case, this is an even simpler task, since the locks appearing in an SCC can be easily identified. However, since the algorithm must also track runtime information to avoid inserting new deadlocks, we had to implement it at runtime.

4.1   Experimental Results for Deadlock Healing

We implemented the healing algorithm for Java programs. Our implementation uses bytecode instrumentation and consists of code that performs healing and runtime analysis of potential deadlocks involving wrapper locks, as described above. Similarly to the deadlock exhibiting code, we use ConTest for the bytecode instrumentation and its listener architecture for the runtime code. We listen to entry and exit of synchronization blocks and calls to `wait`, and activate the healing and analysis code immediately before and after these events. Releasing and acquiring locks after returning from `wait`, which is a necessary step in our healing solution, are not trivial to implement for implicit locks: this is not possible in the Java language. However, it is possible in Java bytecode, so we created the appropriate bytecode methods in ConTest, that can be called directly from the healing listener code.

We return to the Rover Executive example. To test the effectiveness of the healing algorithm, we ran it together with the deadlock exhibiting algorithm. Otherwise, we never see a deadlock occurring and it is hard to evaluate the effectiveness of healing. We note that ConTest's listener architecture enables running multiple listeners without interfering each other, and so we ran the Rover Executive with both the deadlock exhibiting and deadlock healing listeners. For the deadlock exhibiting we used the same parameters that previously lead to exhibiting a deadlock in 35 out of 100 runs. With healing, a deadlock never occurred. The healing was never aborted – no new SCCs were discovered, and there were no cases where a thread called `wait` while holding another lock from the same SCC as the lock it waited on. There were numerous calls to `wait`, in many of them a thread that returned from `wait` then tried to nestedly acquire another lock from the same SCC. These cases could be handled correctly by our solution as described above.

We now return to the Java 1.4 Collection Library. We reran all tested modes that appear in Table 1 from Section 3.1, with 100 runs for each mode, this time with the addition of healing (the "no noise" mode now uses instrumentation for healing purposes but no noise injection). A deadlock never occurred. No calls to `wait` were encountered, and the healing was never aborted.

We also measured the healing runtime overhead for the Rover Executive and for the Java 1.4 List tests, that did not tend to deadlock without noise insertion. For the Rover Executive we observed an average runtime overhead of 15%, whereas for the List tests we observed an average overhead of 30%. The runtime overhead stems both from the dynamic lock graph computation and from the fact that our healing solution increases the thread serialization. The List tests are very short and the lock operations consume a significant part of their runtime. Thus, for these tests, the dynamic lock graph computation is much more costly than for the Rover Executive. As for the performance overhead due to thread serialization, it is more evident since the runs were performed on a dual core machine. A possible future direction to reduce this overhead is to identify decompositions of the SCCs, so it is sufficient to generate a new wrapper lock for each part of the decomposition to guarantee the absence of deadlocks. In addition, we can reduce the performance overhead due to the dynamic lock graph computation by using online algorithms for cycle detection, instead of the DFS-based algorithm for detecting strongly connected components. Overall, more experience with industrial programs is needed to better estimate the runtime overhead.

To conclude, for both examples, the healing mechanism worked with 100% success.

5   Conclusions

In this paper we have looked at exhibiting and healing deadlocks. Our work assumes that deadlock detection is already done. The case for using deadlock exhibiting in testing is straightforward because detection suffers from the problem of false alarms (a killer for analysis tools) while exhibiting does not. We showed a practical deadlock exhibiting technique with very little intervention and small performance impact. We think we found the right balance, where our technique is a lot more effective than the next simplest thing (applying noise to nested synchronization calls) and a lot more practical than trying to force the program into deadlocks using partial replay schemes.

Healing, on the other hand, requires more research. A possible future direction is to combine the computation of the SCCs using dynamic analysis with a conservative over-approximation using static analysis. This should be done with care, as an over-approximation may be too coarse, leading to thread serialization, as mentioned in Section 4.1.

One use case for healing is when there is a program in the field and we want it to run correctly, even though deadlocks are possible. Correct healing, while simple in concept (involves simply adding a wrapper lock to strongly connected components), needs to pay careful attention to a wide variety of issues. Some are language dependent such as the exact type of locks used, some depend on the risk of working with partial information, and some are related to the semantics of different synchronization primitives. Our experience with implementing deadlock healing showed us that there are many pitfalls that need to be avoided, and some of them may cause new deadlocks. We have resolved many of the issues in the context of Java 5, and have shown that healing is a viable technique. However, anyone who would like to translate our work to a different context will need to consider carefully the issues raised in this paper.

We are now starting to deploy deadlock exhibiting in customer sites. For healing, the technology is ready and we are looking for users and use cases for which it can make a difference.

Acknowledgement. We thank the reviewers for their useful suggestions.

References

1. http://msdn2.microsoft.com/en-us/library/ms792855.aspx
2. Agarwal, R., Stoller, S.D.: Run-time detection of potential deadlocks for programs with locks, semaphores, and condition variables. In: PADTAD 2006: Proceeding of the 2006 workshop on Parallel and distributed systems: testing and debugging (2006)
3. Agarwal, R., Wang, L., Stoller, S.D.: Detecting potential deadlocks with static analysis and run-time monitoring. In: Proceedings of the Parallel and Distributed Systems: Testing and Debugging track of the 2005 IBM Verification Conference (2005)
4. Holliday, J., El Abbadi, A.: Distributed deadlock detection. In: Encyclopedia of Distributed Computing. Kluwer Academic Publishers, Dordrecht (accepted for publication)
5. Banaszak, Z.A., Krogh, B.H.: Deadlock avoidance in flexible manufacturing systems with concurrently competing process flows. IEEE Transactions on Robotics and Automation 6(6) (1990)
6. Belik, F.: An efficient deadlock avoidance technique. IEEE Trans. Comput. 39(7) (1990)
7. Ben-Asher, Y., Eytani, Y., Farchi, E., Ur, S.: Noise makers need to know where to be silent - producing schedules that find bugs. In: International Symposium on Leveraging Applications of Formal Methods, Verification and Validation (ISOLA) (2006)

8. Bensalem, S., Fernandez, J.-C., Havelund, K., Mounier, L.: Confirmation of dead-lock potentials detected by runtime analysis. In: PADTAD 2006: Proceeding of the 2006 workshop on Parallel and distributed systems: testing and debugging (2006)

9. Bensalem, S., Havelund, K.: Dynamic deadlock analysis of multi-threaded pro-grams. In: Ur, S., Bin, E., Wolfsthal, Y. (eds.) HVC 2005. LNCS, vol. 3875. Springer, Heidelberg (2006)

10. Edelstein, O., Farchi, E., Nir, Y., Ratsaby, G., Ur, S.: Multithreaded Java program test generation. IBM Systems Journal 41(1) (2002), http://alphaworks.ibm.com/tech/contest

11. Farchi, E., Nir, Y., Ur, S.: Concurrent bug patterns and how to test them. In: IPDPS 2003: Proceedings of the 17th International Symposium on Parallel and Distributed Processing. IEEE Computer Society, Los Alamitos (2003)

12. Farchi, E., Nir-Buchbinder, Y., Ur, S.: Cross-run lock discipline checker for Java. In: PADTAD / Haifa Verification Conference (2005)

13. Giannakopoulou1, D., Pasareanu, C.S., Lowry, M., Washington, R.: Lifecycle verifi-cation of the NASA Ames K9 Rover Executive. In: ICAPS 2005: Workshop on Ver-ification and Validation of Model-Based Planning and Scheduling Systems (2005)

14. Havelund, K.: Using runtime analysis to guide model checking of java programs. In: Proceedings of the 7th International SPIN Workshop on SPIN Model Checking and Software Verification. Springer, Heidelberg (2000)

15. Nir-Buchbinder, Y., Ur, S.: ConTest Listeners: a concurrency-oriented infrastruc-ture for java test and heal tools. In: Fourth International Workshop on Software Quality Assurance (2007)

16. Sánchez, C., Sipma, H.B., Manna, Z., Gill, C.D.: Efficient distributed deadlock avoidance with liveness guarantees. In: EMSOFT 2006: Proceedings of the 6th ACM & IEEE International conference on Embedded software (2006)

17. Savage, S., Burrows, M., Nelson, G., Sobalvarro, P., Anderson, T.: Eraser: a dy-namic data race detector for multi-threaded programs. In: SOSP 1997: Proceedings of the sixteenth ACM symposium on Operating systems principles (1997)

18. Sen, K., Agha, G.: Cute and jcute: Concolic unit testing and explicit path model-checking tools. In: Ball, T., Jones, R.B. (eds.) CAV 2006. LNCS, vol. 4144. Springer, Heidelberg (2006)

19. Terekhov, I., Camp, T.: Time efficient deadlock resolution algorithms. Information Processing Letters 69(3) (1999)

20. Williams, A., Thies, W., Ernst, M.D.: Static deadlock detection for Java libraries. In: Black, A.P. (ed.) ECOOP 2005. LNCS, vol. 3586. Springer, Heidelberg (2005)

A Scalable, Sound, Eventually-Complete Algorithm for Deadlock Immunity

Horatiu Jula and George Candea

EPFL – Swiss Federal Institute of Technology, Lausanne,
Switzerland

Abstract. We introduce the concept of *deadlock immunity*—a program's ability to avoid all deadlocks that match patterns of deadlocks experienced in the past. We present here an algorithm for enabling large software systems to automatically acquire such immunity without any programmer assistance. We prove that the algorithm is sound and complete with respect to the immunity property. We implemented the algorithm as a tool for Java programs, and measurements show it introduces only modest performance overhead in real, large applications like JBoss. Deadlock immunity is as useful as complete freedom from deadlocks in many practical cases, so we see the present algorithm as a pragmatic step toward ridding complex concurrent programs of their deadlocks.

1   Introduction

Writing concurrent software is a challenging task, because it requires careful reasoning about complex interactions between concurrently-running threads. Programmers consider concurrency bugs to be some of the most insidious. An important category of such bugs result in deadlocks—situations in which a set of threads cannot make forward progress because each thread is waiting to acquire a lock held by another thread in that set. Avoiding the introduction of deadlock bugs during development is challenging, because large software systems are developed by multiple teams totaling hundreds to thousands of programmers. Testing is not a panacea either, because exercising all possible execution paths and thread interleavings is still infeasible for large programs; the result is that deadlock bugs do slip into most large production software. Unfortunately, debugging deadlocks is tedious, because they are hard to reproduce and diagnose.

We expect deadlocks to become more frequent, as multi-core CPUs lead to higher degrees of concurrency and encourage new software systems to be increasingly more parallel. There have been proposals for making concurrent programming easier, such as transactional memory [6], but issues concerning I/O and long-running operations still make it difficult to provide atomicity transparently (ironically, several transactional memory implementations resort to locking for implementing efficient transactions and can thus lead to application deadlocks). We believe that locks will continue being a primary vehicle for synchronization in multi-threaded applications.

M. Leucker (Ed.): RV 2008, LNCS 5289, pp. 119–136, 2008.

Several approaches detect and prevent the introduction of deadlocks before a program runs, by using various forms of static analysis [3,4,7,16]. These approaches typically aim to find deadlock bugs in the source code and either let the programmer fix them, or automatically instrument the application with new locks that introduce serialization in the deadlock-prone code. The challenge faced by static approaches is that they either generate many false positives (i.e., wrongly identify deadlock bugs) and burden programmers with sifting through the reports to pick out the true bugs, or they do not scale to large applications due to resource consumption that is exponential in the size of the analyzed program. In fact, false positives vs. scalability appears to be an essential tradeoff in static techniques for finding deadlocks.

Dynamic approaches [2,5,12,15,17] often face a different challenge: false negatives. Since they rely exclusively on runtime information from the present execution (e.g., a lock trace), deadlocks may still occur, because they cannot be predicted. In fact, the pure version of the deadlock avoidance problem is generally undecidable, because it can be reduced to the halting problem [9][1]. One way to simplify the problem and circumvent undecidability is to save deadlock information that persists across executions, and leverage this knowledge to avoid solely the already-encountered deadlocks.

Our proposed approach detects deadlocks at runtime and saves the *contexts* in which they occurred, in order to avoid the contexts in future runs. This constitutes achieving "immunity" against the corresponding deadlocks. To avoid previously-seen deadlocks we employ program steering [10] and automatically change the scheduling of threads. A program with deadlock immunity will progressively eliminate the manifestations of its deadlocks bugs, by automatically avoiding a monotonically increasing set of deadlock contexts. We expect this approach to result in fewer false positives, because it relies on deadlock patterns that actually manifested, not on inferred deadlocks that may occur in the future. However, if a deadlock does not have a pattern similar to an already encountered one, our approach will not avoid it (false negative). To be precise, the false negative rate of our approach is exactly one per deadlock context, because all runs after the first occurrence will be free of the corresponding deadlock pattern.

Fortunately, deadlock immunity is often as useful as complete deadlock avoidance in practice, since the only difference is that one occurrence per deadlock pattern. Thus, software users now have the option of employing a tool based on our approach, instead of waiting for the manifest deadlock bugs to be fixed by software vendors. In fact, deadlock immunity must not be only an interim solution, but could also provide permanent immunity against those deadlocks, without having to risk the system destabilization often associated with patching.

This paper makes three main contributions: (a) An algorithm for developing deadlock immunity with no assistance from programmers or users; (b) Proof that the algorithm is sound (i.e., avoids deadlocks while preserving liveness) and eventually complete (i.e., avoids all deadlocks after a finite number of steps); and

---

[1] In the limited space here we cannot do justice to all the prior work that has provided us with inspiration; we therefore include a more extensive survey in [9].

(c) Preliminary evidence that the algorithm can scale to large programs (over 350,000 lines of code) and large degrees of concurrency (up to 280 threads).

In the rest of this paper we describe the deadlock immunity algorithm (§2), describe a proof of its soundness and completeness (§3) and analyze its complexity (§4). We present an implementation for Java programs and a preliminary evaluation of effectiveness and performance in real systems (§5), after which the paper concludes (§6).

2 Algorithm for Deadlock Immunity

In this section we present the algorithm per se. After an overview and necessary definitions (§2.1), we describe in detail the instrumentation needed to intercept lock/unlock requests (§2.2). Afterward, we present the two main parts of our approach: the avoidance algorithm (§2.3) and the detection algorithm (§2.4).

2.1 Overview and Definitions

The deadlock immunity algorithm applies to the following abstract model of a multi-threaded program: there is a finite number of threads performing synchronization operations (i.e., lock and unlock) on a finite number of shared mutex locks. When a thread t performs a *lock(l)* on mutex l, it follows 3 steps: (1) t requests lock l; then (2) t waits until l becomes free, i.e., not held by any other thread; and finally (3) t acquires l. A thread can request only one lock at time, and a lock can be held by only one thread at a time. When t performs *unlock(l)*, it releases l, which becomes available to other threads for acquisition. A code region protected by a lock l (i.e., situated between a *lock(l)* and *unlock(l)*) is called a *critical section*. When a thread performs *lock(l')* within the critical section of lock l, we say the thread is doing a *nested lock* (if $l' \neq l$) or a *reentrant lock* (if $l' = l$). Both reentrant and nested locking is supported. We identify the *program position* p at which a thread requests or acquires a lock as the offset of the corresponding instruction within the program source code or binary.

A set of threads is deadlocked iff every thread from that set is waiting (step 2 above) for a lock held by another thread in that set. The immediate cause of a deadlock (or, alternatively, its context) is a given sequence of lock acquisitions that have led to the situation described above. A deadlock avoidance mechanism generally tries to predict impending deadlocks and dynamically reorder the lock acquisitions in order to avoid the predicted deadlocks.

The deadlock immunity algorithm consists of two parts, one that detects deadlocks and another that avoids them by forcing threads to yield (in step 1 above) when they are approaching a previously-seen deadlock. In order to detect deadlocks, we maintain a standard *resource allocation graph* $RAG=[V, E]$. The vertices $v \in V$ can be threads or locks, and the edges $e \in E$ can be request, hold, grant, or yield edges.

A *request edge* $t \rightarrow_r l$ represents thread t requesting permission to wait for lock l (step 1 above). A *grant edge* $t \xrightarrow{p}_g l$ represents the fact that thread t was granted permission by the algorithm to wait for lock l at position p in the program (i.e., to enter step 2). A *hold edge* $t\xleftarrow{p}_h l$ indicates that t has acquired lock l at position p (step 3). A group of *yield edges* $t\xrightarrow{p_1}_y t_1, ..., t\xrightarrow{p_n}_y t_n$ indicates that thread t was forced to yield because threads $t_1, ..., t_n$ had acquired (or were granted) locks at positions $p_1, ..., p_n$; the usefulness of yield edges will become clear later on. In summary, a request edge is the manifestation in the RAG of a lock request and a hold edge the manifestation of a lock acquisition. A grant edge reflects the algorithm's decision to allow a thread to do a blocking wait for a lock, while a yield edge captures the immunity algorithm's decision to pause a thread in order to avoid a potential deadlock. In terms of notation, when the value of an edge label or an endpoint is irrelevant, we mark it with $*$ (as in $v_1\xrightarrow{*}_y v_2$, or $v_1\xrightarrow{*}_y *$).

A deadlock appears as a cycle in the RAG, involving exclusively request, grant, and hold edges (i.e., no yield edges). When avoiding deadlocks using thread yields, livelocks can arise; e.g., when a thread t_1 is forced to yield because of thread t_2, while thread t_2 waits for a lock held by thread t_1. We call such livelocks *avoidance-induced livelocks*.

Avoidance-induced livelocks appear as *yield cycles* in the RAG—a cycle is a yield cycle iff all yield edges emerging from its nodes belong to yield cycles. One can think of avoidance-induced livelocks as a group (conjunction) of yield cycles that intersect in a vertex v of the RAG *as well as* in all yield edges that emerge from v. The yield cycle construct enables the algorithm to detect and avoid

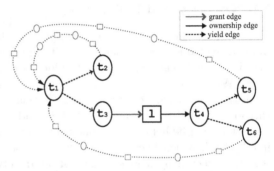

Fig. 1. Livelocked threads and yield cycles

all avoidance-induced livelocks the same way it detects and avoids deadlocks.

To illustrate the concept, consider Figure 1: for thread t_1 to be livelocked, all of its yield edges must be part of cycles, as well as all of t_4's yield edges, since t_4 is in one of t_1's yield cycles. If the RAG had solely the $(t_1, t_2, ..., t_1)$ and $(t_1, t_3, l, t_4, t_6, ..., t_1)$ cycles, then there would be no livelock, because t_4 could "evade" livelock through t_5, allowing t_1 to "evade" through t_3. If, as in Figure 1, cycle $(t_1, t_3, l, t_4, t_5, ..., t_1)$ is also present, then the threads have no way to make forward progress and are thus livelocked.

We use instruction location information to capture and save templates of deadlocks and induced livelocks. Remember, the program position p is an abstraction that denotes the location of an instruction in the source code or binary. A *template* is the set of program positions (edge labels) corresponding to the edges of a cycle in the RAG; remember that only grant, hold, and yield edges carry labels. For example, the template of the cycle $t_1 \rightarrow_r l_1 \xrightarrow{p_1}_h t_2 \rightarrow_r ...l_n \xrightarrow{p_n}_h t_1$ is $\{p_1, ..., p_n\}$. Templates capture the "contexts" in which deadlocks occur. A *template instance* is an instantiation of a template in a program execution, i.e., a set of *(thread, position)* tuples, representing distinct threads that are currently holding or have been granted locks at positions corresponding to the template, that cover all positions in the template; e.g., the instantiation of $\{p_1, ..., p_n\}$ in the current state of a program would take the form $\{(t_1, p_1), ..., (t_n, p_n)\}$.

Templates are analogous to "antibodies"—the algorithm saves them to persistent storage and avoids their re-instantion in all future executions. Since both deadlocks and avoidance-induced livelocks have their templates saved to the same template history, we will refer to all of them as simply *templates*, the unified deadlock and induced livelock history simply *history*, and the deadlocks and avoidance-induced livelocks simply *cycles* when no distinction needs to be made.

An immunizing tool based on the proposed algorithm instruments programs such that all lock and unlock operations are intercepted and relayed to the immunity algorithm's *avoidance module*. This module shares an event queue and the history with the *detection module*, as illustrated in in Figure 2.

The *avoidance module* runs synchronously with the application, in that it is invoked on every lock request, acquisition or release; avoidance decisions are made only for lock requests. This module is responsible for avoiding cycles, based on the templates stored in history. The avoidance module notifies asynchronously the detection component about events (lock request/acquisition/release) and decisions (grant/yield) using an event queue. On every lock request, this module checks whether any templates in the history would be instantiated by granting the requested lock. If not, the thread is allowed to proceed with locking; otherwise, the thread must yield.

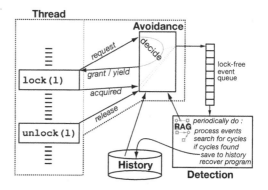

Fig. 2. Architecture of an immunizing tool

The *detection module* runs asynchronously, in parallel with the program's threads. It periodically updates the RAG based on notifications received from the avoidance module, detects cycles in the RAG, and saves these cycles' templates to the history. It then restarts the deadlocked application's threads.

In summary, the proposed approach has three key features: (1) it captures execution-independent templates of previously-encountered deadlocks and avoids future instantiations of these templates; (2) detects and avoids livelocks induced by avoidance in exactly the same way as deadlocks (yield cycles allow us to cast a liveness property into an easily detectable safety property); (3) detects cycles asynchronously in a separate thread, in order to remove this expensive computation from the critical path. Given that a deadlocked application is not making any progress anyway, the only drawback of asynchrony is a potentially longer recovery time; the latter can easily be tuned by selecting a suitable period.

2.2   Instrumentation

The code or binary of the original program needs to be instrumented such that all lock and unlock operations are intercepted. The instrumentation replaces each call to a native lock/unlock with corresponding code that relays events to the avoidance module and exercises control over the scheduling of the calling thread, as shown in Figure 3. We discuss the instrumentation here as much as necessary for understanding the mechanics of the runtime system; the details appear in the next section.

When an immunized thread t wants a lock l at position p, it asks for permission from the avoidance module, which could ask the thread to yield, in which case the thread will sleep until permitted to proceed. When the avoidance module allows the thread to proceed, t uses the native locking mechanism to acquire l and then notifies the avoidance module of the acquisition event. An unlock operation is analogous, but simpler. This form of instrumentation is just one possible design choice—it could also be implemented inside the runtime, the operating system kernel, etc.

2.3   Avoidance

The avoidance module is responsible for controlling the schedule of threads to avoid previously-encountered deadlocks and avoidance-induced livelocks. The interface offered by this module to the instrumented threads consists of three operations: *Request*, *Acquired* and *Release*, that process lock requests, acquisitions and releases, respectively. We developed both a synchronized version of the algorithm, which uses a global lock to ensure atomicity of *Request* and *Release*, as well as a lock-free version, which eliminates this global lock, but requires additional checks in *Request*, *Release* and in the instrumentation of lock operations. We present here the lock-free version of the algorithm; the synchronized version appears together with the lock-free one in [9].

The *Request*, *Acquired* and *Release* operations are described in Figure 5. The core avoidance occurs in *Request*, whose return value determines whether a thread is paused or allowed to proceed. But, before discussing the algorithms in any more detail, we describe the data structures they employ.

Since avoidance is performed synchronously with calling threads, we aim to minimize the amount of work performed in the critical path; for this we choose fine-grain, efficient data structures in the avoidance module. The avoidance module shares only two data structures with the cycle detector: an event queue (updated by the avoidance module and read by the detector) and the template history (updated by the detector and read by the avoidance module). Cycle detection requires a consistent view of the RAG, thus requiring exclusive access to it, but is also a complex operation, thus holding the RAG locked for extended periods of time. We therefore opted to have all RAG updates be performed in the detection module, based on the events received through the queue. This provides optimal decoupling between the two modules.

The avoidance module uses the following data structures:

- *lockGrantees*[p] is a multiset[2] containing the threads that hold (or are granted) locks at position p; it is initially empty. This is the data structure used in searching for template instantiations.

- *history* is the set of templates of previously-encountered cycles. It is persistent, in that all updates are saved on disk, to be available in subsequent executions. At program startup, *history* is loaded in memory.

- *yieldCause*[t] is the cause of thread t's yield; *yieldCause*[t] has the same structure as a template instance, because it is in effect a subset of a real template instance. It is initially null.

- *yielders*[t, p] is the set of threads that are currently paused and have (t, p) in their *yieldCause*; the *yielders* map is initially empty.

- *yielders*[t, p] is the set of threads that are currently paused and have (t, p) in their *yieldCause*; the *yielders* map is initially empty.

- *owner*[l] is the thread currently holding lock l; it is initially null.

- *acqPos*[l] is the program position where lock l was acquired by its current owner; it is initially null.

- *nLockings*[l] is the number of times lock l was reentrantly locked; it is initially 0.

- *yieldLock*[t] is the lock (condition variable) used for pausing or waking up thread t.

The instrumentation for the lock operation (Figure 3) performs avoidance iff the current thread t does not already hold the lock l it is currently requesting

```
lock_wrapper( l )
1   t := current thread ID
2   p := current program position
3   if owner[l] ≠ t then
4       events := events + [request(t,l,p)]
5       yCause := Request(t,l,p)
6       if yCause ≠ null then
7           foreach (t', p') ∈ yCause do
8               native_lock_for_read( (t',p') )
9           if ∀(t', p') ∈ yCause :
                    1_{lockGrantees[p']}(t') > 0 then
10              native_lock( yieldLock[t] )
11              foreach (t', p') ∈ yCause do
12                  yielders[t',p'] :=
                            yielders[t',p'] ∪ {t}
13                  native_unlock_for_read((t',p'))
14              yieldCause[t] := yCause
15              events := events +
                        [yield(t, yieldCause[t])]
16              yieldLock[t].wait()
17              native_unlock( yieldLock[t] )
18          else
19              foreach (t', p') ∈ yCause do
20                  native_unlock_for_read((t',p'))
21              goto 5
22  native_lock( l )
23  Acquired( t, l, p )

unlock_wrapper( l )
1   t := current thread ID
2   Release( t,l )
3   native_unlock( l )
```

Fig. 3. Lock/Unlock Instrumentation

---

[2] A multiset is a set whose elements can be present more than once. An element x is added to a multiset M using the $\uplus$ operator and removed from M using the $\setminus$ operator. For a multiset M and an element x, $1_M(x)$ represents the number of times x was added to M ($M := M \uplus \{x\}$) less the number of times it was removed ($M := M \setminus \{x\}$). x is deleted from M only when $1_M(x)$ reaches zero.

(line 3). To perform the avoidance, the cycle detector is first notified of the request (line 4). Then lines 5-6 check if it is safe for t to proceed with locking l. If yes, t uses the native locking mechanism to acquire l (line 22), notifies the avoidance module of the acquisition event (lines 23) and is done. If unsafe, i.e., the avoidance module returned a non-null *yield cause* on line 5, we must check if the yield cause is still current (lines 7-9). If yes, a yield is required: register t in all (thread, position) pairs from the yield cause (lines 11-12), store the yield cause (line 14), notify the detector about the yield decision (line 15), and wait until a thread from the yield cause releases all required locks and wakes t up (line 16). If the yield cause is no longer valid (line 18), we need to re-check whether it is safe to proceed (line 21). The immunity algorithm influences the thread schedule via a simple wait mechanism that relies on the condition variable $yieldLock[t]$; an alternative choice would have been to call yield in a loop, but that is more CPU-intensive.

When a thread requests a lock, the avoidance module checks whether granting that lock would instantiate any of the templates currently in *history*. An *instantiation* of template $T = \{p_1, ..., p_n\}$ is a set of (*thread, position*) tuples representing distinct threads t that hold (or are granted) locks at positions p from T (i.e., $t \in lockGrantees[p]$), with all positions being covered (i.e., $\forall p \in T : lockGrantees[p] \neq \emptyset$). Thus, a template T would be instantiated by thread t being granted a lock at position p iff $p \in T$ and $T - \{p\}$ is already covered by threads different from t (i.e., $instance(T - \{p\}, \{t\}) \neq null$).

The *templateInstance(t,p)* helper, shown in Figure 4, returns a template instantiation that would occur, if thread t granted a lock at position p (lines 2-4).

If no potential template instantiations are found, *templateInstance(t,p)* returns null. The *instance(T,exclThreads)* helper returns an instantiation of template T that does not involve any thread from *exclThreads* (line 8), or *null* if such an instantiation does not exist (line 9). If *templateInstance*(t, p) returns an instantiation $\{(t_1, p_1) ..., (t_n, p_n)\}$, then it means that $yieldCause[t] = \{(t_1, p_1) ..., (t_n, p_n)\}$, i.e., thread t has to wait until t_1 releases all the locks it acquired at p_1, or ..., or t_n releases all the locks it acquired at p_n. Whenever a thread t releases all locks acquired at position p, it wakes up all yielding threads t_i for

```
templateInstance( t,p )
1  foreach T ∈ history where p ∈ T do
2     templInstance := instance( T − {p}, {t} )
3     if templInstance ≠ null then
4        return templInstance
5  return null


instance( T, exclThreads )
1  if T = ∅ then
2     return ∅
3  else
4     pos := choose p ∈ T
5     foreach t ∈ lockGrantees[pos]
              where t ∉ exclThreads do
6        match :=
           instance(T \ {pos}, exclThreads ∪ {t})
7        if match ≠ null then
8           return {(t, pos)} ∪ match
9     return null
```

Fig. 4. Helpers for matching templates

which $(t, p) \in yieldCause[t_i]$ by performing a notify on the corresponding condition variable (i.e., on $yieldLock[t_i]$).

Figure 5 presents the core operations of the avoidance module.

When *Request(t,l,p)* is invoked, thread t is intially granted lock l (line 1). Then, one checks if thread t can safely proceed, i.e., if no template can be instantiated (line 2). If it is unsafe, the lock grant is canceled (line 6) and thread t must be forced to wait and the yield cause is returned (line 7). If it is safe, one lets t execute the lock by returning a null yield cause (line 7) and notifies the cycle detector about this decision (line 4).

However, a group of threads may still simultaneously instantiate a template after being granted on line 1 the locks they required. If this occurs, at least one thread in the group will notice the instantiation during the check from line 2.

In *Acquired(t,l,p)*, if thread t does not own l, then l is marked as acquired by t (line 2), the position p where l was acquired is saved (line 3), and the detector is notified (line 4). If t already holds l, a counter for reentrant locking of l is incremented (line 5).

In *Release(t,l)*, we decrement the counter associated with t (line 1). If l can be released (line 2), the owner and acquisition position for l must be reset (lines 4-5), the cycle detector notified

Request(t,l,p)
1 lockGrantees[p] :=
             lockGrantees[p] ⊎ {t}
2 yieldCause := templateInstance(t,p)
3 **if** yieldCause = null **then**
4   events := events + [$grant(t,l,p)$]
5 **else**
6   RemoveGrant(t,p)
7 **return** yieldCause

Acquired(t,l,p)
1 **if** $owner[l] \neq t$ **then**
2   owner[l] := t
3   acqPos[l] := p
4   events := events + [$acquired(t,l,p)$]
5 nLockings[l] := nLockings[l] + 1

Release(t,l)
1 nLockings[l] := nLockings[l] - 1
2 **if** nLockings[l] = 0 **then**
3   p := acqPos[l]
4   owner[l] := null
5   acqPos[l] := null
6   events := events + [$release(t,l)$]
7   RemoveGrant(t,p)

RemoveGrant(t,p)
1 **if** $1_{lockGrantees[p]}(t) = 1$ **then**
2   native_lock_for_write((t,p))
3 lockGrantees[p] :=
             lockGrantees[p] \ {t}
4 **if** $1_{lockGrantees[p]}(t) = 0$ **then**
5   **foreach** $t' \in yielders[t, p]$ **do**
6   native_lock(yieldLock[t'])
7   yieldLock[t'].notify()
8   native_unlock(yieldLock[t'])
9   yielders[t,p] := ∅
10   native_unlock_for_write((t,p))

Fig. 5. The avoidance module

(line 6), and the lock grant given to t removed by deregistering t from $acqPos[l]$ (line 7).

In *RemoveGrant(t,p)*, if t is about to release all locks from p (line 1), lock (t, p) in write mode (line 2) to ensure consistency of the operations performed in the instrumentation, and remove the grant given to t for position p (line 3). If t

released all locks from p (line 4), then wake up (notify) all yielders, i.e., threads that have (t, p) in their yield cause, and finally unlock (t, p) on line 12.

2.4 Detection

The detection module finds cycles in the RAG—deadlocks and avoidance-induced livelocks—and saves their templates to history. As illustrated in Figure 7, it periodically fetches and processes the notifications—RAG events and avoidance decisions—sent by the avoidance module, updates the RAG, and looks for cycles in the RAG. If cycles are found, their templates are computed and saved, after which the threads (or a subset thereof) are restarted. The detection module looks only for RAG cycles containing threads with pending lock requests, because only *request* events can introduce new cycles in the RAG (see proof in §3).

These actions are performed with a period of τ (e.g., 1 second). In principle, the value of τ does not affect correctness, given that it merely introduces a delay between the moment the program becomes deadlocked/livelocked and when this condition is detected. In practice, however, τ is a "knob" for tuning the tradeoff between computation overhead and recovery time: a higher τ reduces the CPU time consumed on updating the RAG and detecting cycles, while a lower τ

waitCycles(v)
1 **foreach** $x \in rag$ **do**
2   x.color := white
3 endings := $\emptyset$
4 hasCycles(v, endings)
5 **return** $\bigcup_{x \,\in\, endings}$ $waitChains(x, x)$

hasCycles($v, endings$)
1 **if** $v.color = black$ **then**
2   **return false**
3 **if** $v.color = grey$ **then**
4   endings := endings $\cup \{v\}$
5   **return true**
6 v.color := grey
7 **if** $\exists\, v \xrightarrow{\ *\ }_{r/g/h} v' \in rag$ s.t. $hasCycles(v', endings)$
        $\vee\ \forall\, v \xrightarrow{\ *\ }_y v_i \in rag$: $hasCycles(v_i, endings)$ **then**
8   **return true**
9 **else**
10   v.color := black
11   **return false**

template(C)
1 **return** $\{e.pos \mid e \in C \wedge (e = * \xleftarrow{\ *\ }_h * \ \vee\ e = * \xrightarrow{\ *\ }_y *)\}$

waitChains (v_1, v_2)
1 cycles := $\emptyset$
2 **if** $\exists e = v_1 \xrightarrow{\ *\ }_{r/g/h} v \in rag$ s.t. $v.color = grey$ **then**
3   **if** $v = v_2$ **then**
4   cycles := cycles $\cup \{\{e\}\}$
5   **else**
6   cycles := cycles $\cup\, (\bigcup_{c \,\in\, waitChains(v, v_2)} \{e\} \cup c)$
7 **if** $\forall v_1 \xrightarrow{\ *\ }_y v_i \in rag$: $v_i.color = grey$ **then**
8   **choose** $e = v_1 \xrightarrow{\ *\ }_y v_i \in rag$
9   **if** $v_i = v_2$ **then**
10   cycles := cycles $\cup \{\{e\}\}$
11   **else**
12   cycles := cycles $\cup\, (\bigcup_{c \,\in\, waitChains(v_i, v_2)} \{e\} \cup c)$
13 **return** cycles

Fig. 6. Helpers for the detection module

leads to more prompt detection and, thus, faster recovery from deadlock/livelock, which improves the availability of the program.

The detection module uses two data structures, rag (the resource allocation graph) and $events$ (the event queue used to receive RAG events and avoidance decisions from the avoidance module), which is initially empty. A RAG event can be $request(t, l, p)$, $yield(t, yieldCause)$, $grant(t, l, p)$, $acquired(t, l, p)$ or $release(t, l)$, corresponding to adding a request edge, adding a yield edge, converting a request edge into a grant edge, converting a grant edge into a hold edge, and removing a hold edge, respectively. $requestingThreads$ is the set of threads having pending lock requests.

As in the case of the avoidance module, we make use of helpers, defined in Figure 6. We only give a high-level description of these helpers, because the underlying algorithms are well-known. The $waitCycles$, $waitChains$, and has-$Cycles$ helpers are used for cycle detection, and $template(C)$ is used to extract the template of a cycle C. $hasCycles(v, endings)$ is easiest implemented using colored-DFS [11], in which all explored nodes are marked "grey" or "black", depending on whether they are involved in deadlocks/livelocks. $hasCycles(v, endings)$ finds out whether v is involved in deadlocks/livelocks and returns the nodes in which the deadlocks/livelocks (if any) end. $waitCycles(v)$ retrieves cycles involving v by exploring the "grey" nodes, starting from the endings returned by

$hasCycles(v, endings)$.

A RAG node of type thread can have multiple edges emerging from it: up to one request edge and zero or more yield edges. Thus, a node can be involved in more than one cycle, which means $waitCycles(v)$ could re-

main_loop

```
1  while stop = false
2      sleep τ milliseconds
3      processEvents()
4      foundCycles := ∅
5      foreach t ∈ requestingThreads do
6          foundCycles :=
               foundCycles ∪ waitCycles(t)
7      if foundCycles ≠ ∅ then
8          foreach c ∈ foundCycles do
9              history := history ∪ template(c)
10         restart program
```

processEvents()

```
1  while events ≠ ∅ do
2      evt := events.head
3      events := events.tail
4      switch evt do
5          case request(t, l, p)
6              rag := rag ∪ {t→ᵣl}
7              requestingThreads :=
                   requestingThreads ∪ {t}
8          case yield(t, yCause)
9              rag := rag \ {t→*ᵧt'|t→*ᵧt' ∈ rag}
                   ∪{t→ᵖᵧt'| (t',p) ∈ yCause}
10         case grant(t, l, p)
11             rag := rag \ {t→ᵣl} ∪ {t→ᵖₓl}
12         case acquired(t, l, p)
13             rag := rag \ {t→ᵖₓl} ∪ {t←ᵖₕl}
14             requestingThreads :=
                   requestingThreads \ {t}
15         case release(t, l, p)
16             rag := rag \ {t←*ₕl}
```

Fig. 7. The detection module

turn more than one cycle. However, it is not necessary to retrieve, save and avoid the templates of all cycles containing a particular node: to avoid an induced livelock, it is sufficient to avoid one of its corresponding yield cycles. Thus, if a thread t is involved in an avoidance-induced livelock, it is enough for $waitCycles(t)$ to return just one yield cycle of the livelock.

The two core algorithms are shown in Figure 7. As long as it is not asked to stop, the cycle detector periodically (every τ msec) processes the notifications from the avoidance module (line 3), finds all cycles containing threads with pending requests (lines 4-6) and, if cycles found (line 7), adds the templates of the detected cycles to the history (lines 8-9) and recovers the program (line 10).

3   Soundness and Completeness

In this section we outline the proof of the deadlock immunity algorithm's soundness and refer the reader to [9] for the details. The proof shows soundness by demonstrating *safety*, i.e., that the algorithm indeed avoids previously-seen deadlocks, and *liveness*, i.e., that all threads will eventually make progress. The algorithm is also proven to be *eventually complete*, i.e., that it eventually detects and avoids all cycles, i.e., deadlocks and avoidance-induced livelocks.

In proving soundness and completeness of our algorithm, we make the following assumptions:

- All avoidance routines (*Request, Acquired, Release*) are thread-safe. This depends on implementation: in the synchronized version of the algorithm [9], atomicity (and therefore thread-safety) is ensured by a global lock. In the lock-free version (Figure 5), thread-safety (consistency) is preserved via the additional check performed in the *Request* routine.
- The number of threads in a program and the number of possible program positions (i.e., program size) are finite.
- All existing deadlock bugs in a program and avoidance-induced livelocks eventually manifest.
- All critical sections eventually terminate, except in cases of deadlock or livelock.
- The native thread scheduler is fair.
- All lock/unlock statements performed in the program are instrumented as shown in Figure 3.
- The position within the program of lock operations previously involved in deadlocks or livelocks does not change from one execution to another, i.e., templates are execution-independent. This assumption could be invalidated by a program upgrade or patch.

We first prove completeness of the cycle detection algorithm. The detection module looks only for cycles containing threads with pending requests, so we first prove that, indeed, only the *request* events can introduce new cycles in the RAG; we do this by proving that the remaining RAG events — *acquired* and *release* — cannot introduce new cycles in the RAG. Second, we prove that the detection module detects all cycles required to perform avoidance.

To prove safety (i.e., that we achieve deadlock immunity), we split *history* into its version before the current execution (*history$_{old}$*) and the additions made during the current run ($history_{new}$), i.e., $history = history_{old} \cup history_{new}$. We then prove that the following invariant is maintained: $\forall T \in history_{old} :$ $instance(T, \emptyset) = null$, i.e., the algorithm avoids the instantiation of all templates from $history_{old}$. Then, we prove the invariant $\forall C \in waitCycles(t) :$ $template(C) \notin history_{old}$, i.e., no newly-detected cycle has its template in $history_{old}$. Finally, we prove the invariant $history_{new} \cap history_{old} = \emptyset$, i.e., templates do not repeat in different runs.

To prove completeness (i.e., that an application instrumented with our algorithm eventually develops immunity against all possible deadlocks and avoidance-induced livelocks), we first prove that the number of possible templates is finite. Then we prove that every program instrumented according to Figure 3, after a finite number of restarts, eventually reaches a point beyond which all subsequent executions become free of deadlocks and avoidance-induced livelocks. Finally, we prove that the deadlock immunity algorithm preserves liveness, i.e., all lock requests are eventually granted by our algorithm. The detailed proofs, for both synchronized and lock-free implementations, are presented in [9].

4   Complexity Analysis

In this section, we discuss the theoretical complexity of the algorithm, and in the next section we analyze its empirically measured performance. For conciseness, we highlight here the main results of the complexity analysis and direct the reader to [9] for the details.

For the avoidance module, assume an immunized program is running with a history containing N templates, containing N_P positions on average, and for each position p in a template, $|lockGrantees[p]| = N_G$, on average. Let N_W be the average number of yields (waits) performed by a thread before being granted a lock, and C_{wait} the cost of a $wait()$ system call. Let $|yielders[t, p]| = N_Y$ on average, and C_{notify} the cost of a $notify()$ call. The complexity of the $Request$ operation, which is the most expensive in the avoidance module, is $O(N_W \cdot (C_{wait} + N \cdot (N_P + (N_P - 1)! \cdot N_G^{N_P-1})) + N_Y \cdot C_{notify})$.

Note that we expect N_P to be small in practice, on the order of $N_P = 2...4$, since deadlocks normally involve no more than 4 threads. This is justified by the fact that, for a group of threads to deadlock, first they have to simultaneously perform nested locks, and then to perform the inner locks in such a way that a circular wait occurs. As far as induced livelocks are concerned, note that an avoidance-induced livelock is a conjunction of yield cycles (§2.4) and a yield cycle will mirror one of the already-encountered deadlocks. Thus, since N_P is small, we expect that the exponential term in N_P to not be dominant in practice.

For the detection module, consider $RAG = [V, E]$, with $|requestingThreads| = N_R$, on average; say we have on average N_E events in the event queue. The complexity of the detection module is $O(N_E + N_R \cdot (|V| + |E|))$, because every event is processed in constant time, and we use the optimal colored DFS algorithm (§2.4) for detecting RAG cycles starting from each thread in $requestingThreads$.

For the complete derivation of the two modules' complexities, please see [9].

5   Evaluation

In order to verify the practicality of deadlock immunity, we built a prototype of the deadlock immunity algorithm for Java programs. After describing the implementation and experimental setup, we evaluate effectiveness (§5.1), performance overhead in a real application server (§5.2), as well as discuss the effect of false positives (§5.3). The interested reader can additionally find in [9] the evaluation of performance overhead using a lock-intensive microbenchmark.

In our implementation, we rely on AspectJ [1], an aspect-oriented compiler, to instrument Java programs. We instrument the bytecode-level calls to *monitorenter* (corresponding to the start of Java synchronized blocks) and to *monitorexit* (corresponding to the end of synchronized blocks). The instrumentation is embodied by advices that capture lock requests (*before-monitorenter* advice), lock acquisitions (*after-monitorenter* advice), and lock releases (*before-monitorexit* advice). Lock positions are represented as *file:line* strings corresponding to the line of code containing the statement in the source file.

The experiments reported here were run on computers with 2 x 4-core Intel Xeon E5310 1.6GHz CPUs, 4GB RAM, WD-1500 hard disk, 2 NetXtreme II GbE interfaces, interconnected by a dedicated GbE switch, running Linux Fedora Core 7 with kernel 2.6.20, Java HotSpot Server VM 1.6.0, and Java SE 1.6.0.

5.1   Effectiveness

The first question we wanted to answer was whether the proposed approach will avoid deadlocks in real applications. We scoured bug reports for the MySQL database system [13] and, of the various reports of deadlocks or hangs, we were able to reproduce four (#21427, #14972, #31126, and #17709). They all occur in the connector that allows Java programs to interact with the database engine. We wrote test programs that deterministically reproduce these bugs. The immunized test programs detected each deadlock the first time it occurred, saved the template to history, and successfully avoided it in subsequent executions. Since extensive repeated runs never deadlocked, we cite this as an empirical proof point that the immunized programs had developed immunity against the deadlock bugs. MySQL users encountering these bugs face the option of waiting for the MySQL team to fix them, or to use an immunization tool right away.

While in some cases deadlocks can be eliminated by fixing the root cause, in other cases this is not a reasonable option. For example, a number of synchronized classes in the Java runtime environment can cause deadlocks in the applications that call them. Consider two vectors v_1, v_2 in a multithreaded program—since Vector is a synchronized class, programmers allegedly need not be concerned by concurrent access to vectors. However, if one thread wants to add all elements of v_2 to v_1 via $v_1.addAll(v_2)$, while another thread concurrently does the reverse via $v_2.addAll(v_1)$, the program can deadlock, because underneath the covers, the JDK locks v_1 then v_2 in one thread, and v_2 then v_1 in the other thread. This is a general problem for all synchronized `Collection` classes in the JDK, of which there are dozens. It is difficult for developers to knowingly steer clear of deadlocks resulting from the implementation of an opaque interface, and deadlocks hidden underneath the runtime interface are some of the most insidious. At the same time, it is tenuous to precisely document in this interface all possible usage scenarios that could lead to deadlock.

We wrote test cases for six such deadlock traps and immunized them. After encountering the respective deadlocks for the first time, all subsequent executions were free of deadlocks. This resolution requires no programmer intervention and no JDK modifications.

5.2   Performance Overhead in Real Applications

We applied our immunization tool to JBoss [8], a J2EE application server. JBoss is a piece of middleware that allows enterprise and Web applications to be written in Java, with all complexities of transactions, persistence, group communication, replication, etc. being handled transparently on the applications' behalf. Behind virtually every e-commerce Web site today lies an application server. JBoss is one of the most widely used J2EE servers and, at over 350,000 lines of code (excluding comments), it is likely one of the largest systems written in Java.

To benchmark performance on the immunized JBoss, we used the RUBiS benchmark [14], an online auction application modeled after eBay. In our measurements, we used the servlet version of RUBiS with the browse workload.

We ran JBoss+RUBiS, the corresponding MySQL database tier, and the RUBiS clients on

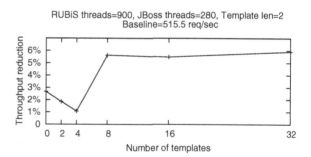

Fig. 8. JBoss throughput drop at 280 threads

separate nodes. We operated the auction site just below its saturation point (900 RUBiS client threads); below and above this level we found the impact of our algorithm to be virtually unmeasurable. The JBoss console reported that 280 threads were running inside JBoss. In Figure 8, we show the measured reduction in throughput introduced by our immunization tool for history sizes ranging from 0 to 32 templates of length 2. The templates are random combinations of program locations at which JBoss performs synchronization.

The conclusion is that the cost of immunity against up to 32 templates is a penalty of < 6% in request throughput on an e-commerce workload, which suggests that our approach offers an efficient deadlock avoidance solution even for the largest production systems.

5.3   Effects of False Positives

An important question is whether, by pruning executions that might lead to deadlock, the immunity algorithm is not being too conservative. Said otherwise, paths that once led to deadlock may not deterministically lead to deadlock. For example, if wrapper methods are used to perform locking (instead of direct calls to *native_lock*), all the lock positions may end up being the same (the location of the lock statement in the wrapper) resulting in overly aggressive serialization of the threads. Exaggerated conservativeness might lead to performance degradation by reducing parallelism, or even to the elimination of some functionality through the persistent avoidance of deadlock-prone executions paths.

While we do not know yet how to quantify the true effect of false positives, or how to measure them directly, our initial experimentation indicates that functionality does not get eliminated for some of the largest programs. Moreover, the low performance overhead suggests that, for the systems we measured, even if loss of parallelism influences negatively the performance, it does so to a small degree. Nevertheless, further experimentation is required, as well as further theoretical analysis of the false positives introduced by deadlock immunity.

The way to reduce false positives is by improving the precision of avoidance. We are currently experimenting with storing more contextual information in the template, such as a suffix of the call path that led to the deadlock-forming lock statements. The added information defines more precisely the particular execution that led to the observed deadlock, thus allowing the algorithm to better distinguish an execution heading for a similar deadlock from one that will not deadlock. Such increase in precision (reduction in false positive rate) will hurt, however, the convergence rate—the less general the avoided templates are, the longer it takes to develop immunity against all the existing deadlock bugs. Said differently, increased precision makes the "eventual" in eventual completeness longer.

We are also exploring techniques for dynamically adjusting (learning) the ideal length of call path suffixes, in order to achieve an optimal precision vs. generality tradeoff. We are also considering saving the sequence of lock positions traversed along the call paths.

Another area we wish to explore further is the use of static analysis and symbolic execution as a way to complement deadlock immunity. In particular, we want to use look-ahead static analysis to help predict deadlocks that are similar to ones we have already seen. Using bounded symbolic execution, on the order of a few instructions ahead of the current state, we can identify unsafe states without having to actually reach them. Performing such analyses at runtime could harness the "free parallelism" made available by the advent of multi-core CPUs. We could also use static analysis for detecting lock statements that would never lead to deadlocks. We could avoid instrumenting these lock statements, thus reducing the intrusiveness and therefore the overhead of our algorithm.

Our empirical evaluation indicates that the deadlock immunity approach is effective at developing immunity against deadlocks, scales to real programs with hundreds of thousands of lines of code, and introduces low overheads on a real e-commerce workload. There are still some questions to be answered with respect to the effect of false positives, and this is the subject of future work.

6   Conclusion

We described an algorithm for imparting deadlock immunity to software systems, that helps avoid deadlocks with no assistance from programmers or users. We showed that, once an immunized program encounters a deadlock, it avoids in all future executions all deadlocks with that same template. We proved the algorithm's soundness and eventual completeness; we also showed empirically that the algorithm is effective against deadlocks in real software like MySQL JDBC and Java JDK. Preliminary results indicate that the algorithm scales gracefully to large software systems: in JBoss, a >350 KLOC application server with 280 threads, worst-case overhead introduced by immunization was a drop of $<6\%$ in request throughput while avoiding up to 32 deadlock templates.

While pure deadlock avoidance is undecidable, deadlock immunity is decidable, to the extent imposed by the definition of similarity between deadlocks. Our technique builds upon and complements prior work by addressing the challenges of real systems: code size scalability, correctness in the face of program I/O, and performance overhead. We believe deadlock immunity is a practical way to eventually run production systems deadlock-free despite the deadlock bugs that lurk within.

References

1. Aspectj (2007), http://www.eclipse.org/aspectj
2. Boronat, P., Cholvi, V.: A transformation to provide deadlock-free programs. In: Intl. Conf. on Computational Science (2003)
3. Engler, D., Ashcraft, K.: RacerX: Effective, static detection of race conditions and deadlocks. In: 19th ACM Symp. on Operating Systems Principles (2003)
4. Flanagan, C., Leino, K.R.M., Lillibridge, M., Nelson, G., Saxe, J.B., Stata, R.: Extended static checking for Java. In: Conf. on Programming Language Design and Implementation (2002)
5. Habermann, A.N.: Prevention of system deadlocks. Communications of the ACM 12(7) (1969)
6. Herlihy, M., Moss, J.E.B.: Transactional memory: architectural support for lock-free data structures. In: 20th Intl. Symposium on Computer Architecture (1993)
7. Java pathfinder (2007),
   http://javapathfinder.sourceforge.net/doc/
   What_can_be_checked_with_JPF.html
8. JBoss, http://jboss.org
9. Jula, H., Candea, G.: A scalable, sound, eventually-complete algorithm for deadlock immunity. Technical Report EPFL-DSLAB-2007-002, EPFL, Lausanne, Switzerland (2007), http://dslab.epfl.ch/pubs/dimmunix-algo
10. Kim, M., Viswanathan, M., Kannan, S., Lee, I., Sokolsky, O.: Java-MaC: A run-time assurance approach for java programs. In: Formal Methods in System Design (2004)

11. Knuth, D.E.: The Art of Computer Programming, vol. III: Sorting and Searching. Addison-Wesley, Reading (1998)
12. Li, T., Ellis, C.S., Lebeck, A.R., Sorin, D.J.: Pulse: A dynamic deadlock detection mechanism using speculative execution. In: USENIX Annual Technical Conference (2005)
13. MySQL bug database, http://bugs.mysql.com/
14. RUBiS (2007), http://rubis.objectweb.org
15. Singhal, M.: Deadlock detection in distributed systems. IEEE Computer 22(11) (1989)
16. Williams, A., Thies, W., Ernst, M.D.: Static deadlock detection for Java libraries. In: 19th European Conference on Object-Oriented Programming (2005)
17. Zeng, F., Martin, R.P.: Ghost locks: Deadlock prevention for Java. In: Mid-Atlantic Student Workshop on Programming Languages and Systems (2004)

Property Patterns for Runtime Monitoring of Web Service Conversations*

Jocelyn Simmonds[1], Marsha Chechik[1], Shiva Nejati[1],
Elena Litani[2], and Bill O'Farrell[2]

[1] University of Toronto, Toronto ON M5S3G4, Canada
{jsimmond,chechik,shiva}@cs.toronto.edu
[2] IBM Toronto Lab, Markham ON L6G 1C7, Canada
{elitani,billo}@ca.ibm.com

Abstract. For a system of distributed processes, correctness can be ensured by statically checking whether their composition satisfies the properties of interest. However, web services are distributed processes that *dynamically* discover properties of other web services. Since the overall system may not be available statically and since each business process is supposed to be relatively simple, we propose to use runtime monitoring of conversations between partners as a means of checking behavioral correctness of the entire web service system. Specifically, we identify a subset of UML 2.0 Sequence Diagrams (SD) as a property specification language. We show how our language can be used to specify the patterns in the Specification Property System (SPS) [1]. By formalizing this subset using automata, we can check finite execution traces of web services against various complex properties. Finally, we discuss our experience using our language for runtime monitoring of an existing application, and conclude with a description of existing tool support.

1 Introduction

Web services are collections of components which discover and bind to other components using published interfaces, with support of Service-Oriented Architectures (SOA). The goal of SOA is to increase the flexibility of business interactions. Each web service component can be written in a traditional compiled language such as Java®, or in an XML-centric language such as BPEL [2].

Consider, for example, a web-based Loan Application system (LA), distributed as a sample application with the IBM® Websphere® Integration Developer v6.0.2. Users enter loan application information (name, taxpayer id, loan amount) through a web page, and are eventually informed of the status of their applications. The LA workflow first checks the user's credit score and declines a loan if the user has a bad credit score, i.e., less than 750. If the credit score is good, the workflow then checks the loan amount: loans for $50,000 or less are automatically approved; loans for larger amounts are earmarked for manual approval.

---

* © Copyright 2008, International Business Machines. All Rights Reserved.

M. Leucker (Ed.): RV 2008, LNCS 5289, pp. 137–157, 2008.
© Springer-Verlag Berlin Heidelberg 2008

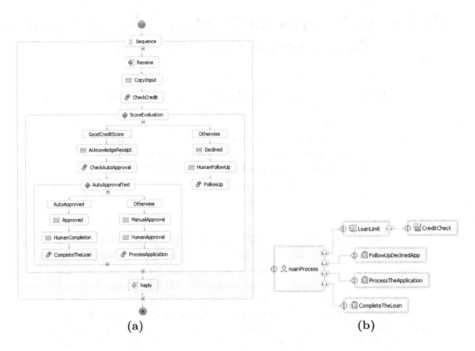

(a)   (b)

Fig. 1. The LA system: (a) workflow, describing the high level steps of the LA system; (b) assembly diagram, describing how the main process of the LA system interacts with its partners

The workflow diagram in Fig. 1(a), which is described as a BPEL specification, shows high level steps that are executed in a loan application system, and Fig. 1(b) shows an assembly diagram describing how the main process of the LA system invokes its *partners*, such as CreditCheck (implemented in Java), rule groups (LoanLimit), or human tasks (FollowUpDeclinedApp, CompleteTheLoan and ProcessTheAppli— cation). Specifically, the CheckCredit activity in Fig. 1(a) invokes the CreditCheck partner in Fig. 1(b), and the conditional activities ScoreEvaluation and AutoApproval— Test invoke the LoanLimit partner. The partners in Fig. 1(b) implement the following functions: CreditCheck uses the taxpayer id to retrieve the corresponding credit score; the LoanLimit rule group checks the credit score and the loan amount. The human tasks CompleteTheLoan, ProcessApplication and FollowUp follow the application results Approved, ManualApproval and Declined, respectively.

Since the LA system is a composition of several distributed business processes, its correctness depends on the correctness of its partners and their interactions. For example, the system should guarantee that every request is eventually acknowledged and none are lost or blocked indefinitely, or that loans are only given to customers with a good credit score. However, in the provided LA application, the CreditCheck module assigns a credit score at random, without using the customer id, thus preventing the overall system from satisfying this property.

Table 1. Some properties of the LA system

P_1	The loan amount must be always greater than zero.
P_2	The credit score should eventually be checked if the loan amount is greater than zero.
P_3	A loan cannot be granted if the loan amount is less than or equal to zero.
P_4	After checking that the applicant has a good credit score, a loan cannot be granted if the loan amount is less than or equal to zero.
P_5	Noone can get a loan without first going through a credit check.

Since each web service is a relatively simple process, analysis can concentrate on the message exchange between partners – their *conversations*. While static techniques for checking partner composition against properties of interest, such as [3,4,5,6,7], are appealing, they have a number of limitations: the problem is decidable only under certain conditions [8], since the partners communicate via infinite-sized channels, and existing techniques are unable to deal with complex message interactions and heterogeneity of partners.

Instead, we concentrate on the dynamic analysis via runtime monitoring. This approach has been shown effective for the webservice domain [9,10,11]. Our goal is to build on the success of this technique to create an industrial-strength (with partnership with the IBM Toronto Lab) monitoring framework that is non-intrusive, supports the dynamic discovery of web services, deals with synchronous and asynchronous communication and partners implemented in different languages, allows for specifying and efficient monitoring of a variety of temporal behaviour, and is usable by practitioners.

In [12], we chose a subset of UML 2.0 Sequence Diagrams [13] as our specification language. This language allows specification of events, has an explicit emphasis on components, and is able to deal with positive and negative scenarios of interaction as well as global properties. We have shown that this subset is sufficiently expressive for capturing *safety* (nothing bad can ever happen) and *liveness* (something good will eventually happen) properties. For example, for the LA system described earlier, possible safety and liveness properties are P_1 and P_2, respectively (see Table 1). While liveness properties are not monitorable in general, they can be effectively checked for web services with finitely terminating behaviours. For example, we can check whether the LA process terminates without giving feedback to the customer. Specifically, for finite behaviours, liveness can be seen as the dual of safety: liveness properties are expressed as finite positive traces, and safety properties as finite negative traces.

To enable monitoring, [12] formalized the chosen subset of Sequence Diagrams using finite-state automata. These automata are then used in the implementation of our non-intrusive monitoring framework which runs in parallel with the system being monitored, intercepting events from web service conversations. The resulting system enables conformance checking of finite execution traces against their specifications expressed in our subset of Sequence Diagrams.

In [12], we showed that *assert* and *negate* operators in UML 2.0 [13] can be used to describe *simple* safety and liveness properties, namely, invariants, e.g., P_1 in Table 1, and request-response properties, e.g., P_2 in Table 1. However, in [12], we assumed that only one assert or negate operator can be applied to a sequence diagram, always as the outermost operator. To conveniently specify and verify various system properties that arise in practice, e.g., P_4 and P_5 in Table 1, we need a more expressive language. In this paper, we extend this language by allowing certain nested applications of *assert* and *negate* operators. Furthermore, we enriched the language with several operators, adopted from UML 2.0 [13] and other scenario-based languages [14]. Examples of these operators include *critical*, *ref* (which allows to reuse portions of sequence diagrams in other diagrams) and message complementation. We show that the resulting language can not only be converted into finite-state automata for monitoring, but is also sufficiently expressive to capture a wide variety of frequently used properties, captured and catalogued in the Specification Pattern System (SPS) [1]. This approach also gives basis for tool support to enable usable specification of runtime conversations.

The rest of this paper is organized as follows. We describe syntax of the subset of UML 2.0 sequence diagrams used for expressing properties of webservice conversations in Section 2. Such properties are then converted into monitoring automata using the techniques discussed in Section 3. We then show how our specification language can be used to specify the complete set of temporal logic property patterns in Section 4. We describe the implementation of the runtime monitoring framework and report on the result of applying our framework to the LA system in Section 5. Finally, we conclude the paper in Section 6 with a summary of the paper, comparison with related work, and an outline of future research directions.

2   A Language for Specifying Conversations

We choose a subset of UML 2.0 Sequence Diagrams as our language for specifying web service conversations. Sequence Diagrams [13] is a popular formalism for modeling behavioural scenarios by describing sequences of messages communicated between different objects over time. Sequence Diagrams have two dimensions: vertical, representing time, and horizontal, representing objects. Each object is illustrated by a rectangle with a vertical dashed line, called a *lifeline*. Lifelines are connected by horizontal arrows denoting messages that are sent from one object to another, synchronously or asynchronously. We refer to Sequence Diagrams with these features as *basic*.

An example sequence diagram describing a scenario of the LA system is shown in Fig. 2(a). The diagram contains three objects, MnPs, CtCk, and LnLt. Object MnPs corresponds to the main workflow of the LA system, and CtCk and LnLt correspond to components CreditCheck and LoanLimit, respectively. The diagram in Fig. 2(a) shows two alternative scenarios: In the first alternative, MnPs first sends a check credit score request, i.e., ckCtSe, to CtCk and then a check loan amount request, i.e., ckLnAt, to LnLt. In the second alternative, LnLt receives a check loan amount request from MnPs. Since the credit score has not yet been checked, LnLt sends a check credit score request to CtCk.

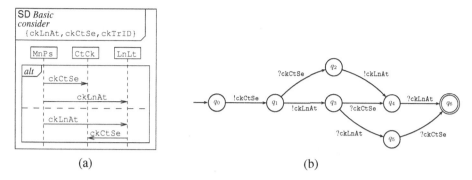

(a)   (b)

Fig. 2. (a) An SD describing a scenario of the LA example; and (b) the NFA corresponding to the first argument of the *alt* operator in Fig 2(a)

Basic Sequence Diagrams can be augmented by a number of operators to capture more sophisticated scenarios. We use the operators described below in our property specification language, and refer to our language as *SD*.

Compositional operators: Operators *parallel (par)* and *alternatives (alt)* are used to compute intersection and union of two SDs, respectively. The operator *loop* is used for repeating the scenario described by an SD multiple times, *opt* – for denoting an optional scenario, equivalent to *alt* with only one argument.

Alphabet changing operators: Operators *consider* and *ignore* are used for modifying the communicating alphabet of SDs.

Critical operator: The *critical* operator is used to ensure atomicity of the enclosed sequence.

Assertion and negation operators: Operators *assert* and *negate* allow users to express mandatory and forbidden system scenarios, respectively.

Interaction use operator: SDs can be shared by references, using the *ref* operator. This is a shorthand for copying the contents of the referred SD where the *ref* operator occurs, and is a new feature in UML 2.0.

To describe system scenarios, we often need to express complementation of an individual message or a set of messages appearing on the same arrow. The *negate* operator is unsuitable for this: it captures negative sequences of messages rather than set complementation. Instead, we use the *message complementation* operator, originally introduced in the Property Sequence Charts (PSC) language [14]. We denote the complement of a message m by $\neg m$ and define it as the set of all messages that are potentially exchanged between objects of the system except for m.

Basic Sequence Diagrams, denoted *BasicSDs*, are the building blocks of our language. The *critical*, alphabet changing, interaction use, *assert*, and compositional operators, except for *par*, can be intermixed and applied any number of times to BasicSDs. The use of *negate* and *par* operators, however, is restricted to sequence diagrams which do not use an *assert* operator. We discuss this assumption and the rationale behind it in Section 3.1 and show in Section 4 that even with this restriction, the resulting language remains very expressive.

$$
\begin{aligned}
\text{SD} ::= & \; \mathit{BasicSD} \mid \texttt{unaryOp SD} \mid \text{SD } \mathit{alt} \text{ SD} \mid \mathit{assert} \text{ SD} \mid \\
& \; \texttt{NotAssertedSD } \mathit{par} \texttt{ NotAssertedSD} \mid \mathit{negate} \texttt{ NotAssertedSD} \mid \\
\texttt{NotAssertedSD} ::= & \; \mathit{BasicSD} \mid \texttt{unaryOp NotAssertedSD} \mid \mathit{negate} \texttt{ NotAssertedSD} \mid \\
& \; \texttt{NotAssertedSD } \mathit{alt} \texttt{ NotAssertedSD} \mid \\
& \; \texttt{NotAssertedSD } \mathit{par} \texttt{ NotAssertedSD} \\
\texttt{unaryOp} ::= & \; \mathit{consider}_E \mid \mathit{ignore}_E \mid \mathit{loop} \mid \mathit{critical} \mid \mathit{opt} \mid \mathit{ref}
\end{aligned}
$$

Fig. 3. Grammar of the SD language

The grammar for our language, SD, is given in Fig. 3 where *BasicSD*, *par*, *alt*, *loop*, *critical*, *opt*, *negate*, *assert*, *consider*, *ignore* and *ref* are terminal symbols, and E is a set of SD messages. Since operators *consider* and *ignore* change the communicating alphabet of SDs, they take a set E of messages as an input argument. In what follows, we denote by SD the set of Sequence Diagrams generated by the above grammar.

3   From SDs to Automata

We define the formal semantics of SD by translating it into *non-deterministic finite automata (NFAs)*, following the approach of [15]. This translation allows us to not only formalize our language but also to study its expressiveness. Specifically, in [12], we have shown that certain scenarios in SD can be captured by particular forms of NFAs known as *Safe* and *Live* automata [16], indicating that SD is capable of expressing safety and liveness properties. In what follows, we briefly review the translation of basic sequence diagrams and the operators described in Section 2 into NFA. We then discuss that the *negate* and *assert* operators allow us to express safety and liveness properties, respectively.

Basic sequence diagrams, i.e, diagrams describing a sequence of events without any additional operator, can be translated into NFAs using the procedure in [15]. Consider the scenario in the first argument of the *alt* operator in Fig 2(a). This basic sequence diagram shows that MnPs first sends event ckCtSe to CtCk and then event ckLnAt to LnLt. We denote the sending of a message m by !m and its receiving by ?m. Thus, the set of events of the sequence diagram in Fig. 2(a) is {!ckCtSe, ?ckCtSe, !ckLnAt, ?ckLnAt}. Intuitively, lifelines and message arrows in a sequence diagram define a partial order on the set of events of that diagram. Given a basic sequence diagram S, an NFA A_S is equivalent to S iff A_S accepts exactly the set of traces that respect the partial order of S. For example, the automaton A_S corresponding to the scenario in the first argument of the *alt* operator in Fig 2(a) is shown in Fig 2(b).

The semantics of the compositional operators can be given in terms of the standard operations defined on NFAs (e.g., see [17]). For example, *alt* corresponds to the union operator and *loop* corresponds to the Kleene star operator.

Operators *consider* and its dual, *ignore*, are used to change the set of communicating alphabets of an SD. Both of them receive an SD S and a set of events E as input, but *consider* adds the elements in E to the set of events of S, whereas *ignore* removes the elements in E from the set of events of S.

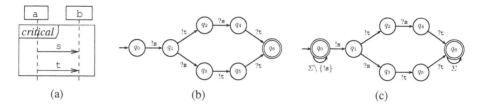

Fig. 4. (a) A basic SD enclosed by a *critical* operator and its corresponding NFAs: (b) before applying *critical*; (c) after applying *critical*

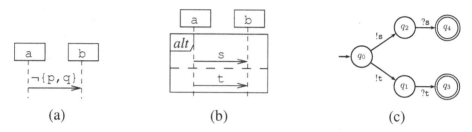

Fig. 5. (a) An SD with message complementation; (b) the same SD after eliminating the *complement* operator, if the underlying alphabet Σ is $\{p, q, s, t\}$; and (c) its corresponding NFA.

We can specify a critical region in a sequence diagram using the *critical* operator. A critical region means that the traces of the region cannot be interleaved by other messages and thus should be treated atomically. We treat this operator to mean that if the first message of the critical region is observed, then the rest of the behavior must be observed as well.

For a sequence enclosed by a critical operator, once the first symbol of the sequence has been seen, the entire sequence should be seen as well. For this reason, the self-loop at the initial state of an automaton corresponding to a critical region is labelled by Σ minus the initial symbols of the expected sequences. For example, Fig. 4(a) shows a sequence diagram with a critical operator, and Fig. 4(c) – its corresponding automaton.

The operator *ref* is used for sharing portions of SDs between several others. Our treatment of *ref* is to inline the SD being referenced, applying the necessary translation rules to the result in order to obtain the corresponding NFA, as illustrated in Fig. 6.

The message complement operator has been adopted from [14]. If Σ is the set of messages exchanged in an SD, and $m \in \Sigma$, then $\neg m$ is $\Sigma \setminus \{m\}$. For a set $\{m, n\}$ of messages, $\neg\{m, n\} = \Sigma \setminus \{m, n\}$. For example, let $\Sigma = \{p, q, s, t\}$. Then, $\neg p = \{q, s, t\}$ and $\neg\{p, q\} = \{s, t\}$.

This operator, although not being part of UML 2.0, can be expressed in terms of UML operators as follows: Let $S \subseteq \Sigma$ be a set of messages. We replace $\neg S$ by an SD fragment in which the operator *alt* is applied to individual messages in

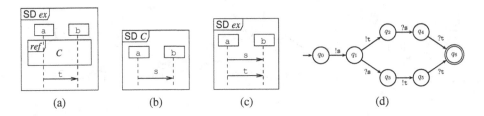

Fig. 6. (a) An SD which references SD C; (b) SD C; (c) SD ex after copying the content of SD C; and (d) its corresponding NFA

$\Sigma \setminus S$. For example, consider the SD in Fig. 5(a) with a message $\neg\{p, q\}$, and let $\Sigma = \{s, t, p, q\}$. This SD is equivalent to the one in Fig. 5(b) where $\neg\{p, q\}$ is replaced by an *alt* fragment in which s and t are two alternative messages. The NFA for the sequence diagram without message complement operators can be generated in a straightforward way following the translation for the *alt* operator (see Fig. 5(c)).

3.1   Assertion and Negation Operators

The *negate* operator provides a mechanism for specifying undesirable (negative) scenarios, and the *assert* operator allows us to specify desirable (positive) scenarios. The former operator can be used to express safety properties, e.g., P_1 in Table 1, and the latter – finitary liveness properties, e.g., P_2.

Various formal treatments of the semantics of the *assert* and *negate* operators are given in the literature, e.g., [16,18,19]. These operators have a rich expressive power, and yet their arbitrary combinations are not well understood. In particular, it is unclear whether negating an asserted scenario should mean that this scenario is not required to occur or that its negation has to occur. In this section, we define the semantics of *assert* and *negate* operators in terms of NFAs. Our formalization allows us to arbitrarily combine these operators as long as we never attempt to apply a *negate* operator to a sequence diagram containing an *assert*ed fragment.

Representing safety properties. The *negate* operator over SDs is equivalent to the complementation operator of NFA. Given an SD S and its corresponding automaton A_S, we first add a self-loop transition labeled Σ, i.e., the underlying alphabet of S, to the initial state of A_S in order to enable A_S to guess when a satisfying run begins. For example, Fig. 7(b) illustrates the automaton corresponding to the SD in Fig. 7(a) after adding this self-loop and before complementation. Note that after adding this self-loop, A_S becomes non-deterministic. To obtain the automaton for the negated SD, we need to first determinize A_S, and then complement the result.

As mentioned above, *negate* allows us to express safety properties. By applying *negate* to a SD S, we indicate that the scenario represented by S is a forbidden one, and therefore, a safe system should never produce this

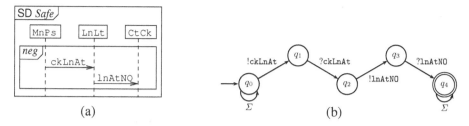

Fig. 7. (a) An SD describing P_1 in Table 1 and its corresponding NFAs: (b) before applying *negate*

scenario [16]. For example, Fig. 7(a) shows a *negate* operator applied to the sequence !ckLnAt.?ckLnAt.!lnAtNo.?lnAtNo, representing the safety property P_1 in Table 1.

Representing liveness properties. The meaning of the *assert* operator is given by the UML standard as follows [13], *"the sequences of the operand are the only valid continuations. All other continuations result in invalid behaviour"*. This interpretation has been formalized in different ways [18,16]. The one that we have adopted is that of [18] which is described as follows: given an asserted behaviour $\sigma = \sigma_0 \ldots \sigma_n$ and a system behaviour σ', every occurrence of σ_0 in σ' should be followed by the rest of σ. Thus, an SD with an *assert* is interpreted universally: "for every run, once it satisfies the start of the sequence, it must complete the sequence before termination". Note that the difference between *assert* and *critical* is that the former checks all possible suffixes of the input run to probe the sequence, whereas the latter only checks the first occurrence of its sequence.

In [18], *alternating* automata with *universal* initial states are used to capture this meaning of *assert*. Such automata accept a trace if *all* of the runs emanating from their initial states are accepting. NFA, however, accept a trace when *there exists* an accepting run emanating from the initial state. Rather than moving outside NFA (and thus complicating the monitoring framework), we chose to reinterpret the acceptance for the *assert* operator instead: an NFA for an asserted trace σ checks all suffixes of the system traces, and if one is not accepted, a failure is reported. This "universal" treatment is given to the entire sequence diagram, not just the part containing *assert*. This works correctly as long as such NFAs are not complemented or composed (in parallel) – the negation and parallel composition operators over automata with universally interpreted acceptance are different from those operators of NFA. While negation and parallel composition operators for NFA are computed via subset construction and cross-product, respectively, these operators for the alternating automata simply convert universal states into existential or add an additional universal state, respectively [20]. Thus, we restrict the application of *negate* and *par* to SDs that contain an *assert* described in Section 2.

Since alternating automata can be converted into NFA with a possibly exponential blow-up in size, we could have translated the *assert* operator directly into

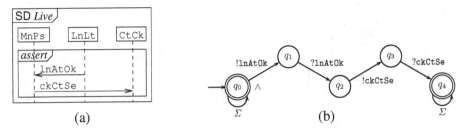

Fig. 8. (a) An SD describing P_2 in Table 1 and its corresponding NFAs: (b) after applying *assert*

NFA. However, we chose not to do it to preserve the succinctness and relatively small size of our monitoring automata.

Given the above discussion, the translation of *assert* operator is straightforward: After deriving the NFA A_S for SD S and adding a self-loop labelled Σ at its initial state, the automaton for *assert* S is obtained by interpreting the initial state as universal (we follow the notation of [18], denoting this state with a "$\wedge$") and making it accepting. For example, the SD in Fig. 8(a) describes the liveness property P_2 in Table 1 – the desirable scenario is enclosed in the scope of an *assert* operator. Fig. 8(b) shows the automaton corresponding to this SD.

Complexity of the Translation. The size of an automaton A_S corresponding to a basic sequence diagram S is $O(n^k)$ where n is the number of events and k is the number of processes [15]. Applying the sequence diagram operators does not cause a significant increase in the size of the resulting automata except for the cases that involve a determinzation step which can be exponential in the number of states of A_S. However, we note that in practice, the automata we have generated are relatively small, less than 9 states and 30 transitions [12]. Obviously, it remains to be seen whether the approach remains feasible for larger web service systems and more complex properties.

4   SD Templates for Temporal Logic Property Patterns

In this section, we introduce several templates expressed in the SD language for describing temporal logic property patterns [1]. We first provide an overview of these patterns in Section 4.1. We then describe our templates in the SD language in Section 4.2 and show how they can encode the property patterns.

4.1   Temporal Logic Property Patterns

The *Specification Pattern System* (SPS), proposed by Dwyer et al. [21], is a pattern-based approach to the presentation, codification, and reuse of property specifications. The system allows patterns like "event P is absent between events Q and S" or "S precedes P between Q and R" to be easily expressed in and

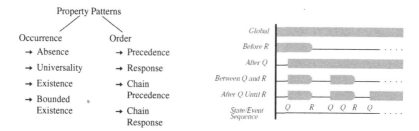

Fig. 9. Pattern Hierarchy   **Fig. 10.** Pattern Scopes

translated between linear-time temporal logic (LTL) [22], computational tree logic (CTL) [22] and other state-based and event-based formalisms. SPS has been advocated as a standard tool for measuring the practical usefulness and expressive power of specification languages, e.g., [14] and [23].

The property patterns are organized into a hierarchy based on the kinds of system behaviors they describe (see Fig. 9): *Occurrence* patterns talk about the occurrence of a given event/state during system execution, and *Order* patterns specify relative order in which multiple events/states occur during system execution. The patterns are described below in detail:

Absence	An event does not occur within a given scope;
Existence	An event must occur within a given scope;
Bounded Existence	An event can occur at most a certain number of times within a given scope;
Universality	An event must occur throughout a given scope;
Response	An event must always be followed by another within a scope;
Response Chain	A chain of events must always be followed by another chain of events within a scope;
Precedence	An event must always be preceded by another within a scope;
Precedence Chain	A chain of events must always be preceded by another chain of events within a scope.

Each pattern is associated with *scopes* – the regions of interest over which the pattern must hold. There are five basic kinds of scopes (depicted in Fig. 10):

Global	The entire program execution;
Before R	The execution up to event R;
After Q	The execution after event Q;
Between Q **and** R	All parts of the execution between events Q and R;
After Q **until** R	Similar to *between*, except that the designated part of the execution continues even if the second event does not occur.

For example, consider a property that says between every *enqueue* and *empty* messages, there must be a *dequeue* message. This property falls into the "Existence" pattern group because it indicates the occurrence of an event within a scope. The scope of this property is that of "Between" shown in Fig 10. Looking

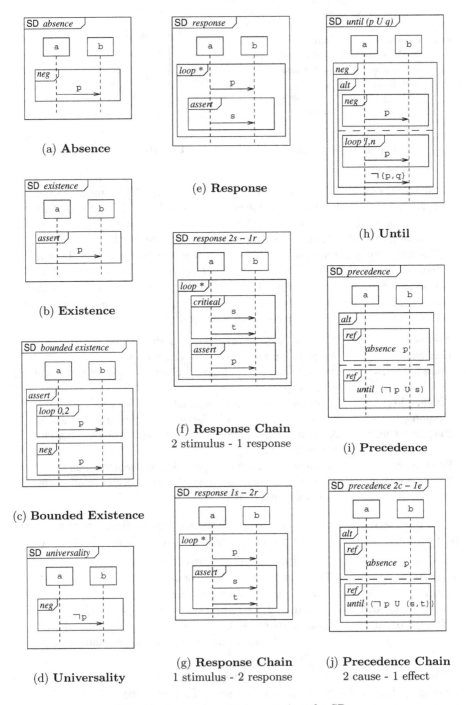

Fig. 11. Property pattern mappings for SDs

up the LTL formalization of this pattern/scope combination from the catalogue and substituting our event names, we obtain the formula $\Box((\mathtt{enqueue} \wedge \neg\mathtt{empty}) \Rightarrow (\neg\mathtt{empty} \; W \; (\mathtt{dequeue} \wedge \neg\mathtt{empty})))$.

4.2 Mapping Property Patterns to SDs

In this section, we provide several SD templates for the SPS patterns (see Fig. 11), and show how these tempolates are used to express patterns in the SPS hierarchy. Selected mappings are described below; the remainder can be found in Appendix A.

Absence: Message p cannot occur in a given scope. This can be expressed as shown in Fig. 11(a).

Existence: Message p must occur in a given scope. This can be expressed as shown in Fig. 11(b).

Until: This pattern is not part of the SPS; however, it is used to specify the **Precedence** patterns. A sequence p* of messages occurs until the first occurrence of message q, in a given scope (see Fig. 11 (h)). This pattern, formalized using a single "until" temporal operator [22], can be refuted in one of two ways: a) p never occurs, or b) after seeing a finite number of p messages (expressed using *loop 1, n* in Fig 11(h)), neither a p nor a q message occurs (expressed as $\neg\{\mathtt{p}, \mathtt{q}\}$ in Fig 11(h)).

Precedence: Message s (cause) precedes message p (effect), as shown in Fig. 11 (i). Note that this pattern allows the cause part to occur without the effect part. We describe this pattern in SD by expressing the two possible cases that this pattern specifies: a) p never occurs, or b) p never occurs before s. The first case corresponds to checking *absence* of p; the second – to checking $\neg\mathtt{p} \; U \; \mathtt{s}$, since we want to be sure that *no* p messages are sent before the first s message.

In the SDs in Fig. 11, symbols p, q, s, and t can denote more complex SDs, not just individual messages. In this case, we treat these symbols as place holders and use a *ref* operator for the SDs that should be inserted in their place, and replace message complementation by negation. In Section 4.4, we provide detailed examples of how these patterns are used to specify properties of the LA system.

4.3 Mapping Property Scopes

We now show how to express property patterns involving scopes which are used to define the traces over which a property will be monitored. Scopes can be simple messages or more complex scenarios in our specification language. The *ref* operator is used to introduce scope delimiters in the corresponding locations. For example, to apply the **Before** R scope to a property, the scope delimiter R is inserted after the property we wish to verify (see Fig. 12(a)). In the case of the **After** Q scope, the delimiter is inserted before the property (see Fig. 12(b)). Finally, both the **Between** (see Fig. 12(c)) and the **After-until** (see Fig. 12(d)) scopes

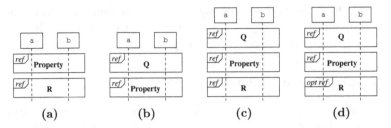

Fig. 12. Scope mapping for sequence diagrams: (a) **Before** R; (b) **After** Q; (c) **Between** Q and R; and (d) **After** Q **until** R

add before/after delimiters. In the **After-until** scope, the property is valid even if the "until" part does not occur. Therefore, the second delimiter in this scope is optional. Thus, there is an implicit *opt* operator in each scope delimiter.

4.4   Specifying Properties of the Loan Application

The following examples show how property patterns can be used to specify example properties of the LA system given in Table 1. Properties P_1 and P_2 are described in Figs 7 and 8, respectively. The rest of the properties in that table are discussed below.

Property P_3: "A loan cannot be granted if the loan amount is less than or equal to zero."

We express this property using the **Absence** pattern (see Fig. 11(a)): our property holds if there are no scenarios where a loan is granted after the system has been warned that the loan amount is less than or equal to zero. In the LA system, the LnLt component sends a `loanAmountNotOkay` (`lnAtNO`) message when the loan amount is less than or equal to zero. A loan is considered granted if it is manually or automatically approved, which can be monitored by checking if the main workflow MnPs sends a `completeTheLoan` (`ceLn`) or `processTheApplication` (`psAn`) message. See Fig. 13(a) for the corresponding SD; the resulting monitor is shown in Fig. 13(b).

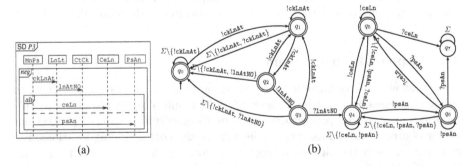

Fig. 13. P_3: **Absence** pattern. (a) SD describing the LA property P_3 and (b) the resulting monitor.

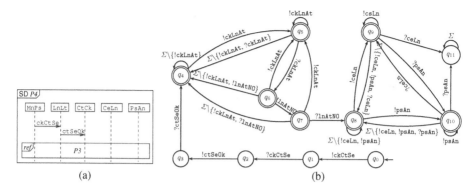

Fig. 14. P_4: **Absence** pattern, Scope **After**. (a) SD describing the LA property P_4 and (b) the resulting monitor, obtained by concatenating the NFAs for the scope and P_3.

Property P_4: "After checking that the applicant has a good credit score, a loan cannot be granted if the loan amount is less than or equal to zero."

This property is equivalent to the property P_3 with the **After** Q scope, where Q is "checking for a good credit score". To express it, we introduce the scope delimiter Q before the property P_3, as seen in Fig. 12(b). The SD corresponding to P_4 is shown in Fig. 14(a) and consists of two parts: (1) scope Q and (2) property P_3, i.e., the fragment specified by a *ref* operator which should be replaced by the SD for P_3. The resulting monitor is shown in Fig. 14(b).

Property P_5: "Noone can get a loan without first going through a credit check."

At this point, we have identified common scenarios that occur in the LA system: SDs *creditCheck* (Fig. 15(a)) and *loanGranted* (Fig. 15(b)). We can now express property P_5 using the **Precedence** pattern: SD *creditCheck* must precede SD *loanGranted*. Note that the SD *creditCheck* is not optional and must occur for the property to hold. The SD for P_5 is shown in Fig. 15(c).

5   Tool Support and Experience

Tool Support. We have implemented our runtime monitoring framework within the IBM WebSphere® business integration products [24]. In what follows, we describe the architecture of our solution and its intended use. We also report on preliminary experience of using this framework to check correctness of web services. For implementation details, see [12].

Our solution uses the WebSphere Process Server (WPS) [25] and the WebSphere Integration Developer (WID) [26]. The former provides a BPEL-compliant process engine for executing BPEL processes and a built-in Service Component Architecture (SCA), which is a particular instantiation of SOA. The latter provides a development environment for building web service applications and a graphical package for creating UML Sequence Diagrams.

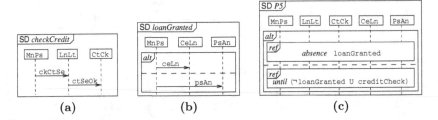

Fig. 15. P_5: The **Precedence** pattern. (a) SD for *checkCredit*; (b) SD for *loanGranted*; (c) SD showing application of the **Precedence** pattern.

During and after application development, users can create UML SD specifications for their web service applications within the WID environment. If monitoring is enabled, our framework translates these diagrams into monitor automata using the techniques in Section 3. During the execution of the web service, interaction events from the WPS are sent to our framework using sockets. These events are immediately used to update the state of every active monitor automaton, until an error has been found or all partners terminate. This provides an *online* feedback mechanism through the SD editor to report violations.

Our patterns are available as editable UML sequence diagrams (`.dnx` files). Users must first add these files to the WID project of the application they wish to monitor. These patterns can now be modified to create actual system properties, using our Sequence Diagram editor.

Violations in our framework are either due to the occurrence of a negative trace (safety violation), or the absence of a positive trace (liveness violation). To report violations, we display the causes in the Sequence Diagram editor by highlighting the beginning of the negative trace for safety violations (see Fig 16 (a)), and the termination location for liveness violations (see Fig 16 (b)).

Experience. We applied our framework to the Loan Application system, with the goal of specifying and checking the properties mentioned in Table 1. On normal execution traces of this system, these properties should never fail, as this application implements the workflow shown in Fig 1(a). As it is a *sample* application, some details have been simplified. For example, the **CreditCheck** component generates random credit scores.

We ran the system on two different taxpayer ids (**tpid**) and three different loan amounts (**la**), with the following specific input configurations:

c_1 = <tpid = 1234, la = \$10,000>, c_2 = <tpid id = 1234, la = \$60,000>,
c_3 = <tpid id = 1888, la = -\$1,000>.

As the system is supposed to generate random credit scores, we ran the system 10 times with each configuration. For configuration c_1, we expected to see some automatic approvals of the loan, and some declines, based on whether the good or the bad score is generated. For c_2, we expected some manual approvals of the loan (the loan amount is above the automatic approval limit), and some declines. Finally, since the loan amount in c_3 is invalid, we expected to see only loan declines.

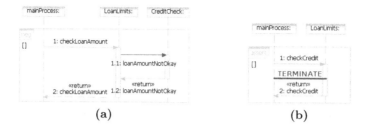

Fig. 16. Reporting errors: (a) A complete (negative) trace; (b) An incomplete sequence: violation of a liveness property.

For configurations c_1 and c_2, the behavior we observed was as expected: P_1, P_2, P_5 always held and P_3, P_4 held when the loan was granted. However, for all executions of c_3, the system automatically approved the loan, meaning that properties P_1, P_3 and P_4 were violated. For all executions of c_3, the system produced the following faulty execution trace:

$$FT = (\text{MnPs, ckCtSe, LnLt}), (\text{LnLt, ctSeOK, CtCk}), (\text{MnPs, ckLnAt, LnLt}),$$
$$(\text{LnLt, lnAtNO, CtCk}), (\text{MnPs, ceLn, CeLn}).$$

where each triple $(Sender, m, Receiver)$ denotes partner $Sender$ sending a message m to partner $Receiver$. This trace depicts a failure of P_1 because the loan amount is not greater than zero, as indicated by the triple $(\text{LnLt, lnAtNO, CtCk})$. This trace also shows a violation of P_3 because it includes an invalid behaviour, acceptance of the invalid loan, indicated by the subtrace

$$(\text{MnPs, ckLnAt, LnLt}), (\text{LnLt, lnAtNO, CtCk}), (\text{MnPs, ceLn, CeLn}).$$

Finally, P_4, being the scoped version of the property P_3, fails on this trace as well.

To identify the cause of the violations, we examined the BPEL diagram in Fig. 1 (a) to see that the trace FT is produced if the LA system obtains the taxpayer's credit score, checks if the credit score is greater than 750 (`ScoreEvaluation`), checks if the loan amount is greater than zero (input validation), and checks if the loan amount is less than $50,001 (`AutoApprovalTest`). The `ScoreEvaluation` should only occasionally be true, as the `CreditCheck` component generates random credit scores. However, we obtained trace FT every time the system was run with the taxpayer id 1888, i.e., the system always approved a negative loan.

We traced this behaviour to two problems. The first, identified after looking at the BPEL code of the LA system, was that the application did not use the results of the input validation, allowing requests for negative loans to go through. The second, identified only after examining the source code for the `CreditCheck` partner, was that the partner was distributed with hard-coded logic: an applicant with a taxpayer id that ends with "888" was always given a good credit score instead of a random one. Combined, these two problems yielded the approval of the loan for configuration c_3 every single time.

Overall, our experience showed that the system can handle simultaneous failure of several monitors and allowed us to specify interesting properties which led to the discovery of two real faults in the LA system.

6 Conclusion

In this paper, we described our framework for runtime monitoring of web service conversations developed as part of an industrial-strength system. The framework is an aggregation of existing runtime verification techniques and is a continuation of [12]. It is non-intrusive, running in parallel with the monitored system and intercepting interaction events during run time. Thus, it does not require any code instrumentation, does not significantly affect the performance of the monitored system, and enables reasoning about partners expressed in different languages. Furthermore, the use of a subset of UML 2.0 SDs as a specification language ensures that the framework is usable by practitioners to specify a wide range of properties. By formalizing this subset using automata, we can check finite execution traces of web services against these properties. Liveness becomes finitary, where user-specified time limits or the process termination act as the stopping conditions.

We have successfully mapped all the Specification Property System patterns into our SD subset. The availability of customizable patterns should improve the usability of our specification language. More complex conversations can be checked, as it is easy to build properties through SD composition. Using SD references, our properties are also easier to read, since details can be hidden. Finally, we have created a library of such sequence diagram patterns and showed how patterns can be used to specify monitors which lead to discovery of bugs in real webservice applications.

Future Work. While the initial experience using the framework has been positive, we need to address a number of issues before it becomes fully usable. The first set of issues deals with increasing the range of properties that can be specified and monitored. In the examples presented here, all objects were unique, whereas in practice, users may be interested in verifying interactions between multiple processes of the same type. For example, a user with a good credit score may concurrently apply for two loans, each for less than $50 001, to bypass the manual approval required for a loan for the total amount. In this case, two bank branches may want to communicate to avoid this kind of situation. We feel that the problem can be easily solved by encoding process IDs into the specification, the automata transition relation, and interaction events.

We also plan to begin investigation of techniques to help locate cause of errors from seeing results of successful and unsuccessful runs of the system. For example, given a monitor violation, we would like to produce similar conversations that do not cause a violation, so as to help pinpoint cause of the violation (as the place signaled with the violation is not necessarily the cause). We will experiment with the techniques in [27,28] for this task.

On a side note, our work so far has been built on a basis that all partners operate within the same process server and thus a centralized monitor is a viable option. In practice, most web services are distributed, requiring a distributed monitoring framework. We plan to investigate techniques used in the DESERT project [29] to turn a centralized monitor into a set of distributed ones, running in different process servers.

Acknowledgements and Trademarks

We thank Yuan Gan and Jonathan Amir for implementing several parts of the monitoring framework, and Simon Moser and Axel Martens for generating many useful discussions. This work is financially supported by the IBM Toronto Centre for Advanced Studies, Ontario Graduate Scholarship and NSERC.

IBM and WebSphere are trademarks or registered trademarks of International Business Machines Corporation in the United States, other countries, or both. Java and all Java-based trademarks are trademarks of Sun Microsystems, Inc. in the United States, other countries, or both. Other company, product, and service names may be trademarks or service marks of others.

References

1. Dwyer, M., Avrunin, G., Corbett, J.: Patterns in Property Specifications for Finite-State Verification. In: Proceedings of 21st International Conference on Software Engineering (ICSE 1999) pp. 411–420 (May 1999)
2. IBM: Business Process Execution Language for Web Services,
   http://www-128.ibm.com/developerworks/library/specification/ws-bpel/
3. Fu, X., Bultan, T., Su, J.: Conversation Protocols: A Formalism for Specification and Verification of Reactive Electronic Services. In: H. Ibarra, O., Dang, Z. (eds.) CIAA 2003. LNCS, vol. 2759, pp. 188–200. Springer, Heidelberg (2003)
4. Fu, X., Bultan, T., Su, J.: Analysis of Interacting BPEL Web Services. In: Proceedings of the Thirteenth International World Wide Web Conference (WWW 2004), New York, pp. 621–630 (May 2004)
5. Kazhamiakin, R., Pistore, M.: A Parametric Communication Model for the Verification of BPEL4WS Compositions. In: EPEW/WS-FM, pp. 318–332 (2005)
6. Baldoni, M., Baroglio, C., Martelli, A., Patti, V., Schifanella, C.: Verifying the Conformance of Web Services to Global Interaction Protocols: A First Step. In: EPEW/WS-FM, pp. 257–271 (2005)
7. Foster, H., Uchitel, S., Magee, J., Kramer, J.: Model-based Verification of Web Service Compositions. In: Proceedings of 18th IEEE International Conference on Automated Software Engineering (ASE 2003), pp. 152–163. IEEE Computer Society, Los Alamitos (2003)
8. Ghafari, N., Gurfinkel, A., Klarlund, N., Trefler, R.: Algorithmic Analysis of Piecewise FIFO Systems. In: Proceedings of 7th International Conference on Formal Methods in Computer-Aided Design (FMCAD 2007), Austin, Texas, LNCS, pp. 45–52 (November 2007)
9. Baresi, L., Ghezzi, C., Guinea, S.: Smart Monitors for Composed Services. In: ICSOC 2004, pp. 193–202 (2004)

10. Robinson, W.N.: Monitoring Web Service Requirements. In: Proceedings of RE 2003, pp. 65–74 (2003)
11. Mahbub, K., Spanoudakis, G.: Run-time Monitoring of Requirements for Systems Composed of Web-Services: Initial Implementation and Evaluation Experience. In: Proceedings of ICWS 2005, pp. 257–265 (2005)
12. Gan, Y., Chechik, M., Nejati, S., Bennett, J., O'Farrell, B., Waterhouse, J.: Run-time Monitoring of Web Service Conversations. In: Proceedings of CASCON 2007 (November 2007)
13. Object Management Group (OMG): Unified Modeling Language (UML 2.0), http://www.uml.org/
14. Autili, M., Inverardi, P., Pelliccione, P.: A Scenario Based Notation for Specifying Temporal Properties. In: Proceedings of SCESM, ICSE 2006 Workshop (2006)
15. Alur, R., Yannakakis, M.: Model Checking of Message Sequence Charts. In: Baeten, J.C.M., Mauw, S. (eds.) CONCUR 1999. LNCS, vol. 1664, pp. 114–129. Springer, Heidelberg (1999)
16. Grosu, R., Smolka, S.A.: Safety-Liveness Semantics for UML 2.0 Sequence Diagrams. In: ACSD 2005, pp. 6–14 (2005)
17. Hopcroft, J.E., Ullman, J.D.: Introduction to Automata Theory, Languages and Computation. Addison-Wesley, Reading (1979)
18. Harel, D., Maoz, S.: Assert and Negate Revisited: Modal Semantics for UML Sequence Diagrams. In: Proceedings of SCESM, ICSE 2006 Workshop, pp. 13–20 (2006)
19. Störrle, H.: Assert, Negate and Refinement in UML 2 Interactions. In: Stevens, P., Whittle, J., Booch, G. (eds.) UML 2003. LNCS, vol. 2863, pp. 79–94. Springer, Heidelberg (2003)
20. Vardi, M.: An Automata-Theoretic Approach to Linear Temporal Logic. In: Moller, F., Birtwistle, G. (eds.) Logics for Concurrency. LNCS, vol. 1043, pp. 236–266. Springer, Heidelberg (1996)
21. Dwyer, M.B., Avrunin, G.S., Corbett, J.C.: Property Specification Patterns for Finite-state Verification. In: Proceedings of 2nd Workshop on Formal Methods in Software Practice (March 1998)
22. Clarke, E., Grumberg, O., Peled, D.: Model Checking. MIT Press, Cambridge (1999)
23. Yu, J., Manh, T.P., Han, J., Jin, Y., Han, Y., Wang, J.: Pattern Based Property Specification and Verification for Service Composition. In: Aberer, K., Peng, Z., Rundensteiner, E.A., Zhang, Y., Li, X. (eds.) WISE 2006. LNCS, vol. 4255, pp. 156–168. Springer, Heidelberg (2006)
24. IBM: WebSphere Business Integration Software, http://www-306.ibm.com/software/info1/websphere/index.jsp?tab=products/businessint
25. IBM: WebSphere Process Server, http://www-306.ibm.com/software/integration/wps/
26. IBM: WebSphere Integration Developer, http://www-306.ibm.com/software/integration/wid/
27. Zeller, A.: Isolating cause-effect chains from computer programs. SIGSOFT Softw. Eng. Notes 27(6), 1–10 (2002)
28. Groce, A., Chaki, S., Kroening, D., Strichman, O.: Error explanation with distance metrics. Int. J. Softw. Tools Technol. Transf. 8(3), 229–247 (2006)
29. Inverardi, P., Mostarda, L., Tivoli, M., Autili, M.: Synthesis of Correct and Distributed Adaptors for Component-Based Systems: an Automatic Approach. In: Proceedings of ASE 2005, pp. 405–409 (2005)

A Other Property Patterns

$k-$**Bounded Existence:** Message p can occur at most k times in a given scope. We can check the existence of at most k messages using the *loop* operator. After the loop, we need to check that p does not occur, which corresponds to the absence pattern (see Fig. 11 (c)).

Universality: Only a sequence p^* of messages can occur in a given scope. This is equivalent to checking for the absence of complement messages (see Fig. 11 (d)).

Response: Message p (stimulus) must be followed by message s (response), in a given scope. A response can occur without stimuli, so the stimulus is represented using a regular message, whereas the response is mandatory. The existence of stimulus/response pairs are checked in an infinite *loop*, as there can be many stimulus/response pairs in one execution trace (see Fig. 11 (e)).

Response Chain: A sequence $p_1, \ldots, p_n$ of messages must be followed by the sequence $q_1, \ldots, q_m$ of messages, in a given scope. We show two examples of this pattern: p responds to s, t (see Fig. 11 (f)), and s, t responds to p (see Fig. 11 (g)). Response chain patterns have the same basic form of the response pattern.

  - p responds to s, t: 2 stimulus – 1 response. The *critical* operator is used to enclose the message sequence s, t, to ensure atomicity of this sequence. An *assert* cannot be used since the stimulus sequence is optional.
  - s, t responds to p: 1 stimulus – 2 response. The message sequence now occurs within the *assert* operator, so an additional *critical* operator would be superfluous).

Precedence Chain: A sequence $p_1, \ldots, p_n$ of messages must precede the sequence $q_1, \ldots, q_m$ of messages, in a given scope. We show an example of this pattern, 2 cause – 1 effect, p is preceded by s, t (see Fig. 11 (j)). This pattern is mapped using the *absence* and *until* patterns, just like in the *precedence* pattern. The implicit *negate* operators in the *absence* and *until* patterns handle the message sequences, so there is no need to add *critical* operators.

Runtime Monitoring of Object Invariants with Guarantee

Madhu Gopinathan[1] and Sriram K. Rajamani[2]

[1] Indian Institute of Science
gmadhu@csa.iisc.ernet.in
[2] Microsoft Research India
sriram@microsoft.com

Abstract. High level design decisions are never captured formally in programs and are often violated as programs evolve. In this paper, we focus on design decisions in which an object o works correctly only if another object p is in some specific states. Such decisions can be specified as the object invariant of o.

The invariant of o must hold when control is not inside any of o's methods (i.e. when o is in a steady state). From discussion forums on widely used APIs, it is clear that there are many instances where o's invariant is violated by the programmer inadvertently changing the state of p when o is in a steady state. Typically, o and p are objects exposed by the API, and the programmer (who is the user of the API), unaware of the dependency between o and p, calls a method of p in such a way that o's invariant is violated. The fact that the violation occurred is detected much later, when a method of o is called again, and it is difficult to determine exactly where such violations occur.

We propose a runtime verification scheme which guarantees that when o is in a steady state, any violation of o's invariant is detected exactly where it occurs. This is done by tracking dependencies automatically and validating whether a state change of an object p breaks the invariant of any object o that depends on p. We demonstrate that our tool INvCOP, which implements this scheme, can accurately pinpoint violations of invariants involving multiple objects that were reported in discussion forums on widely used APIs.

1 Introduction

Design decisions impose constraints on both the structure and behavior of the software. Typically, these decisions are described informally in comments embedded within code, or in documents. These documents are seldom updated as the software evolves. As a result, valuable design information is missing in most complex software. A promising approach to solve this problem is to capture design decisions formally as rules, and build tools that automatically enforce that programs obey these rules.

Data types are the only rules that are formally captured in programs, and enforced by programming languages. Over the past decade, we have witnessed

M. Leucker (Ed.): RV 2008, LNCS 5289, pp. 158–172, 2008.

practical tools and type systems that extend this type of checking to allow state-ful protocols on objects [1,2,3]. All these systems treat the state associated with each object independently. For example, they can check if every lock in the program is acquired and released in strict alternation, or if every file is opened before read, and then closed before the program exits. However, they are not capable of expressing rules that involve multiple inter-related objects. Since objects usually depend on other objects, such rules are common:

> "... no object is an island. All objects stand in relationship to others, on whom they rely for services and control" [4]

In this paper, we present a runtime verification approach for enforcing the following **inv-rule**: *The invariant of object o (which can refer to the state of other objects p) must hold when control is not inside any of o's methods.* The unique feature of our approach is that we track dependencies between objects automatically, and guarantee that violations of the **inv-rule** are detected exactly when they occur.

Example 1: Iterators for collection classes. Consider the Java code fragment below that uses an iterator to access the integers in a list sequentially.

```
1   //list is of type ArrayList<Integer>
2   //with integers 1,2,3 added
3   for(Iterator<Integer> i = list.iterator(); i.hasNext(); ) {
4     int v = i.next();
5     if(v == 1)
6       list.remove(v);
7     else
8       System.out.println(v);
9   }
```

On execution, a `ConcurrentModificationException` (CME) (the name is misleading as it occurs in single threaded programs also) is thrown at line 4. The API documentation for `ArrayList` [5] states the following:

> *If list is structurally modified at any time after the iterator is created, in any way except through the iterator's own remove or add methods, the iterator will throw a ConcurrentModificationException.*

The `Iterator` i depends on the `list` to not change during iteration. This can be specified as the invariant of `Iterator`:

```
List myList = ..;
int expectedVersion = ..;

//object invariant of Iterator
public boolean Inv() {
  return myList != null &&
         expectedVersion == myList.version;
}
```

Since `list.remove` (line 6) removes an element from the list and changes `list.version` as a side-effect, the invariant of the iterator is violated at this point. However, this violation is detected only when the `next()` method is called at line 4. Hence CME is thrown at line 4.

Example 2: Statement and Connection. Consider the code below that uses JDBC(Java Database Connectivity) API to access a database.

```
1    Connection con = DriverManager.getConnection(..);
2    Statement stmt = con.createStatement();
3    ResultSet  rs1 = stmt.executeQuery("SELECT EMPNO
4                                 FROM EMPLOYEE");
5    ..
6    con.close();
7    ..
8    ResultSet rs2 = stmt.executeQuery("SELECT EMPNAME
9                                 FROM EMPLOYEE");
```

A statement depends on the connection used to create it for executing SQL statements. Closing a connection will invalidate any statement created by that connection. Calling any method of an invalid statement other than `isClosed` or `close` results in a `SQLException`. To avoid such errors, a connection must not be closed before closing any statement created by that connection. This can be specified as the invariant of `Statement`.

```
Connection connection = ..;
boolean isClosed = ..;

//object invariant of Statement
public boolean Inv() {
  return isClosed ||
    (connection != null && !connection.isClosed());
}
```

The invariant of `stmt` is violated at line 6 as `con` is closed before closing `stmt`. When the `executeQuery` method is called later, this is detected. Hence `SQLException` is thrown at line 8.

The **inv-rule** is difficult to enforce, since it requires keeping track of the state of related objects. In Example 1, a programmer may not be aware that iterator i depends on the list, and that changing the list will break the iterator's invariant. Similarly, in Example 2, a programmer may not be aware that closing the connection will break a statement's invariant. Such violations routinely occur in large programs [6,7,8]. Debugging such violations is hard. In Example 1, an exception is thrown at line 4, and the stack trace of the exception does not refer to line 6, which violated the rule. In Example 2, an exception is thrown at line 8, and the stack trace does not refer to line 6, which violated the rule.

Our goal is to enable providers of APIs to document the **inv-rule** precisely and provide a tool to help users of the API to detect exactly where violations occur in the user code. Thus, we can rely on the **inv-rule** being enforced in any program using the API.

We are not the first to consider rules involving multiple objects. Several "ownership" type systems have been invented to enable objects to own other objects they depend on [9,10]. However, these require making changes to the programming language, and there is still a lot of debate on the pros and cons of various ownership type systems [11]. Also, program verification tools to check such invariants have been proposed, which force programmers to follow a particular methodology [12]. While this methodology works naturally for certain ownership structures, they need to be extended to handle cases where multiple objects depend on the same object [13] (as in Example 2 where multiple statements depend on the connection used to create them).

In this paper, we show how to enforce the **inv-rule**. The paper has two main contributions:

- We guarantee that in every run of a program, either a violation of the **inv-rule** is reported exactly where it occurs, or the run indeed satisfies the **inv-rule** (see Theorem 1 in Section 2.3 for a precise statement). This distinguishes our work from other runtime monitoring approaches to rule enforcement such as MOP [14], Tracematches [15] and JLo [16], where no such guarantees can be given if critical events from the program are missed by the monitor (see Section 4 for an example).
- Our approach is implemented in a tool called INVCOP. We demonstrate that rules involving objects exposed by the API are not violated by detecting usage errors previously reported in discussion forums on two commonly used APIs.

2 Approach

In this section, we explain the key features of our approach in stages, motivating the need for each feature. Consider Example 2 in Section 1. Our goal is to enforce the rule that in any program, a connection cannot be closed unless all the statements created using that connection are closed. We have seen that this can be specified as the object invariant of `Statement`.

```
public boolean Inv() {
  return isClosed ||
    (connection != null && !connection.isClosed());
}
```

Similarly, we can capture the dependency of iterator on list using the object invariant of iterator. Consider designing a reusable monitor object which reports an assertion violation if the **inv-rule** is violated. For every object that registers with the monitor, we require a side-effect free public method `boolean Inv()` returning a boolean, that checks the actual invariant (depending on the implementation of the object). To capture this requirement, we introduce the role *ObjWInv* (object with invariant).

```
role ObjWInv {
  boolean Inv();
}
```

For every object o of role *ObjWInv* (i.e. a subtype of *ObjWInv*), we add a boolean auxiliary field *inv*. Our goal is to ensure that for every object o of role *ObjWInv* in the program, whenever $o.inv$ is true, `o.Inv()` returns true. In the monitor, $o.inv$ is set to true only by using *CheckAndSetInv(o)* that asserts $o.Inv()$ before setting $o.inv$ to true:

```
CheckAndSetInv(ObjWInv o) {
  assert o.Inv();
  o.inv = true;
}
```

The goal of the monitor is to report an assertion violation whenever a state change of p breaks the invariant of any o that depends on p. For this, the monitor must know the dependents of p. Therefore, we introduce another auxiliary field *ObjWInv.dependents* of type *Set* of *ObjWInv*. To register an object o, the monitor's *Init* method must be called which initializes $o.inv$ to false and $o.dependents$ to empty set.

```
Init(ObjWInv o) {
  o.inv := false;
  o.dependents := nullset;
}
```

The monitor must be informed of dependencies (e.g. when a statement is created using a connection) by calling its *Add* method.

```
Add(ObjWInv o, ObjWInv p) {
  assert(o.inv = false);
  p.dependents.Add(o);
}
```

The monitor must be informed that o is in a steady state and $o.inv$ must be monitored by calling its *Start* method. Before executing a method of o, *Stop* must be called to indicate that $o.inv$ need not be monitored.

```
Start(ObjWInv o) {              Stop(ObjWInv o) {
  assert(o.inv = false);          assert(o.inv = true);
  CheckAndSetInv(o);              o.inv := false;
}                               }
```

Whenever the state of an object p changes, we should check with the monitor by calling its *Validate* method. This method checks whether the state change of p breaks the invariant of any o that depends on p.

```
Validate(ObjWInv p) {
  for(o in p.dependents) {
    if(o.inv = true)
      CheckAndSetInv(o);
  }
}
```

Next, we need to instrument the program with appropriate calls to the monitor. Consider again, the JDBC user code given below. The calls to the monitor methods are shown in italics.

```
1   Connection con = DriverManager.getConnection(..);
2   Init(con); // register con
3
4   Statement stmt = con.createStatement();
5   Init(stmt); // register stmt
6   Add(con, stmt); // inform monitor that stmt depends on con
7   Start(stmt); //start monitoring stmt.inv
8   ..
9   Stop(stmt);   //stop monitoring stmt.inv
10  ResultSet  rs1 = stmt.executeQuery("SELECT EMPNO FROM EMPLOYEE");
11  Start(stmt); //start monitoring again
12  ..
13  con.close();
14  Validate(con); // inform monitor that con's state changed
15  ..
16  ResultSet rs2 = stmt.executeQuery("SELECT NAME FROM EMPLOYEE");
```

With this added instrumentation, the call to *Validate* (line 14) reports an assertion violation as closing con breaks the invariant of **stmt** which is still open. Without the monitor, the error manifests subsequently, on line 16, when **stmt** is used. In this example, this is close to line 13, but in large programs the manifestation could be arbitrarily far away from the cause, resulting usually in long hours of debugging. With the monitor, we can detect the error at the point where **inv-rule** is violated (line 13).

However, there are two problems with the approach above:

1. Adding calls to monitor methods in the program creates a tight coupling between the monitor and the program bound to the rule. It is not easy to disable the monitor during deployment.
2. Errors can be missed if a call to an appropriate monitor method is omitted. For example, if the call to *Validate(con)* is omitted on line 13 above, then the error in the program is not detected by the monitor. The API programmer must ensure that the monitor knows about dependencies (by calling *Add*) and state changes of *p* are validated (by calling *Validate*). As new methods are added to *p*'s class, the API programmer must ensure that appropriate calls to *Validate* are made. This process is error prone.

Sections 2.1 and 2.2 give solutions to problems 1 and 2.

2.1 Specifying Bindings Using AOP

Aspect oriented programming (AOP) [17] enables the various *concerns* (in this case, the JDBC specific code and the monitor specific code) to be specified separately. A description of the relationships of the two separate concerns enables an AOP implementation such as AspectJ [18] to compose them together. Thus, if the relationship is correctly specified, then the appropriate monitor methods are implicitly invoked.

Any class in the program with a public method `boolean Inv()` can be bound to the role *ObjWInv* (i.e. it becomes a subtype of *ObjWInv*). The API programmer can bind the classes `Statement` and `Connection` as shown below (the binding below uses AspectJ syntax).

```
declare parents: Statement implements ObjWInv;
declare parents: Connection implements ObjWInv;
```

In AspectJ, a *join point* is an identifiable point, such as a call to a method or an assignment of a field, in the execution of a program. All join points have an associated context. For e.g., a method call has the context caller, target and arguments. These are the points at which the monitor specific code can be composed with the JDBC code. A *pointcut* is a set of join points. *Advice* is the code to be executed at the join points in a particular pointcut. At runtime, a *before* advice is triggered before the join point and an *after advice* after the join point.

The initialization of *ObjWInv* occurs before the constructor body of a class implementing *ObjWInv* executes. After this point, the auxiliary state of *o* is initialized by calling the monitor method *Init(o)*.

```
pointcut init(ObjWInv o) : initialization(ObjWInv.new(..))
                           && this(o);
after(ObjWInv o) : init(o) {
  Init(o);
}
```

After the field `Statement.connection` is set (during the construction of `Statement`), the target `Statement` *o* and the argument `Connection` *p* are collected and *o* is added as a dependent of *p*.

```
pointcut setConnection(ObjWInv o, ObjWInv p) :
                       set(Connection Statement.connection)
                       && target(o)
                       && args(p);
after(ObjWInv o, ObjWInv p) : setConnection(o,p) {
  Add(o,p);
}
```

After statement is created, the monitor is asked to start monitoring its invariant.

```
pointcut create() : call(Statement.new(..));
after() returning(ObjWInv o) : create() {
  Start(o);
}
```

Before closing the statement, the monitor is asked to stop monitoring its invariant.

```
pointcut stmtClose(ObjWInv o) : call(public void Statement.close())
                              && target(o);
before(ObjWInv o) : stmtClose(o) {
  Stop(o);
}
```

After closing the connection p, we must validate whether this change breaks the invariant of any statement o that depends on the connection p.

```
pointcut conClose(ObjWInv p) : call(public void Connection.close())
                             && target(p);
after(ObjWInv p) : conClose(p) {
  Validate(p);
}
```

It is easy to see that the `Iterator`/`List` code can be composed with the same monitor in a similar fashion. Mistakes can be made in the binding: suppose the pointcut `conClose` does not list the call to `Connection.close`. Then the monitor misses the critical event that a connection with an associated open statement is closed in the program. Other runtime monitoring approaches using AOP [14,16] rely on the programmer to correctly specify all the events that create dependencies and change relevant state in the program. In section 2.2, we show how to improve upon this by automatically tracking dependencies (as o.Inv() executes) and calling *Validate* whenever a relevant state change occurs.

Note that in many cases, a default binding such that $Stop(o)$ is called before and $Start(o)$ is called after every public method execution on o suffices. Then with automatic dependency tracking and validation, the API programmer need not write a binding description at all. However, in some cases, a custom binding is needed (see section 3).

2.2   Automatic Dependency Tracking with Validation

The key insight we have is that for any object o, the objects p on which o's invariant depends can be computed when o.Inv() executes using AOP techniques. Thus, if we compute these dependencies, we can check whether o.Inv() holds every time an object p that o depends on changes, and flag a violation of the **inv-rule** exactly where it occurs. In this section, we show how to track dependencies and validate relevant state changes automatically.

Definition 1. $(o, p, f) \in \mathcal{D}$ *iff the object invariant of o depends on the value of the field $p.f$.*

We must have $(o, p, f) \in \mathcal{D}$ iff the field $p.f$ is read during the last execution of o.Inv() (i.e. o is a dependent of p). Suppose the value of $p.f$ changes. It can potentially break the invariant of some o iff $(o, p, f) \in \mathcal{D}$ and $o.inv$ is true. *Validate* is invoked to check whether the change in value of $p.f$ breaks any such o's invariant.

The fields read during the execution of o.Inv() can be captured using AOP. We require that all such fields f must be either of a built-in type or of a subtype

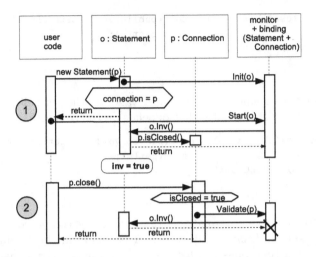

Fig. 1. Automatic dependency tracking with validation

of *ObjWInv*. This restriction is imposed so that we can register with the AOP execution environment for changes to these fields. We rely on the AOP execution environment to get a notification when the value of such a field f changes. More details on the implementation are given in section 3.

Consider Figure 1. In scenario 1, after the statement o is constructed, $Start(o)$ is invoked. Since *Start* calls *CheckAndSetInv(o)*, o.Inv() is called, and we compute all the fields $p.f$ that o depends upon. Therefore, $(o, p, isClosed) \in \mathcal{D}$. In scenario 2, after the field `Connection.isClosed` is set to false in `Connection.close`, *Validate(p)* is called. As *o.inv* is true and o.Inv() returns false, an assertion violation occurs. We now show that our approach always catches such errors subject to certain restrictions and assumptions.

2.3   Correctness

We consider sequential programs only. To summarize, the following restrictions on the program enable us to automatically track dependencies and validate state changes that may violate object invariants.

R1 Every field f read during the execution of o.Inv() must be either of a built-in type or of a subtype of *ObjWInv*.

R2 The execution of o.Inv() cannot modify any state.

These restrictions are checked by INVCOP using AOP, and if they are violated, an assertion violation is thrown.

The assumptions made on the AOP environment are:

A1 Every read access of a field $p.f$, where p is an object of type *ObjWInv*, can be detected.

A2 Every change of a field $p.f$, where p is an object of type *ObjWInv*, can be detected.

A3 The initialization of an object of type *ObjWInv* can be detected.

Assuming **A3**, we can ensure that every object o of type *ObjWInv* is registered with the monitor by calling *Init(o)*. Note that *Init(o)* sets *o.inv* to false. The following theorem relates the auxiliary field *o.inv* to the actual invariant of the object o.Inv().

Theorem 1. *Let r be any run of program P composed with the monitor using binding B. Suppose r does not have any assertion violations. Then, the following holds in all states of r:*

$$\forall o \in ObjWInv.(o.inv = true) \implies (o.Inv() = true)$$

Proof. The auxiliary field *o.inv* is set to true only using *CheckAndSetInv(o)*. Therefore, o.Inv() must have returned true. Let f be a field declared in a class P. Consider the assignment of a new value to $p.f$, where p is an instance of P. If this assignment violates the object invariant of o (i.e. o.Inv() now returns false and its previous execution returned true), then, the previous execution of o.Inv() must have accessed $p.f$. By assumption A1, we have $(o, p, f) \in \mathcal{D}$. By assumption A2, the assignment of $p.f$ is detected and *Validate(p)* is called. Since *o.inv* is true and $(o, p, f) \in \mathcal{D}$, *CheckAndSetInv(o)* is called. Since we assume that r does not have assertion violations, and *CheckAndSetInv(o)* calls assert o.Inv(), we have that o.Inv() = true.

3   Implementation

We have implemented the above approach in a tool called INVCOP. We first present the tool description followed by experimental results. The components of INVCOP are:

Monitor. As we have discussed in section 2.

Depend. Compute $\mathcal{D}$ during the execution of o.Inv(). Invoke the monitor method *Validate* when a state change is detected.

Aspect Generator. Generate an aspect combining the above two components and a binding. In most cases, a default binding suffices. However, in certain cases (given below), the API programmer may need to provide a custom binding.

The Depend component uses AOP to to compute the dependency relation $\mathcal{D}$. The execution of o.Inv() is captured using a pointcut. Then using a control flow pointcut (cflow), any read operation of a field $p.f$ during the execution of o.Inv() can be captured. If a joinpoint specified by such a pointcut is reached, then (o, p, f) is added to $\mathcal{D}$. A call to p.Inv() during the execution of o.Inv() can be captured similarly to add (o, p, inv) to $\mathcal{D}$, i.e. o depends on $p.inv$.

The Aspect Generator generates an aspect A by combining the Monitor, Depend and binding. The binding is attached verbatim. For binding a class C to the role $A.ObjWInv$, AspectJ compiler modifies the inheritance hierarchy of C to introduce $A.ObjWInv$ as a parent. Currently, this is possible only if the byte code of C is under its control. Therefore, we cannot bind the collection classes in `java.util` to $ObjWInv$. Our prototype implementation uses proxy objects to keep track of the relationship between iterators and collection classes. At runtime, a singleton instance of the generated aspect is created in the virtual machine. This instance enforces the **inv-rule** by validating state changes of objects of type $A.ObjWInv$.

Custom Binding. In the default binding, $Start(o)$ is invoked after the object o is constructed. Before the execution of every public method on o, $Stop(o)$ is invoked and after such an execution, $Start(o)$ is invoked again. However, in some cases, the API programmer may need to specify explicitly when $Start$ and $Stop$ are to be invoked. Consider the following example [12].

```
class T {                          public float method2() {
  public boolean Inv() {             return 1/(y-x);
    return 0 <= x && x < y;        }
  }                                }

}

public void method1() {          class User {
  x++;                             public void m(T t,..) {
  y++;                             //callback
  //invoke method m on user object   t.method2();
  user.m(this,..);                 ..
  ..                             }

}                                }
```

If the API programmer allows the user to call back the method `T.method2` during the execution of `m`, then $Start(t)$ must be invoked before the call `user.m(this,..)`. Otherwise, $Stop(t)$ (called before executing `method2`) will report an assertion violation as $t.inv$ is false.

Experimental Results. We first illustrate the difficulty faced by an API user using a real world scenario [7]. Figure 2 shows the usage of class `Document` in JDOM, a library for in-memory representation of XML documents.

A document iterator for navigating an XML document (in the form of a tree) uses a stack of list iterators where each list iterator is used for iterating over nodes at each level in the tree. An element in the tree is returned by the list iterator on top of the stack. If the user code calls `detach` on an element, then it is removed from the list of nodes at that level. An exception is thrown if user code invokes `detach` during iteration followed subsequently by `next` as shown in the stack trace below. The user code in the stack trace is shown in italics.

```
java.util.ConcurrentModificationException
    at java.util.AbstractList$Itr.checkForComodification(Unknown Source)
    at java.util.AbstractList$Itr.next(Unknown Source)
    at org.jdom.DescendantIterator.next(DescendantIterator.java:134)
```

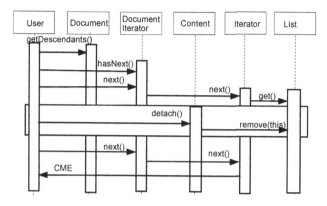

Fig. 2. Navigating a XML tree

```
at org.jdom.FilterIterator.hasNext(FilterIterator.java:91)
at OrderHandler.processOrder(OrderHandler.java:26)
```

From the above trace, it is not clear to the API user where exactly the invariant of iterator has been violated. After compiling with the aspect generated by INVCOP, the stack trace is as shown below.

```
java.lang.AssertionError: Invariant does not hold
    at rules.Inv_jdom.CheckAndSetInv(Inv_jdom.aj:122)
    ..
    at org.jdom.Element.removeContent(Element.java:885)
    at org.jdom.Content.detach(Content.java:91)
    at ItemHandler.processItem(OrderHandler.java:12)
    at OrderHandler.processOrder(OrderHandler.java:29)
```

This clearly points out that the user code *processItem* violated the iterator's invariant by calling `Content.detach`.

Table 1 shows some libraries for which we used INVCOP to detect **inv-rule** violations. Each scenario was modeled after usage violations reported in discussion forums. For each scenario, the columns show the total number of classes in the library and the number of classes bound to *ObjWInv*. We have already discussed the first scenario. Scenario 2 is based on an error report filed for MySQL JDBC library [8]. In scenario 3, user code first associates an implementation of Key with some value using a dictionary (implemented as a binary search tree). Then the key is modified violating the tree invariant.

With our prototype implementation, the time for each run with the generated aspect was 2-3 times that of the run without the aspect. However, this is insignificant compared to the amount of human effort spent in debugging these problems without a tool like INVCOP. Instead of documenting the reason for an exception in a FAQ (as in [6]), API users can be asked to use a tool such

Table 1. Detected **inv-rule** violations

API	Scenario	Total # of classes	Classes bound to *ObjWInv*
JDOM	Figure 2 [7]	69	IteratorProxy ListProxy
MySQL	[8]	95	Statement Connection
Binary Search Tree	[19]	5	BinarySearchTree Node Key

as INVCOP so that the violations of API rules can be detected quickly. Even if the API programmer has not formally captured all the API rules, as problems are reported, API rules can be captured incrementally. Once the violations have been found and fixed, the generated aspect can be removed during deployment.

4   Related Work

The SLAM toolkit [1] checks if C programs obey interface rules specified as state machines in the SLIC rule language. Powerful type systems have been designed to track a state machine as part of an object's type [2,3,20]. However, all these systems treat the state associated with each object independently. In this work, we focus on rules involving the states of multiple objects.

Contracts [21] identified behavioral compositions and obligations on participants as key to object oriented design. Recently, [22] has pointed out the need to enforce framework constraints (which typically involve multiple objects) so that plugin writers cannot violate them. These papers point to the need to automatically enforce constraints involving multiple objects in large programs.

Several "ownership" type systems have been invented to track dependencies between objects [9,10]. The proposals in the literature differ in how they constrain programs: for example, some allow ownership transfer whereas some others do not. Program verification tools have been built to check if programmers follow particular programming methodologies [12]. When multiple objects depend on a shared object (many Statements may depend on the same Connection), the methodology needs to be extended [13]. Also, these systems do not work with existing programming languages.

JML [23] requires that an invariant must hold at the end of each constructor's execution, and at the beginning and end of all public methods. Our approach ensures that this is indeed the case during runtime.

MOP [14], Tracematches [15] and JLo [16] also use aspects for runtime verification. Consider the MOP specification (from [14]) for ensuring that a vector v is not modified when enumeration e is being used for enumerating the elements of the vector:

```
1   SafeEnum (Vector v, Enumeration+ e) {
2   [String location = "";]
3   event create<v,e>: end(call(Enumeration+.new(v,..))) with (e);
4   event updatesource<v>: end(call(* v.add*(..))) \/
5                          end(call(* v.remove*(..))) \/ ...
6                          {location = @LOC;}
7   event next<e>: begin(call(* e.nextElement()));
8   formula : create next* updatesource+ next
9   }
10  validation handler { System.out.println("Vector updated at "
11  + @MONITOR.location); }
```

In this MOP specification, a faulty pattern is specified using a formula which encodes incorrect sequences of events. After the event `create<v,e>` occurs, `e` depends on `v` to not change. The event `updatesource<v>` signals that the vector is modified. The formula `create next* updatesource+ next` specifies the faulty pattern: the enumeration is created, then vector is modified, followed by a `next` method call on the enumeration.

Suppose the specification of the event `updatesource<v>` inadvertently omits the method `v.remove()` (line 5 above). Then, an error similar to the one in Example 1 cannot be detected by MOP. In contrast, INVCOP does not require explicit specification of events that signal dependencies or state changes. With INVCOP, the programmer merely specifies that the enumerator depends on the vector's state. Whenever the state of the vector changes, automatic dependency tracking helps to check whether the invariant of the enumerator is violated. Thus, we believe that automatic dependency tracking is a useful feature that can be added to tools such as MOP to give guarantees such as the one offered by Theorem 1.

For us to track state changes of an object p that may affect the invariant of another object o, o must refer to p directly or indirectly. The AOP based monitoring approaches mentioned above do not place any such restrictions. However, the advantage of our approach is that we can enforce the **inv-rule** without the programmer having to list all methods that change object state and potentially break some other object's invariant.

5   Conclusion

We have presented an approach to formally capture design decisions which require an object o to constrain the state changes of another object p. We have also shown that our tool INVCOP guarantees to enforce such design decisions. Compared to other runtime verification approaches based on AOP, our approach reduces the specification burden on API programmers for the kind of design decisions we focus on in this paper. This is due to our novel dependency tracking and validation mechanism.

We have used our tool INVCOP to accurately pinpoint several usage violations that involved inter-related objects, reported in discussion forums on widely used

APIs. Extending our work to concurrent programs, handling subclasses, and building a modular and scalable static analysis scheme for enforcing such design decisions require further research, and are beyond the scope of this paper.

References

1. Ball, T., Rajamani, S.K.: The SLAM project: Debugging system software via static analysis. In: POPL, pp. 1–3. ACM, New York (2002)
2. DeLine, R., Fähndrich, M.: Enforcing high-level protocols in low-level software. In: PLDI. ACM, New York (2001)
3. Chin, B., Markstrum, S., Millstein, T.: Semantic type qualifiers. In: PLDI, pp. 85–95. ACM, New York (2005)
4. Beck, K., Cunningham, W.: A laboratory for teaching object-oriented thinking. In: OOPSLA, pp. 1–6 (1989)
5. http://java.sun.com/j2se/1.5.0/docs/api/
6. JDOM FAQ – http://www.jdom.org/docs/faq.html#a0390
7. http://www.jdom.org/pipermail/jdom-interest/2005-March/014694.html
8. http://bugs.mysql.com/bug.php?id=2054
9. Clarke, D.G., Potter, J., Noble, J.: Ownership types for flexible alias protection. In: OOPSLA, pp. 48–64 (1998)
10. Boyapati, C., Liskov, B., Shrira, L.: Ownership types for object encapsulation. In: POPL, pp. 213–223. ACM, New York (2003)
11. Boyland, J.: Why we should not add readonly to java (yet). JOT 5(5), 5–29 (2006)
12. Barnett, M., DeLine, R., Fähndrich, M., Leino, K.R.M., Schulte, W.: Verification of object-oriented programs with invariants. JOT 3(6), 27–56 (2004)
13. Barnett, M., Naumann, D.A.: Friends need a bit more: Maintaining invariants over shared state. In: MPC, pp. 54–84. Springer, Heidelberg (2004)
14. Chen, F., Rosu, G.: Mop: an efficient and generic runtime verification framework. In: OOPSLA, pp. 569–588 (2007)
15. Avgustinov, P., Bodden, E., Hajiyev, E., Hendren, L.J., Lhoták, O., de Moor, O., Ongkingco, N., Sereni, D., Sittampalam, G., Tibble, J., Verbaere, M.: Aspects for trace monitoring. In: FATES/RV, pp. 20–39 (2006)
16. Stolz, V., Bodden, E.: Temporal assertions using aspectj. Electr. Notes Theor. Comput. Sci. 144(4), 109–124 (2006)
17. Kiczales, G., Lamping, J., Mendhekar, A., Maeda, C., Lopes, C.V., Loingtier, J.M., Irwin, J.: Aspect-oriented programming. In: ECOOP, pp. 220–242 (1997)
18. AspectJ –, http://www.eclipse.org/aspectj/
19. http://www.ibm.com/developerworks/java/library/j-jtp02183.html
20. Foster, J.S., Terauchi, T., Aiken, A.: Flow-sensitive type qualifiers. In: PLDI, pp. 1–12. ACM, New York (2002)
21. Helm, R., Holland, I.M., Gangopadhyay, D.: Contracts: Specifying behavioural compositions in object-oriented systems. In: OOPSLA/ECOOP, pp. 169–180 (1990)
22. Jaspan, C., Aldrich, J.: Checking framework plugins. In: OOPSLA Companion, pp. 795–796 (2007)
23. Leavens, G., Cheon, Y.: Design by contract with jml (2003)

A Lightweight Container Architecture for Runtime Verification

Hakim Belhaouari and Frédéric Peschanski

Laboratoire d'Informatique de Paris 6
UPMC Paris Universitas
`first.last@lip6.fr`

Abstract. We present in this paper a runtime verification architecture that enforces formal contracts for component-based systems. The contracts are based on logical assertions combined with state-transition systems. They are expressed separately from the implementation logic. A set of static analyses can be applied on the contracts but ultimately further verifications have to be performed on-line. This is the main purpose of the monitoring system we describe in this paper. The monitoring architecture is based on a model of lightweight hierarchical containers that exhibits a high-level of flexibility and extensibility. For instance, containers can be dynamically composed and unplugged on a per-instance basis. Beyond runtime verification, the monitoring architecture is reused for other purposes such as QoS monitoring and component hot-swapping. A performance comparison with other design by contract environments is also proposed.

1 Introduction

Lightweight formal methods represent a privileged way to increase the overall quality of software without impacting too strongly the mainstream development methodologies. *Design by contract* (DbC) is a particularly representative lightweight formalism [1]. In the classical DbC approach, contracts are specified by annotations of the (object-oriented) source code using simple Hoare-style logic assertions. The contracts are then verified at runtime. Recent works introduce more expressive logics together with tools performing partial static analyses of the contract, e.g. in Java Modeling Language (JML) [2] and Spec# [3].

In this paper, we present Tamago, a platform that supports the design by contract methodology in the development of software components [4]. The platform provides a contract specification language, a set of analysis tools and a runtime verification infrastructure. The contract language tries to offer a good balance between the expressivity of the proposed constructs, their potential for static analysis and, ultimately, the efficient verifications of the remaining contracts at runtime. The specifications of contracts are based on classical DbC assertions (extended with first-orders quantifiers) combined with state-transition systems. An important aspect is that unlike most related approaches the contracts are expressed and verified separately from the implementation logic.

M. Leucker (Ed.): RV 2008, LNCS 5289, pp. 173–187, 2008.

The present paper mostly discusses the monitoring architecture that performs the verification of the contracts at runtime. While most runtime verifiers employ *code injection* to weave the implementation code on the one side and the verifier logic on the other side, we introduce a container-based architecture for the same purpose. A first advantage of this approach is that the containers performing the runtime verifications are *non-intrusive* wrt. the implementation code. This is clearly a *safer* approach in that there is far less opportunity of breaking the underlying implementations. Moreover, the approach is more *flexible*: the Tamago containers can be composed and even plugged/unplugged at runtime. We show, also, that beyond runtime verification other kinds of containers can be developed. A further contribution is that despite the increase in flexibility, the runtime monitoring delivers good performances if compared to other DbC environments based on code injection.

The outline of the paper is as follows. In section 2 the overall Tamago platform is presented. We briefly describe the contract specification language and the static analyses that can be applied on the contracts. The contract compiler is then presented in section 3. We emphasize the support of multiple *percolation patterns* and the pre-compilation of product automata. The container-based monitoring architecture is described in section 4. We illustrate, in particular, its use as a runtime verifier for contracts. Two extensions are also discussed: a support for component hot-swapping and a QoS monitoring system. Section 5 gives a performance comparison between Tamago and other related DbC frameworks. A panorama of related work, conclusion and bibliography follow.

2   The Tamago Platform

We overview in this section the Tamago platform. We first describe briefly the language for contract specifications and then present the tool-suite we develop to assist the enforcement of contracts from both a static and dynamic point of view.

2.1   Contract Specifications

One of the key characteristics of Tamago is the separation of concerns between the contract specifications on the one side and the implementations of components on the other side. Instead of source code annotations [2,3,5,6], the contracts in Tamago are specified *separately*. A contracted interface, or *service*, defines a set of *functionalities* that any *provider* of the service must implement. In complement to their signatures, the functionalities are also annotated with preconditions and postconditions expressed in first-order logical assertions. Global invariants can also be expressed separately. Since the assertions do not directly apply to specific implementations but in general to any implementation of the service, the *observable properties* of the service must be precisely characterized. To increase the expressivity of the contract language while preserving good opportunities for static analyses, an automata-theoretic model of *service behavior* (similar to *component protocols* [7]) is proposed.

```
service MessageBufferService {
    property int size;
    property bool isEmpty;
    property Message[] messages;

    invariant (♯size ≥ 0) ∧ [♯isEmpty ⟺ (♯size = 0)];
    invariant ♯messages.length = ♯size

    Message match(MessageType type) {
        pre type ≠ null;
        post ∃m ∈ ♯messages{m.getType() = type }
                ⟹ return = m
                ∨ return = null
    }

    bool put(Message m) {
        pre m ≠ null;
        post return ⟺ ♯size@pre = ♯size + 1;
    }

    bool contains(Message m) {
        post return ⟹ ∃ msg ∈ ♯messages{
                m.equals(msg)
        }
    }

    Message take() {
        pre ¬♯isEmpty;
        post return ∧ contains(m)@pre
                ⟹ ♯size@pre = ♯size − 1;
    }

    behavior {
        init state empty { allow match, put, contains;}
        state notempty { allow all; }
        transition empty to notempty with put when ¬♯isEmpty
        transition notempty to empty with take when ♯isEmpty
    }
}
```

```
service MessageQueueService
    extends MessageBufferService {

    bool put(Message m) {
        post ♯messages[0] = m;
        post ∀i∈ [1; ♯size@pre]
            {♯messages[i] = ♯messages@pre[i − 1]}
    }

    Message take() {
        post return = ♯messages@pre[♯size]
    }
}
```

```
component MessageQueue
    provides MessageQueueService {

    property const int capacity;
    invariant ♯capacity ≥ ♯size;

    bool put(Message m) {
        pre ♯size < ♯capacity;
    }
    void flush() {
        post ♯size <= ♯size@pre
    }

    behavior {
        state notempty { allow flush; }
    }
}
```

Fig. 1. Examples of service and component contracts

Fig. 1 illustrates a simple example of a message buffer specification (for a communication system). We briefly overview the MessageBufferService (on the left side of the figure). All assertions are based on observations made on properties, here the *size* of the buffer, an *empty* flag and an array used to observe the buffered *messages* (the buffer itself, of course, does not have to be implemented using an array). In the assertions, the ♯ operator is used to access the value of a property. The invariants speak for themselves. Each functionality (or method) is specified using a triple: signature, precondition(s) and postcondition(s). The suffix operator **@pre** is used to reference observations made at the time of the precondition. The **behavior** part describes an automaton that imposes further constraints on the activation of functionalities. For the message buffer, there are only two states: empty or not. Each state corresponds to a set of available functionalities. The transitions between the states are triggered by method invocations. A transition can be further *guarded* by logical assertions. For example, while in the notempty state, an invocation of take can trigger a transition to the empty state if the property *isEmpty* becomes true. This automata-theoretic framework plays in fact a prominent role in the approach.

On the right side of Fig. 1 we illustrate the subtyping relation between services. We define a MessageQueueService that inherits from the message buffer service. It strengthens the contracts for two of the functionalities: put and take. The remainder of the specification is inherited from the parent. We should stress the fact that a given service can inherit from multiple parent services. From a DbC perspective, such a subtyping relation relates to *behavioral subtyping* [8,9]. This is further discussed in section 3.

The bottom right of the figure shows an example of a component specification, a MessageQueue component that *provides* the MessageQueueService. A component may in general both *require* and *provide* multiple services [4]. For the purpose of designing by contract, an advantage is that the interactions between the required and provided services may be captured at the component level. Finally the component adds a new method called flush. Tamago also supports specifications at higher level of abstractions. At the *assembly* level a contract for a complete architecture of interconnected components can be specified. Such an assembly can be given the status of a first-class component by defining a *composite* specification.

2.2 Static Analyses

The Tamago contract description language tries to find a compromise between (1) the simplicity of use for real-world situations, (2) the expressivity of the proposed constructs and (3) the possibility of performing thorough static analyses on the contract specifications. While (1) is quite subjective, finding a good balance between (2) and (3) is challenging. In this section we briefly describe the static analysis tools that we develop for the Tamago platform (a more comprehensive overview is proposed in [10]).

The first analysis performs a structural consistency check of the contracts. The automaton underlying the contracts is used to drive the static verification. In case such an automaton is left unspecified, the algorithm generates a default automaton on-the-fly with an unique state that allows every methods. A LeanTap-based first order theorem prover is used to discover symbolic inconsistencies and tautologies [11]. Unreachable states, redundant assertions and invalid transitions are also tracked down. The *structural subtyping* issues [12] are also resolved during this first analysis. In Fig. 1, the precondition of the take method for the message buffer is for example warned as redundant by the analysis (it is subsumed by a transition guard).

In a second phase, a *symbolic interpreter* is used to animate the contract specification resulting from the structural analysis. The algorithm performs a depth-first search of the automaton and exploits a finite-domain constraint resolver to refine the domains of properties' values in preconditions and invariants. The postconditions are used both as next states constraints and as effects on the observable properties. Various fixpoint detection heuristics are used to ensure the termination of the analysis. As an illustration we consider the message queue component of Fig. 1. By default, the domain for the capacity is left unspecified, which avoids any exhaustive verification of the contract. However, the value of such a constant can be specified for the analysis.

The Tamago tool-suite finally provides an automated testing framework, which also uses the animation of the automaton and the constraint resolver. The goal here is to determine the possible domains of the method parameters in the contracts. For the moment, we only provide such an automated generation of test cases for primitives types (i.e. integer, real, boolean and string). However an API is proposed to extend the generation of tests case for user-defined types.

The structural analyzer and symbolic evaluator cannot encompass the whole expressivity of the proposed contract model. Ultimately, the Tamago environment rely on a runtime system that enforces the (remaining) contracts at runtime. This is described in the next section.

3 Contract Compilation

The objective of the Tamago-CC compiler is to generate the code that enforces the behavioral contracts on implementations partly at instantiation and binding times but mostly at runtime. The architecture and behavior of the generated code itself is discussed in the next section. There are at least two aspects worth studying on the compiler itself: the generation of *percolation patterns* and *product automata*.

3.1 Percolation Pattern

A *percolation pattern* describes the generation of the effective pre/post-condition from a contract specifications [13,14]. The presence of behavioral subtyping complicates the mapping between the specified assertions and their effective counterpart. Most approaches follow the Eiffel percolation pattern, which builds assertions by OR-ing preconditions and AND-ing postconditions [1,8,13]. The Eiffel percolator is rather weak since it allows to contradict the preconditions of ancestors at the specification level. In fact, there is no single best solution for the percolation problem and various algorithms have been proposed in the literature: *exact pre/post, exact pre, exact post, plug-in* (Eiffel approach [1]), *weak plug-in* or *guarded plug-in, relaxed plug-in*, etc [13]. Indeed, the choice of one percolation algorithm or another depends on the context of use. For example, the component presented in Fig. 1 adds a precondition to the put functionality. The Eiffel percolator would "forget" about this constraint, which could lead to an inconsistency wrt. the implementation. A *weak plugin* percolator would on the contrary raise an exception in such situation[1]. In the context of a secure environment a restricting percolator may be preferable whereas an open-ended plugin system may benefit from more relaxed assertions.

---

[1] A solution that works for all percolation patterns in the example of Fig. 1 would be to remove the added precondition and report the constraint on the postcondition: $\sharp capacity = \sharp size$**@pre** $\implies$ ¬**return**. In more involved examples, though, such a workaround might be difficult to find in practice. Hence the interest of more precise percolation patterns.

To allow for the maximum flexibility in percolation patterns, Tamago supports the choice of the specific percolator to use at deployment time. The contract compiler can emit verification code for most of the known percolation algorithms. The advantage is that the component implementors are allowed to offer a panel of available percolators, which are then selected by the clients at deployment time depending on their specific contexts of use. Moreover, a dedicated API is provided to develop user-defined percolators.

An advantage of pre-compiling the percolation patterns is to provides increased performances: the work will not be required at runtime anymore. The impact of this is discussed in the section 5.

3.2   Product Behaviors

Beyond the logical assertions, the automata defining the service behaviors play a prominent role in the Tamago platform. Taken in isolation, the enforcement of a single automaton is trivial. However, the possibility to inherit from multiple services requires the possibility to compose automata. Another case is when components provide multiple services. To ensure that the generated automaton may simulate the union of all the automata defined by the provided/inherited services, we implement a product operator that consists in computing all the reachable states of synchronized automata [15].

Informally, the purpose of the algorithm is first to determine the initial merged state from all the initials states of the combined services. Then, the arrival states for all the transitions starting from the initial state must be determined. The algorithm then reiterate the process until all the abstract states and transitions have been taken into account. Various optimization and minimization techniques exist for this problem [15].

We illustrate the operation in Fig. 2, which describes the generation of the automaton for the component MessageQueue of Fig. 1. This component provides the MessageQueueService, which itself is a subtype of the MessageBufferService. There are thus three contracts to combine in this case and two automata. On the left side of Fig. 2 is depicted the automaton of the message buffer service. The second operand is the automaton described for the component, which adds the possibility to invoke the flush method in the notempty state. The result of the product between these automata is shown on the right-side of the figure.

The generation of such a global automaton allows to emit an efficient verification code for the runtime system. It also allows to isolate completely the verification logic on a per-component basis. Even if a component provides a large number of services, there will be only one automaton to "follow".

4   Monitoring

This section investigates the most important characteristics of the runtime verification of contracts in Tamago. Unlike most of other DbC tools [2,3,5,6] the Tamago-CC compiler is *not* based on *code injection* but rather adopts a container-based architecture, which is inspired from the PicoContainer approach [16].

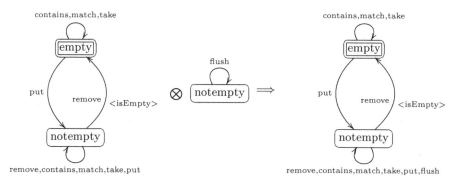

Fig. 2. Example of a product automaton

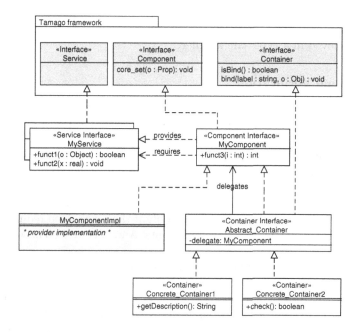

Fig. 3. Runtime Architecture

4.1 Architecture

The container architecture we propose is based on a variant of the *decorator design pattern* [17] that allows the generated code to be specialized for a type, i.e. a component interface composed of provided and required service interfaces.

In Fig. 3, we describe the hierarchy generated for an arbitrary component (named MyComponent on the figure). The root interfaces are inherited from the runtime support libraries. The architecture largely exploits interface inheritance to ensure type compatibility at all levels: service, component and container.

For example, the component interface implements the interfaces of all its provided services. Consequently, an implementation of the component must only implement this single combined interface. The abstract container (technically a kind of decorator) also implements this component interface and by default delegates all the invocations to another implementation of the *same* interface. A delegate can thus be an arbitrary container (that extends the abstract container) or an implementation of the component. It is thus possible to form a chain of *hierarchical, lightweight* containers ultimately ended by real implementations.

An important feature of this framework is to allow the combination of multi-purpose containers, e.g. containers for security, transaction control, etc. We exploit this feature to decompose the issues of contract enforcement at runtime. By default, the Tamago-CC compiler generates two containers: one for automaton checking and the other one for evaluating the logical assertions. The compiler can emit code for containers implementing various percolation patterns. Consequently, Tamago supports several dynamically-selectable percolation patterns. Note that the container architecture also allows containers to be dynamically inserted/removed in a type-safe manner.

4.2   Runtime Verification

The dynamics of the runtime monitoring architecture is illustrated in Fig.4. Here we see a typical chain of containers, consisting in first the behavior manager (that interprets and verifies the product automaton described in section 3.2), followed by the assertion verifier. The chain is ultimately ended by the implementation of the component. All containers (as well as the implementation) are assumed locally independent from each others. It is for example possible to inverse the order between the behavior and assertion checkers. This may result in different errors and diagnostics to be reported but only if there are some redundancy between the automaton and assertion constraints. And of course no false diagnostic may be reported anyway.

Perhaps the most important aspect of this *isolation* policy it that it is impossible for containers to interfere directly with the internals of others containers. Most of all, this makes the approach *non-intrusive* wrt. the implementation code, unlike most of other DbC approaches based on code injection. In Tamago implementations are considered as black boxes, and the whole verification must be performed without direct access to the component internals. Beyond the advantages of dealing with proprietary and/or secured implementation, this makes the extremely sensible and difficult aspect of *semantic preservation* reduces to a much simpler problem of consistent filtering/wrapping.

At runtime, it is possible to dynamically enable/disable a verification container in a transparent way for the client. This is firstly by "playing" with the chain of containers: insertions and removals in the chain. This mechanism is enough to handle enabling/disabling of stateless containers, for example the assertion checker. For stateful containers the enable protocol must also deal with the (re-)activation of the container in a consistent internal state. This is the case of the behavior manager that can be disabled easily but whose reactivation can

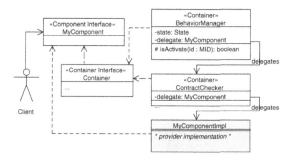

Fig. 4. Default Containers Hierarchy at Runtime

become non-trivial. The idea, in this case, is to implement a consistent state detection heuristics that can be inferred by intercepting the calls from and to the wrapped implementations. If a unique state can be determined in the automaton, then the container goes back to the runtime verification mode. Since the containers must be independent, the heuristics for reactivation must be implemented in the container itself. Of course, disallowing the dynamic reactivation of containers is always safe (albeit sometimes counter-productive).

4.3 Extension Framework

One of the key feature of the proposed container architecture is its *extensibility*. While runtime verification is the main purpose of the monitoring system, we developed early proof-of-concept containers that serve very different objectives.

One of the interest of having separate contract specifications and implementations is that a single specification can be provided by multiple implementations (possibly from different vendors). At deployment-time, it is of course possible to select the implementation as long as it implements the correct interfaces. We developed a further possibility of replacing provider components at runtime, so-called *hot-swapping*, thanks to a dedicated container as well as some conventions for implementors. To make the runtime verification resilient upon hot-swapping, the container proceeds as follow. First, the framework locks the component to be replaced and store all its observables values. Then it injects those values inside the replacing implementation and finally unbinds/rebinds all the required services. Of course, there must exist some convention so that the implementation can find back the correct run state to restart with. One possibility we explore, suggested by [18], is to apply a set of characteristic tests on the plugged component.

The second proof of concept container we developed is a monitoring support for tracking *Quality of Service*. The hierarchical container pattern allows to wrap method calls in both a flexible and efficient way. Depending on where the QoS container is placed in the hierarchy, it can be used for example to measure the execution time of method calls directly on the implementation, or the overhead implied by one of multiple containers, or any combination we might think of (e.g. total response-time).

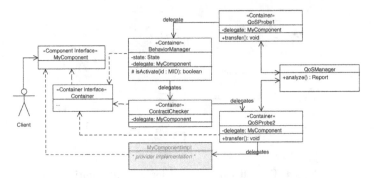

Fig. 5. Disable verification and enabling new monitoring

Fig. 5 illustrates an instantiation of the proposed QoS manager. Two QoS probe containers are deployed, one for measuring the response-time (QoSProbe1) and another for measuring the overhead involved by the verification containers (QoSProbe2). As the figure explains, the QoS manager does not have to be explicitly implemented itself as a container. It can, however, interact with the probe containers, e.g. to allow their reconfiguration at runtime.

5   Performance Evaluation

Most of the tools for runtime verification of software contracts are based on code injection/static weaving. We see at least two explanations for this fact. First, code injection allows to interfere at the most detailed level of implementations. Our opinion is that for many if not all situations this is not strictly required. The price to pay also is very high since the injected code could easily interfere *too much* with the implementation. The second explanation relates to performances, and it is a well accepted fact that in most cases *indirections* are less efficient than injections. To verify this common idea we decided to compare the monitoring system of Tamago with other DbC infrastructures. The experiments are carried out on a Pentium4 computer with 1GB of RAM memory and a 3.6GHz clock speed. The operating system is linux/mandriva and the Java environment is Sun JDK version 1.5.0_06. We compare the code generated by the Tamago compiler with three DbC tools based on Java: JML (release 5.4) [2], jContractor (release 0.1) [6] and STClass (release 4.0) [5].

In a first benchmark we implemented a set of classical examples of the DbC literature. Despite their simplicity, these examples are both representative and relevant for such a benchmark. Indeed, they involve most of the features found in typical DbC platforms (except the advanced features of JML or our own service behaviors). The examples we (re)wrote are: purse (withdraw/deposit of money), bucket and bounded bucket (inspired by a game called Pipe Mania) as well as a classical abstract data type for lists. In each case, the first step is to implement and measure the execution time of a *reference* implementation without contracts. The second step is to enrich a copy of the reference implementation with the contract assertions. In the case of JML and STClass, this means decorating the implementation with special comments. In the case of jContractor, the situation is worst in that the assertions are not specified in a given logic but must be manually implemented in the host java language. Tamago, on the other hand, offers a separate language for the specification of contracts, as described in section 2.1. All the examples are tested with various parameters and the average execution time resulting from a very large number of runs (10000) is finally reported.

Fig. 6 shows the runtime overheads induced by the tested platforms on the four examples. The bottom line, indiced 0, corresponds to the running time of the examples *without* any contract. The overhead is then expressed as a percentage wrt. the basic running time. For example, an overhead of 100% means the run with verification enabled takes twice the running time of the reference implementation. The results obtained are relatively high, which can be explained by the simplicity of the computations performed in each case. More realistic examples would probably lead to better results but it would be cumbersome to maintain a version for each one of the tested platforms. As seen from the figures, Tamago is in general faster than *all* the other platforms, even if it does not perform any code injection. These results are somewhat surprising. We see two possible explanations for this. First, the Tamago-CC compiler performs a thorough analysis of the contracts, which allowed us to implement various optimizations (such as the pre-compilation of percolation patterns and the generation of the product automaton, both explained in section 3). A second (more tentative) explanation is that the indirections induced by the container architecture of Tamago are relatively shallow and static (as long as the containers are not constantly plugged/unplugged), which probably allows many opportunities for the Just-In-Time compiler. This hypothesis should be investigated more thoroughly but we do not see any other meaningful explanation when comparing the code generated by all the platforms. The case of JML also is worth discussing, in that it in average induces a penalty of more than ten times the execution time of the reference implementation. Of course, JML is advertised as a *heavyweight* DbC platform, and is probably not well suited for runtime verification in general.

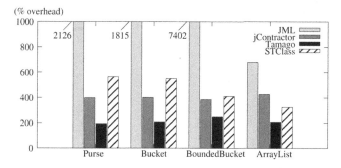

Fig. 6. Performance evaluation for classical DbC examples

In a second benchmark we decided to test the support for behavior suptyping in all the platforms. We only tested the plugin percolator since only Tamago supports more precise percolators. The benchmark example is a simple service with a unique observable property, an invariant and a method surrounded by preconditions and postconditions. Such a service is then inherited by a child service that adds a new invariant, weakens the precondition and strengthens the postcondition. The main parameter is the *depth* of the hierarchy of inherited services.

Figure 7 shows the execution times (in milliseconds) with respect to the depth of the hierarchy. Because of the very poor results of the JML percolator, we use a logarithmic scale. We see an exponential (asymptotic/logarithmic) increase in the JML case, while all the other cases are roughly linear. Once again the Tamago percolator seems to deliver the best performances, which can be explained by the pre-compilation of the percolator. Not that we tested the percolation until a depth of 100, which is not realistic in practice. So, while the curves have a tendency to coincide as depth increases, the difference between Tamago and jContractor/STClass really *is* significant for practical purposes.

In a third benchmark we study the *horizontal* composition of contracts. The parameters in the example are now the number of invariants, preconditions and postconditions to check on a given functionality. We excluded JML from the benchmark because a linear scale is more interesting in this example, and a preliminary run convinced us that JML would not deliver better performances. The case for jContractor, also, is problematic. In fact, jContractor does not support any notion of logic since all the assertions must be written by hand. Put in other terms, the combination of the various assertions also must be written by hand and there is no point in measuring the efficiency of hand-written code in this benchmark. So we are left with STClass and Tamago which both support a logic and deliver acceptable performances.

Fig. 8 shows the absolute response times with relation to the *breadth* of the contracts. Both implementations exhibit a linear overhead wrt. the parameter.

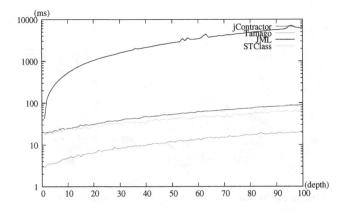

Fig. 7. Benchmarking the plugin percolation pattern

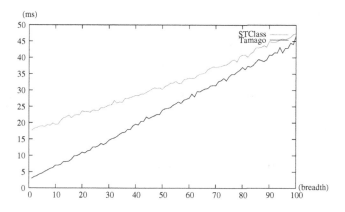

Fig. 8. Horizontal composition of contracts

The absolute times computed in the case of Tamago are below the ones for STClass, but the slope is bigger also at first. So we think that for very large contracts the two platforms should deliver approximately similar performances.

These benchmarks, though of course incomplete and subjective by nature, at least comforts us in thinking that the proposed container architecture is quite efficient in practice. This, together with its increased safety and flexibility, makes this kind of container architecture a better candidate for supporting runtime verification, if compared to code injection/static weaving. Finally, of the tested platforms, only Tamago supports the full disabling of the verification at runtime.

6 Related Works

DbC tools support contract specifications in various forms, e.g. with dedicated language construct [1,3], comments/annotations in the source code [2,5], or directly in the implementation [6]. These approaches do not offer, in general, to separate the contract descriptions and their various possible implementations. It is finally the implementations that take responsibility in enforcing the contracts. Tamago, on the contrary, clearly separates the two aspects, and the platform only is responsible of contract enforcement.

From the point of view of expressivity, the logic proposed in Tamago can be seen as an intermediate between basic Eiffel-like approaches, e.g. STClass [5], and an heavyweight specification language such as JML [2]. The basic boolean conditions are extended with first-order quantifiers, which can be analyzed by a first-order prover [11]. A prominent feature of the Tamago-CDL language is the model of behavior automata it supports. While increasing the expressivity of the language, it also uncovers many interesting static analyses to be performed on the contracts. Similar notions are proposed in other works, e.g. *component protocols* [7], but for a different purpose. In [7] for instance, the protocols (modelled as petri-nets) are used to check the consistent binding of multiple components at runtime, no static analysis is performed.

Most of DbC tools use code injection/static weaving techniques [2,5,6] that are intrusive wrt. the underlying implementation (source or binary). There are several concerns with such intrusive approaches. First, the preservation of the implementations integrity is threatened. In some situations, the injection would even be forbidden for intellectual property/security reasons. The container architecture proposed in Tamago on the contrary is non-intrusive. Beyond the increased levels of flexibility and safety it provides, the containers also deliver good performances.

7   Conclusion and Future Work

The current trend in lightweight formal methods is the integration of static and dynamic analyses of contracts expressed in rich logics. Our experiments with the Tamago platform shows that even relatively simple logical and automata-theoretic contracts are quite complex to handle from a static analysis point of view. Of course, more expressive languages could be introduced, and the tendency is to do so, but this would undoubtedly come at the price of making the end-to-end approach we aim for less realistic.

One direction we explore at the moment is the introduction of higher-level logical modalities (e.g. spatial/temporal) that could be interpreted in our automata framework. A similar example is that of never-claim conditions for linear temporal logic. Another direction is to address concurrency issues by introducing rely/guarantee assertions together with pre and postconditions. Thanks to the flexible container architecture of Tamago, we think that the runtime verification part of the problem could be solved rather effortlessly.

References

1. Meyer, B.: Object-Oriented Software Construction, 2nd edn. Prentice Hall, Englewood Cliffs (1997)
2. Leavens, G.T., Cheon, Y., Clifton, C., Ruby, C., Cok, D.R.: How the design of JML accommodates both runtime assertion checking and formal verification, vol. 55, pp. 185–208. Elsevier, Amsterdam (2005)
3. Barnett, M., Leino, K.R.M., Schulte, W.: The Spec# programming system: an overview. In: Barthe, G., Burdy, L., Huisman, M., Lanet, J.-L., Muntean, T. (eds.) CASSIS 2004. LNCS, vol. 3362, pp. 49–69. Springer, Heidelberg (2005)
4. Szyperski, C.: Component Software: Beyond Object-Oriented Programming. Addison-Wesley Longman Publishing Co., Inc., Boston (2002)
5. Deveaux, D., Jezequel, J.M.: Increase software trustability with self-testable classes in java. In: IEEE Software Engineering Conference (2001)
6. Karaorman, M., Hlzle, U., Bruno, J.: jContractor: A reflective Java library to support design by contract. In: Cointe, P. (ed.) Reflection 1999. LNCS, vol. 1616. Springer, Heidelberg (1999)
7. Reussner, R., Poernomo, I., Schmidt, H.W.: Reasoning about software architectures with contractually specified components. In: Cechich, A., Piattini, M., Vallecillo, A. (eds.) Component-Based Software Quality. LNCS, vol. 2693, pp. 287–325. Springer, Heidelberg (2003)

8. Findler, R.B., Latendresse, M., Felleisen, M.: Behavioral contracts and behavioral subtyping. In: ESEC/FSE-9: Proceedings of the 8th European software engineering conference, pp. 229–236. ACM Press, New York (2001)
9. Liskov, B.H., Wing, J.M.: A behavioral notion of subtyping, vol. 16, pp. 1811–1841. ACM Press, New York (1994)
10. Belhaouari, H., Peschanski, F.: An integrated platform for contract-oriented development. Formal Languages and Analysis of Contract-Oriented Software (2007)
11. Beckert, B., Posegga, J.: leantap: Lean tableau-based deduction. J. Autom. Reasoning 15, 339–358 (1995)
12. Abadi, M., Cardelli, L.: A Theory of Objects. Springer, Heidelberg (1996)
13. Toth, H.: On theory and practice of assertion based software development. Journal of Object Technology 4, 109–129 (2005)
14. Zaremski, A.M., Wing, J.M.: Specification matching of software components, vol. 6, pp. 333–369. ACM Press, New York (1997)
15. Zampunieris, D., Charlier, B.L.: An efficient algorithm to compute the synchronized product, vol. 00, p. 77. IEEE Computer Society, Los Alamitos (1995)
16. Fowler, M.: Inversion of control containers and the dependency injection pattern (2004), http://www.martinfowler.com/articles/injection.html
17. Gamma, E., Helm, R., Johnson, R., Vlissides, J.: Design Patterns. Addison-Wesley, Boston (1995)
18. Chen, F., Rosu, G.: Mop: an efficient and generic runtime verification framework. In: OOPSLA, pp. 569–588. ACM, New York (2007)

Author Index

Lecture Notes in Computer Science

Sublibrary 2: Programming and Software Engineering

For information about Vols. 1– 4709
please contact your bookseller or Springer